*city-pick*

# ST PETERSBURG

Oxygen Books

Published by Oxygen Books Ltd. 2012

This selection and commentary copyright © Heather Reyes 2012

Illustrations © Eduardo Reyes 2012

Copyright Acknowledgements at the end of this volume constitute an extension of this copyright page.

A CIP catalogue record for this book is available from the British Library.

ISBN 978-0-9567876-2-0

Typeset in Sabon by Bookcraft Limited, Stroud, Gloucestershire

Printed and bound in Great Britain by Henry Ling Ltd, Dorset Press, Dorchester

# Praise for the series

'Brilliant ... the best way to get under the skin of a city. The perfect read for travellers and book lovers of all ages'

**Kate Mosse, author of *Labyrinth***

'This impressive little series'          *Sunday Telegraph*

'It's like having your own iPad loaded with different tomes'          *The Times*

'An attractive-looking list of destination-based literature anthologies ... a great range of writers'          *The Independent*

'There are some books that you spot and immediately curse under your breath – "Why didn't I think of that? What a great idea!" ... The editors have scoured the literature and compiled a miscellany of observations by writers, famous and insignificant, which describes the beauty, the unique character and the essence of the chosen city'          *The Sydney Morning Herald*

'The excellent city-pick series which uses descriptions of a city penned by writers, both living and dead, to illuminate the metropolis in question.'

*Condé Nast Traveller*

'All of a sudden the traditional travel guide seems a little dull ... city-pick offers a more soulful guide to the metropolises of the world in the company of journalists, musicians, playwrights, bloggers and novelists past and present.'

*The Good Web Guide*

'An inviting new series of travel guides which collects some of the best writing on European cities to give a real flavour of the place ... Such an *idée formidable*, it seems amazing it hasn't been done before'

Editor's Pick, *The Bookseller*

'The beauty of this clever series is the breadth and reach of its contributors.'

*Real Travel Magazine*

'Wonderful.'          *The Guardian*

'Essential – slip it into your bag alongside a *Rough Guide.*'

*Waterstone's Books Quarterly*

# Contents

# Excellent prospekts

# White nights and dark days

# Contents

## The great and the good, the not so good ... and everybody else

## For art's sake

# Leningrad

# City under siege

## The Sleeping Beauty wakes

# Editor's Introduction

The preparation of this anthology has been one of the most exciting and illuminating reading journeys imaginable. Starting out with few ideas beyond the most basic clichés – snow, ballet, the Hermitage, the storming of the Winter Palace, Dostoyevsky – I have discovered a place that, while younger than most of the world's major cities (it was only founded in 1703), contains more beauty, more suffering, more dreams and nightmares than are packed into cities far more ancient.

The range of non-Russian writers who have engaged with the city has been one source of surprise: rediscovering Malcolm Bradbury's novel *To the Hermitage* has been a great delight, and I have chosen to include a number of extracts from it as it is an informative as well as a highly entertaining and intelligent read. I was previously unaware of H. G. Wells' *Russia in the Shadows* as well as of Sacheverell Sitwell's delightful recreation of the 1868 city in *Valse des Fleurs* (though he never set foot in the place). But the biggest surprise was discovering Truman Capote's account of accompanying an American opera company to Cold War Leningrad for a performance of *Porgy and Bess*, told in the classic Capote style combining crisp humour with vivid description.

I also discovered that Casanova wrote about the city in the famous account of his life, but as the passage mainly concerned his meeting with Catherine the Great, already present in a number of extracts, it didn't make it through to the final selection: but do read it! One of the most delightful discoveries was French travel writer and journalist Olivier Rolin's insightful *En Russie* which has not yet appeared in English. We acquired permission to translate several extracts for this anthology, and I would like to express my great thanks to Professor Amanda Hopkinson for checking and refining the original translations we provided.

We have included only short extracts from some of the great Russian novels of the nineteenth century as we felt these were likely to be already known to many readers and are easily available and that the space would be better given to more recent Russian writing on the city. I am hugely indebted to my co-editor in St Petersburg, Marina Samsonova, for selecting such illuminating material, including much previously unpublished in English. And thanks, too, to James Rann of Academia Rossica for helping to further refine the choice of extracts and for arranging their translation. Both Marina and James have given generous amounts of time to checking and refining the translations and providing much necessary information. We would all like to thank the writers – along with their publishers and agents – who have given permission for us to present their work in this anthology. Needless to say, we also extend our thanks to the translators whose sometimes under-appreciated skills allow us to enter books that would otherwise be closed to us.

Unsurprisingly, a great deal of contemporary and near-contemporary Russian writing on the city engages with its past and the traumas that have seen it change from St Petersburg to Petrograd (1914) to Leningrad (1924) and back to St Petersburg (1991). There has been a great deal to be 'worked through' in writing – both in fiction and non-fiction. This is certainly reflected in the final choice of extracts – but so too are the deep feelings its residents have for their extraordinary city, for its unique achievements and unrivalled beauties. In his essay 'In Petersburg We'll Meet Again', contemporary Russian poet Alexander Kushner writes about the feeling that there have always been two Petersburgs: the formal, magnificent and elegant 'European' city – the Petersburg of Pushkin and Akhmatova – and the 'backstairs' Petersburg of Dostoyevsky and Nakrasov, believing that the two cities still co-exist today, despite the many changes wrought by the last hundred years.

It's true that such a duality is probably present in most large cities, but in St Petersburg the very beauty and magnificence of the historic city centre emphasises the contrast with its darker side. But as Kushner points out, this duality is 'the very stuff of poetry'.

Indeed, there is much wonderful St Petersburg poetry and we urge the reader to seek it out. But this is a prose anthology and the process of selection was already hard enough.

My starting point for researching St Petersburg was one of the books suggested by journalist Tim Stanley – to whom many thanks: *St Petersburg: A History* by Arthur George with Elena George. For anyone who really wants to engage with the city, I can think of no better place to start. I have included a few extracts from the book, but these can scarcely do justice to its scope and depth ... and the fact that it is just a jolly good read, too.

But the very first book I ever read about St Petersburg was Gladys Malvern's children's biography of Anna Pavlova, *Dancing Star*, given to me by my late godmother, Marie Simons, when I was about nine. It was in this book that I first met the words Tsar, Mariinsky Theatre, 'The Imperial School of Dancing', Serge Diaghilev, Nijinsky, Karsavina, Petipa, Bakst, Benois, the Ballets Russes ... A whole new world and a city I fell in love with even then. So it was an act of personal indulgence to include a short extract from a book aimed at much younger readers than those who are likely to pick up this anthology – which we hope you will enjoy, whether you visit St Petersburg or simply create it in your head from the words on the following pages.

Heather Reyes
2012

# A dream of a city

*The founding of St Petersburg in 1703 was Peter the Great's 'I have a dream' moment. He did, indeed, have a clear vision of the elegant, enlightened, European-style city on the River Neva which would displace Moscow as the capital of a reformed Russia. But it was also the sound decision of a military strategist to establish a strong base in an important defensive location – particularly against the troublesome Swedes. For all the city's drawbacks – the damp, the weather, the long dark winters – it has been the quintessential 'dream city' for many visitors and even some residents. So we start with five fragments on the complex beauty of this unique and endlessly fascinating city.*

It floats under the late summer sky, borne up by the light that seems as much to rise from the Baltic as to shine from above. Floating, lyrical, miraculous Petersburg, made out of nothing by a Tsar who wanted everything and didn't care what it cost. Peter's window on Europe, through which light shines. Here's beauty built on bones, classical façades that cradled revolution, summers that lie in the cup of winter.

Helen Dunmore *The Siege* (2001)

✳ ✳ ✳

To walk under this sky, along the brown granite embankments, is itself an extension of life and a school of farsightedness. There is something in the granular texture of the granite pavement next to the constantly flowing, departing water that instils in one's soles an almost sensual desire for walking. The seaweed-smelling head wind from the sea has cured here many hearts oversaturated with lies, despair, and powerlessness. If that is what conspires to enslave, the slave may be excused.

Joseph Brodsky, 'A Guide to a Renamed City' (1979)
in *Less Than One: Selected Essays*

✳ ✳ ✳

I have moved into the very heart of my fantasy of St Petersburg. Each time I step onto the street there is a frisson of enchantment and disbelief. Along to the right is the bridge over the Winter Canal and beyond it the epauletted shoulders of the Winter Palace, sideways on, close up, haveable. At noon each day the cannon of the Peter and Paul Fortress rattles the bedroom windows — it is always a shock but a shock of Ruritanian dalliance. If you walk not into Ulitsa Khalturina but the other way, back through the courtyard, and through another courtyard, you emerge on the Neva Embankment directly opposite the cannon's discharge. I can walk everywhere now — I am at the hub of the wheel.

Duncan Fallowell, *One Hot Summer in St Petersburg* (1994)

\* \* \*

I owe much to my city. I remember how the city rescued me in my difficult and poverty-stricken youth: I never loved it so much as in my bleak student years. It soothed me in the dark hours that are familiar to any young person with a penchant for reflection. It silently came to help me with its 'harmonies austere', reminding me of the paltry scale of my own sufferings. I spent countless hours alone with the city in the misty, icy dusk of winter.

> Mikhail German, 'City Chronotopes' in
> *St Petersburg as Cinema* (2011) (ed. Lubov Arkus)
> translated by Sergei Afonin and Alice Jondorf

\* \* \*

'You are fortunate that you go to Leningrad first. A lovely city,' he said, 'very quiet, really European, the one place in Russia I could imagine living, not that I do, but still … Yes, I like Leningrad. It's not the least like Moscow.'

> Truman Capote, *The Muses Are Heard* (1957)

\* \* \*

12 July 1839

St Petersburg, with its magnificence and immensity, is a monument raised by the Russians to their future power; the hope which produced such efforts seems to me a sublime sentiment. Not since the Temple of Jerusalem has the faith of a people in its own destiny brought forth from the earth a greater marvel than St Petersburg.

> Marquis de Custine, *Letters from Russia* (1839)
> translated by Erica King

\* \* \*

*The apparent 'miracle' of St Petersburg's construction is captured in a legend, recorded here in one of the very best books on the city,* St Petersburg: A History, *by Arthur George with Elena George.*

There is a legend that St Petersburg – too miraculous to be the work of ordinary humans – was created by a Giant. Inspired by the sight of the setting sun over the silvery waters of the Neva as it flows into the Gulf of Finland, he decided to build there his paradise, the city of his dreams. There he built a house, but the Earth swallowed it. Undeterred, he built another house, but the Earth swallowed it too. The Giant furrowed his brow, realising that the task would be harder than he thought, yet he refused to give up. Then, in a stroke of genius, he built the whole city on the palm of his hand and gently lowered it to the ground. This time the Earth sighed, but did not swallow the city. The Giant now had his paradise.

The Giant, of course, was Peter the Great. Indeed, at six feet seven inches tall, Peter towered over everyone else. Yet it was not simply his height that made him a giant. More important was his vision of a new Russia and what he did to bring it about. And central to it all was the creation of St Petersburg, which Peter envisaged and created as the embodiment of all that he stood for, a laboratory and a model for the rest of Russia to follow, a catalyst for changing the national life. He called it his 'paradise' and spared no effort or expense for it, personally supervising the details of its construction and labouring with his own hands to turn his dream into reality.

Peter the Great and St Petersburg are inseparable. To understand Peter takes one far in understanding his city in its proper context and full sense. The story of St Petersburg thus begins with that of its founder: his upbringing, the influences upon him, his friends and helpers, his view of the world, his dreams and goals.

Arthur George with Elena George, *St Petersburg: A History* (2003)

✳ ✳ ✳

*Peter the Great travelled widely in Europe at the time of the Enlightenment and was greatly influenced by all he experienced there. But it was perhaps his stay in Amsterdam that gave the biggest impetus to his vision of a new capital for Russia. The link between the two cities is recorded in this extract from Malcolm Bradbury's hilarious, informative, and touching novel,* To the Hermitage.

For didn't the whole thing start as a dream here, when the young Peter the Great (great already, for he rose up six feet eight in his boots) arrived in his Great Embassy for youthful rest and recreation? A boisterous young man who broke windows, turfed friends, acquaintances, even total strangers into hedges, he drank and whored with the best. He came incognito and in disguise, even though he stood higher than anyone and had a pronounced facial tic, and his retinue of a hundred servants, six trumpeters, two clockmakers, four dwarfs and a monkey, suggested to the shrewder observer he might be a person of consequence. In Amsterdam he studied astronomy and anatomy, found out how to dissect a corpse, was taught how to cast metal, shave a face, pull teeth (the teeth, indeed, of anyone unlucky enough to be to hand). He acquired the trades of carpenter, boat-builder, sail-maker, became noted for his vast and indiscriminate curiosity ('What is dat?').

When he returned to Russia, became Tsar, defeated the Swedes, retook the eastern Baltic, and decided to build a triumphal capital on the Neva, staring dangerously out through storm, ice and foggy winters at the tempting riches of the West, it was Amsterdam he tried to build. Peter's city would not be another Scythian hotch-potch: mud-based buildings, leaking hovels, bearded boyars, rooting pigs and starving serfs. It would have not just cathedrals and monasteries, fortresses, prisons and arsenals, but canals, palaces, academies, museums, and stock exchanges, the glories of trade and war. He summoned Dutchmen to dig out his canals and embankments. When these seemed smaller than the ones in Holland, he had them filled and dug again. Meantime as the new city began to rise, Dutch ships carried the bricks, Dutch painters decorated the salons, Dutch bankers provided the ready. Swedish slaves and gulaged Russian serfs might have dug the foundations, raised the roofbeams, perished in the Finnish swamplands in their hundreds of thousands. But the peerless new city, which some began to name the city of bones, was raised not just on drowned skeletons but jolly Dutch guilders.

Malcolm Bradbury, To the Hermitage (2000)

❊ ❊ ❊

*There's the dream, and there's the reality – the diffi-culties of making that dream come true. An extract from exiled Russian poet, the Nobel laureate Joseph Brodsky (1940–1996) reflecting on the beginnings of his native city.*

Russia is a very continental country; its land mass constitutes one-sixth of the world's firmament. The idea of building a city on the edge of the land, and furthermore proclaiming it the capital of the nation, was regarded by Peter I's contemporaries as ill conceived, to say the least. The womb-warm, and tradi-tional to the point of idiosyncrasy, claustrophobic world of Russia proper was shivering badly under the cold, searching Baltic wind. The opposition to Peter's reforms was formidable, not least because the lands of the Neva delta were really bad. They were lowlands, and swamps; and, in order to build on them, the ground would have to be strengthened. There was plenty of timber around but no volunteers to cut it, much less to drive the piles into the ground.

But Peter I had a vision of the city, and of more than the city: he saw Russia with her face turned to the world. In the context of his time, this meant to the West, and the city was destined to become in the words of a European writer who visited Russia then – a window on Europe. Actually, Peter wanted a gate, and he wanted it ajar. Unlike both his predecessors and his successors on the Russian throne, this six-and-a-half-foot-tall monarch didn't suffer from the traditional Russian malaise – an inferiority complex toward Europe. He didn't want to imitate Europe: he wanted Russia to *be* Europe, in much the same way as he was, at least partly, a European himself. Since his childhood many of his intimate friends and companions, as well as the principal enemies with whom he warred, were Europeans: he spent more than a year working, travelling, and literally living in Europe; he visited it frequently afterward. For him, the West wasn't terra incognita. [...]

When a visionary happens also to be an emperor, he acts ruthlessly. The methods to which Peter I resorted, to carry out his project, could be at best defined as conscription. He taxed everything and everyone to force his subjects to fight the land. During Peter's reign, a subject of the Russian crown had a somewhat limited choice of being either drafted into the army or sent to build St Petersburg.

Joseph Brodsky, 'A Guide to a Renamed City' (1979)
in *Less Than One: Selected Essays*

❖ ❖ ❖

*French journalist and travel writer Olivier Rolin visited Russia just before the fall of Communism. Here is one of the many wonderful word-pictures resulting from the time he spent in St Petersburg (still called Leningrad at the time, of course).*

Along the canals, the globes of the street lamps throw pale circles onto the pastel walls; in the deserted Square of the Decembrists, the Bronze Horseman looks lost, the only complex, human form in the middle of a vast geometric space, standing out in the mist made of mingled water and sky, the receding perspectives of the palaces converging on the shining spire of the Peter and Paul Fortress. 'So, go forth, sublime builder ...' Go forth across the circumflex accents of the bridges, along the dotted lines of the tramways, beneath the electric street-lights. On Palace Square, the semi-circle of the great General Staff building still displays several of the gigantic pictures with which it was covered for the commemoration of the Revolution; a woman goes by, a little silhouette with hurried steps, beneath the vermillion foot of a sailor from the cruiser *Aurora*[1], twice as high as herself. And then the ghostly colonnades of Our Lady of Kazan, the winking globe of the *Dom Knigi*[2], and in the hotel corridors, the smells – of sour apple and of cabbage soup, and another, more acrid, of disinfectant (Cresyl? Creosote?) which succeed in convincing one that it's good to be back in this utopian, freezing place that Nabokov considered 'the world's the most gaunt and enigmatic city'.

Olivier Rolin, *In Russia* (1987)
translated by Erica King

❉ ❉ ❉

*There are many for whom St Petersburg is a night-*
*mare rather than a dream. An extract from R. N.*
*Morris's detective fiction set in the nineteenth century.*

The further they got from Bolshaya Street, the muddier the streets became, and the more disreputable the dwellings. Most of these were tumbledown wooden hovels.

---

1   The refusal of the *Aurora*'s crew to carry out an order to put to sea (on 25 October 1917) was one of the first events of the October revolution. The blank shot fired from one of its guns signalled the assault on the Winter Palace. The ship is now preserved as a museum. (Ed.)

2   Literally 'House of Books'. Situated on Nevsky Prospekt (number 28) and occupying part of the building known as Singer House (from the Singer sewing machine company), 'Dom Knigi' is the city's biggest and most famous bookstore. The 'globe' is set on top of a small, steeple-like tower on one corner of the building. (Ed.)

The Petersburg Quarter had once been the heart of the city, its streets lined with the homes of the wealthy and well-to-do. Peter the Great had built his first palace here, albeit a modest one, as an example to his nobles. But the rich had followed the power south, across the river, closer to the heart, rather than the edge, of Russia. They had left the bleak northern quarter, the unpropitious territory reclaimed from Finnish swamps, to be colonised by the poor.

The streets were mostly unpaved, many not even boarded. Compared to the broad, brightly lit avenues of more southern districts, these were mean, dark, dangerous alleys. In places, the area could feel like nothing more than a maze of filthy dead ends.

Tolya directed the *drozhki*[1] driver down a boarded thoroughfare, which, in the absence of an official name, had been dubbed Raznochinnyi Street — *the street of the classless ones.* The wheels clanked over the loose planks. They bounced in its wake like the bars of one of Gusikov's xylophones. At the far end of the street was Dunkin Lane, more a swamp of conjoined puddles, down which the driver quite sensibly declined to venture. [...]

Lippevechsel's Tenements in Gorokhovaya Street was one of those sprawling apartment blocks that seemed to have grown like an organism rather than built to any rational plan. Ramshackle and crumbling, its various fronts and wings clustered around a series of dirty yards into which sunlight never penetrated. When the wind blew through it, it was felt by every occupant, even those huddled around one of its stoves or samovars, even one buried under a mound of rags or bent double in a cupboard. Close to Kameny Bridge, the building overlooked the Yekaterinsky Canal, which was frozen now, but in the summer served as an open drain. The stench, in those high hot days, seeped in through the gaping cracks in its walls and spread throughout the building. It mingled with the smells of cooking, insinuating itself into the lives of the residents, so that it shared their intimacies and infected their dreams.

---

1   A low, four-wheeled open carriage. (Ed.)

The interior of the building was divided by flimsy partitions and lit here and there by oil lamps. Doors hung open or were lacking altogether. Families lived side by side and almost on top of one another, every room divided and sublet to meet the rent. From one side of a curtain came the cries and cracks of a beating, from the other the frenzied thump of copulation. Everywhere in the background could be heard a gentle snagging sound, as regular and constant as the lapping of the sea, an anonymous, muffled weeping.

R. N. Morris, *A Gentle Axe* (2007)

* * *

*But, in his diary of 1927, composer Sergei Prokofiev records his great pleasure in seeing the city again ... even if the hotel isn't perfect.*

Wednesday 9 February

I jumped out of bed at eight o'clock to shave and look through the window at the environs of Petersburg, which are so familiar to me. And yet the snow was so thick there was quite a lot I didn't recognise. [...]

The familiar railway station flashes by and we are settled in a car. Leningrad is covered with snow; it's a bright day and that gives it a clear and tidy appearance. There is the hippopotamus-like monument of Alexander III[1], which has been left for the edification of communist posterity to show how lacking in grace the tsars were. We drive along the Nevsky Prospekt and I am full of joy and excitement. The monument to Catherine is also there, and this square with the Alexandrinsky Theatre is so beautiful. In the Gostiny dvor (the arcades) I am struck by the number of boarded-up stores. We turn up Mikhailovsky Street. When we reach the hotel the driver asks for an exorbitant price and the commissionaire at the door pays him half.

1 Since moved to a courtyard of the Marble Palace. (Ed.)

A spacious room has been reserved for us in the Hotel Evropeiskaya with a large bathroom and also beds in the same room, separated from it by a curtain. The room is much larger than the one in Moscow, but that was impeccably appointed and moreover the view from the window was stupendous. This hotel seems to have got somewhat run down since the days of its former glory, although it's still the best in town. […]

During the many years of my travels abroad I had somehow managed to forget what Petersburg was really like; it began to seem to me that its beauty was a creation of patriotic feelings on the part of its citizens, and that, essentially, Moscow was the heart of Russia. I began to think that the European charm of Petersburg would pale in comparison with the West and that, on the contrary, the Eurasian beauty of some Moscow lanes was something unique. Now, however, strolling in this particular mood, the grandeur of St Petersburg absolutely took my breath away! It looks so much more elegant and imperial than Moscow. The white snow and the clear weather contributed to this effect.

Sergei Prokofiev, *Soviet Diary 1927 and Other Writings* (1991)
translated by Oleg Prokofiev

✳ ✳ ✳

*We'll end the section with a much more positive view, from Duncan Fallowell's richly rewarding depiction of the post-Soviet city in* One Hot Summer in St Petersburg.

In the course of the night most of the Navy Day flags have been stolen from the Kirovsky Bridge and here, at about mid-stream, we are arrested – by the sky, vast and pale blue, turning white at the eastern horizon to the left, and by the sun, strawberry-coloured, looking too big and pushing up through narrow bands of mist. Only two-thirds of the disc is presently visible above the horizon. But its slow upward slide is detectable with the naked eye.

A fine pearly mist pervades the city, not obscuring any of it but casting all in a pastel soft focus sparkling here and there with jewels. From the western side of the bridge dozens of small boats and yachts can be seen anchored on the river, bobbing but still asleep. The warships are dressed with flags, but it's too early even for them to be awake. It is very quiet. The only sound is the call of landbirds and seabirds. Hugely grand, St Petersburg is nonetheless dwarfed by the greatness of sky and river. No other city is so penetrated to its very heart by the grandeur of nature. This renders it both epic and intimate. The cosiest moments are susceptible to epic intrusion. And vice versa.

In the east the too-big strawberry bulb of the sun continues edging upwards minute by minute, until the whole disc wobbles free of the horizon, and rising on up through the low tiers of mist, it rises free of the mistline also, and attains to a round incandescent orange of godlike assertiveness, although the eye may still look upon it unharmed and the light which pours from it is soft, steady, clear.

On this riverine or indeed maritime summer Sunday at 6 a.m., the city is the most beautiful I have seen it, blessed, shining like new toys in the early morning sun. For the very first time it is not haunted in the slightest degree, but entirely clean and undefiled, entirely healthy, in every way at peace. It is breathing light. Young. Perfect. [...]

They present me with a painted wooden bell which they have made themselves. And a cassette of Sergei Stadler playing the Paganini Caprices. Why, when later I listen to them, do these Caprices sound as though written for, in and about St Petersburg? Because this city claims everything and everyone which comes into its orbit. There is no escape from its sense of place, not even for a minute. Which is how all great cities used to be, but are no longer. They have all now joined at some level that international technoplastic club. All except this one. This is the last to go. The lack of modernisation is a joy. To save it, it must be restored, but a modernised St Petersburg would not be the town I fell in love with. Anyway, whatever happens, I shall never leave it now.

Duncan Fallowell, *One Hot Summer in St Petersburg* (1994)

# Neva-land

*Both Amsterdam and St Petersburg have been called 'the Venice of the north', the character of all three cities being defined not just by the beauty of their architecture but by the particular contribution of water to their exceptional characters. In this section we explore the shaping influence of St Petersburg's watery setting – the relatively short River Neva and many smaller rivers and canals, as well as the Gulf of Finland.*

The rapid growth of the city and of its splendour should be attributed first of all to the ubiquitous presence of water. The twelve-mile-long Neva branching right in the centre of town, with its twenty-five large and small coiling canals, provides this city with such a quantity of mirrors that narcissism becomes inevitable. Reflected every second by thousands of square feet of running silver amalgam, it's as if the city were constantly being filmed by its river, which discharges its footage into the Gulf of Finland, which, on a sunny day, looks like a depository of these blinding images. No wonder that sometimes this city gives the impression of an utter egoist preoccupied solely with its own appearance.

Joseph Brodsky, 'A Guide to a Renamed City' (1979)
in *Less Than One: Selected Essays*

✾ ✾ ✾

The Neva is a beautiful river, about as wide as the Thames at London Bridge; its course isn't long: it runs from Lake Lagoda, nearby, and flows into the Gulf of Finland. A short trip brings us to a granite quay alongside which are lined up a flotilla of little steam boats, sailing ships, schooners and small craft.

On the other side of the river, that is to say on the right as you go up-river, rise the roofs of enormous hangars covering dry construction docks; on the left large buildings with palace-like façades, that we were told are the Institute of Mines and the school for naval cadets, stretch their monumental outlines.

Théophile Gautier, *Travels in Russia* (1867)
translated by Erica King

✾ ✾ ✾

*We have already looked at the founding of the city, in the first section: here it is again in Orlando Figes' masterly cultural history of Russia,* Natasha's Dance *– this time with the emphasis on the difficulties presented by such a soggy location.*

Few places could have been less suitable for the metropolis of Europe's largest state. The network of small islands in the Neva's boggy delta were overgrown with trees. Swept by thick mists from melting snow in spring and overblown by winds that often caused the rivers to rise above the land, it was not a place for human habitation, and even the few fishermen who ventured there in summer did not stay for long. Wolves and bears were its only residents. A thousand years ago the area was underneath the sea. There was a channel flowing from the Baltic Sea to Lake Lagoda, with islands where the Pulkovo and Pargolovo heights are found today. Even in the reign of Catherine the Great, during the late eighteenth century, Tsarskoe Selo, where she built her Summer Palace on the hills of Pulkovo, was still known by the locals as Sarskoe Selo. The name came from a Finnish word for an island, *saari*.

When Peter's soldiers dug into the ground they found water a metre or so below. The northern island, where the land was slightly higher, was the only place to lay firm foundations. In four months of furious activity, in which at least half the workforce died, 20,000 conscripts built the Peter and Paul Fortress, digging out the land with their bare hands, dragging logs and stones or carting them by back, and carrying the earth in the folds of their clothes. The sheer scale and tempo of construction was astonishing. Within a few years the estuary became an energetic building site and, once Russia's control of the coast had been secured with victories over Sweden in 1709-10, the city took on a new shape with every passing day. A quarter of a million serfs and soldiers from as far afield as the Caucasus and Siberia worked around the clock to clear forests, dig canals, lay down roads and erect palaces. Carpenters and stonemasons (forbidden by decree to work elsewhere) flooded into the new capital. Hauliers, ice-breakers, sled-drivers, boatsmen and labourers arrived in search of work, sleeping in the wooden shacks that crowded into every empty space. [...]

Whereas older European cities had been built over several centuries, ending up at best as collections of beautiful buildings in diverse period styles, Petersburg was completed within fifty years and according to a single set of principles. Nowhere else, moreover, were these principles afforded so much space. Architects in Amsterdam and Rome were cramped for room in which to slot their buildings. But in Petersburg they were able to expand their classical ideals. The straight line and the square were given space to breathe in expansive panoramas. With water everywhere, architects could build mansions low and wide, using their reflections in the rivers and canals to balance their proportions, producing an effect that is unquestionably beautiful and grandiose. Water added lightness to the heavy baroque style, and movement to the buildings set along its edge. The Winter Palace is a supreme example. Despite its immense size (1,050 rooms, 1,886 doors, 1,945 windows, 117 staircases) it almost feels as if it is floating on the embankment of the river; the syncopated rhythm of the white columns along its blue façade creates a sense of motion as it reflects the Neva flowing by.

Orlando Figes, *Natasha's Dance: A Cultural History of Russia* (2002)

*Sailing across from Stockholm, the 'Enlightenment pilgrims' in Malcolm Bradbury's* To the Hermitage *approach the great city from the sea. But before that, a short piece from a nineteenth-century visitor also approaching the city from the water.*

10 July 1839

The Baltic Sea, with its none too bright colouring and its not very busy waters, indicates the proximity of a continent depopulated by the rigours of its climate. There the barren coastline is in harmony with the cold, wide sea, while the sadness of the sun and the sky, and the chill colour of the waters, freeze the traveller's heart.

Marquis de Custine, *Letters from Russia* (1839)
translated by Erica King

\* \* \*

We've sailed the seaway past Kronstadt on Kotlin Island, its fortress buildings lost somewhere inside the mist. We've come down the estuary channel, lined with cranes and defences, where rusty-looking warships and submarines lie spliced together at moorings offshore. We've eased gently into the crane-spiked harbour, where the waters are thick, mud-marked and oil-stained. There, Anders tells me as we watch our landing from the bridge deck, is the passenger terminal that sits on the very tip of Vasilievsky Island, and which is no distance at all from the heart of the great old capital. At first glance, seen over the water from a distance, it could not look more smart or hospitable, as good and gleaming a sample of late-modernist space-age architecture as you could wish for. Lit by cold crisp autumnal sunlight, its curves swing and surge in the hi-tech fashion, its aluminium claddings snatch at the sun. Its white cement gleams, its big windows glisten. It has all the appearance of being built at the peak of superpower assertion, when every big building was a symbol of the prevailing regime. Modernist emblems of sailing caravels mural its walls. On the building's end a sign announces, in two different alphabets, SANKT PETERBURG/SZENPETERVAR.

In fact it's only when, siren blaring, the *Vladimir Ilich* begins to receive the embrace of shore – the dock-arms opening, the hawsers swinging over the closing gap, the shore stanchions starting to grip, the probing gangplanks swinging out over the side, the side-ramps dropping down – that some of the flaws and blemishes grow apparent. All is not quite as it seems; what can have happened here? The building is new, surely, its curved lines and modern materials belonging to recent times and the age of sixties heavy cementing. Indeed much of the city, especially this part of it, would have to be new, since most was rebuilt after the horrific nine-hundred-day siege, when German forces surrounded it through several winters and began a night bombardment, vowing to pulp the place to bits. [...]

Today, at the dockside, it's the free market that appears to rule – or maybe rather it's the old world of the souk. At any rate, no sooner are we walking out of the terminal than we're swept up by a turmoil of trade, a frenzy of solicitation. Everything is for sale: all the things you can think of, and then a good few you can't. Youths stand in lines in front of ancient suitcases, which are packed with military medals and lemon peelers; tank-drivers' fur caps and old postage stamps; peasant carvings and old cameras. Old women standing on squares of cardboard hold up worn dresses and old suits. There are glorious CDs of Prokofiev, and the great Gregorian liturgies. There are bronze busts of Lenin at knockdown prices, and others of the slaughtered Tsar Nicholas II. Weapons are everywhere – from small pistols and rusting hand-grenades to an entire armoured car, loaded gun-turret and all – on offer at a price marked in dollars and apparently ready to roll.

Verso and I stop together to inspect the coloured dolls, the *matrioshki*, which are supposed always to carry the latest political news. Well, for the moment at least, it's still a wooden Yeltsin that firmly encases a wooden Gorbachev and a wooden Brezhnev, and no one is yet encasing Yeltsin. On the other side of the world, Clinton too seems to be all right for the moment, holding inside himself the images of Bush, Reagan, Carter, Nixon. Helmut Kohl contains Schmidt and Adenauer. Quiet John Major boxes in Thatcher and Heath. 'Buy now before everything changes,' says Verso, taking out his wallet and virtually disappearing beneath the scrum. Following my own tastes, I look around and find exactly what I'm after. Joseph Brodsky holds Anna Akhmatova, who in turn embraces Mandelshtam, who incorporates Dostoyevsky, who digests Gogol, who has assimilated Pushkin. Pushkin opens up too, and inside him is the very tiniest and most indecipherable something. Who?

Could it possibly be Diderot? Never mind. I'm here and, as they told me at the Kafé Kosmos, it's a writers' city, a set of telescoped images, illusory and ever-shifting, and yet presumably very real and just waiting for us over the other side of this vast dockyard wall.

Malcolm Bradbury, *To the Hermitage* (2000)

* * *

*The Neva may be wide and beautiful but – at least when Duncan Fallowell visited the city – it had other characteristics too ...*

After that we decide simply to walk for a while. Over the Kirovsky Bridge, built in England at the turn of the century but too short — the Russians had to add an extra arch. As you walk across, the great size of the Neva becomes increasingly apparent. Buildings tilt back from each other on opposite banks in accordance with the curvature of the earth. Every seventy feet or so a fisherman stands patiently, hoping to pull out a semi-poisonous sprat with his rod. Very soothing under a pacific blue sky until you look over the parapet and down at the water and see thick muscles of strong currents whipping past the stanchions.

Dima says that not long after the Revolution an English company proposed to clean the Neva free of charge if they could keep everything they found in it: the Soviets refused. In 1917 people threw in jewels and gold, hoping to recover them at a later date. 'I know someone whose father threw in a gold sword! But we have never cleaned the river properly ourselves so — jump in, Dooncan. See what you can find. But be careful. The whole of Mendeleyev's table is in that river!'

Duncan Fallowell, *One Hot Summer in St Petersburg* (1994)

*Even the less obviously attractive waterways can offer their own delights.*

The Obvodny[1] Canal is not the most picturesque conduit in town, but since there is not a corner of Old St Petersburg that is not picturesque, the Obvodny has a charm all its own. The water is sluggish and low, a pale coffee colour, and the inclined concrete banks are littered with junk dried out by the summer's heat. This is a nineteenth-century manufacturing district of redbrick factories with crenellations like forts, a poor area but attractive, with trees and cobbled streets. There is a brightness to the light and a freshness to the air which says that the sea is not far away.

Duncan Fallowell, *One Hot Summer in St Petersburg* (1994)

✣ ✣ ✣

*Contemporary poet Sergei Stratanovsky fills out the picture of the same area.*

When our family moved to the Obvodny area from Nevsky Prospect, my grandmother was heartbroken. Every time she had to travel to the centre, she would say, 'I'm going to the city.' Before the revolution Obvodny was not considered part of the city at all. In 1998 I happened to be in Leiden and found that they have their own Obvodny Canal there, too. Of course, Peter originally designed St Petersburg on a Dutch model, and when Obvodny was being built they bore this in mind. There are a great many western influences here. Obvodny Canal was the principal trading artery of the city, with innovative looms and steam boilers arriving from England, and it was here that the first factories were built. Obvodny was a hive of activity back then, full of barges and ships. I was too late to see any of that. As far back as I can recall it has been silent and dark. Except for intellectual life. There were gatherings every Friday on Kurly-

---

1 literally 'by-pass' (Ed.)

andskaya Street for religious and philosophical readings, and Viktor Sosnora's literary club, which was held right next door to the military academy where Lermontov once studied... It was a good place to lose yourself in, among the drunks, the thugs and the galoshes-makers from the Red Triangle rubber factory.

The old factories are either being pulled down now, or just left empty and falling into ruin, or they are being converted. The archives, the equipment, the very architecture itself is all being destroyed, despite the fact that modern architecture sprang entirely from the industrial, and the factories and plants of the nineteenth century were designed by genuinely superb artists. They were innovators and inventors. They constructed a city within a city, and managed enormous spaces; a whole world that is invisible from the outside. Life inside was entirely self-contained and unique. If you look outside, however, the buildings entirely match the spirit of Petersburg. They are uniform and horizontal. 'Style Moderne' for the tram depots, Classicism for the provisions stores. The chimneys of the Stieglitz factory harmonise with the dome on Smolny Cathedral, and the towers on top of the Red Triangle are as rhythmical as the Admiralty ... Except that nobody sees this. The public eye is untrained. Foreigners see it; they gasp and swoon in amazement. Their own old factories now house museums.

It is primarily the Red Triangle factory that sets the mood of the district. It is quintessentially urbanistic. The blocks closest to the factory make up the most proletarian part of Obvodny. People lived and worked here in my day as though it was still the nineteenth century. Smoke, blackened faces and clods of mud ... When I read the German expressionists I thought immediately of Obvodny. Nowadays they hold rock concerts at the Triangle. But back then it all looked hopelessly gloomy.

Sergei Stratanovsky, 'Obvodny Canal' in *St Petersburg
as Cinema* (2011) (ed. Lubov Arkus) translated by
Sergei Afonin and Alice Jondorf

✳ ✳ ✳

*Andrei Bely's novel* Petersburg *depicts the city at the beginning of the twentieth century, at a time of polit-ical unrest. Bely (1880–1934) often satirizes the styles and 'incompetencies' of other writers – as in the in the first main paragraph below (very windy and misty at the same time; smooth walls criss-crossed with lines …) and greatly influenced the Symbolist and Modernist movements. He is sometimes compared to James Joyce. (Nabokov considered the novels of Bely and Joyce as the highest literary achievements of the twentieth century.) The taster below is from the prize-winning translation by John Elsworth.*

And so Nikolai Apollonovich sat in the darkness.

And while he sat there the Neva still opened out between Alexander Square and Millionnaia; the stone arch of the Winter Canal displayed its lachrymose expanse; the Neva thrust itself from there in an onslaught of moist wind; the fleeting surfaces of its waters glinted from there soundlessly, their pale gleam reflected furiously in the mists. The smooth walls of the four-storeyed palace wing, criss-crossed with lines, glistened with malice in the moonlight.

No one, nothing.

As ever the canal disgorged its choleric water into the Neva: the same bridge still bent over it; as ever a nightly female shadow ran out on to the bridge, to – cast herself into the river? … Liza's[1] shadow? No, not Liza's, but simply – some Petersburg woman's; the woman ran this way, but did not throw herself into the river: crossing the Winter Canal, she ran hurriedly away from a yellow house on the Gagarin Embank-ment, beneath which she would stand every evening, gazing for a long time at the windows.

---

1   A reference to Liza in Tchaikovsky's opera based on Pushkin's *The Queen of Spades.* (Ed.)

The quiet plashing was left behind her: in front a square spread out; endless statues, green-tinged bronze, appeared from all sides above the dark-red walls; Hercules and Poseidon surveyed the expanses by night as well; across the Neva a dark mass rose up – in the outlines of islands and houses; and cast its amber eyes sadly into the mist; and it seemed it was weeping; a row of lights along the bank dropped tears into the Neva.

Andrei Bely, *Petersburg* (1916)
translated by John Elsworth

❋ ❋ ❋

*It is a tradition, on one's wedding day, to go around the city and take photographs at St Petersburg's 'sacred' places: Olivier Rolin records a frequent sight on the Neva's embankment during the lighter evenings.*

Seven o'clock in the evening. The grey waters of the Neva swell around Vasilievsky Island, rising below the rostral columns of raspberry red. At the far end are the low fortifications and the tapering pagoda of the Peter and Paul fortress. Hydrofoils pass beneath the bridges, trailing scarves of spray. Guardsmen are busying about a gun-carriage on the quayside. She poses in a dress of white muslin on the arm of her husband in his blue uniform. She has the jolly red face of a peasant; the muslin blows about in the biting wind; she'll end up catching pneumonia – she'll 'snuff it on her wedding day', as the song goes. Photo. Glasses are unpacked from a bag, a bottle of champagne is opened, glasses are clinked between the fishermen with their rods, in front of the green and white colonnades of the Winter Palace. Above, under the rostral columns, waits the big black 'limousine' from the Palace of Weddings carrying, on its roof, the traditional bells hanging from metallic rings. A sudden shower flattens the muslin against the bride's robust body.

Olivier Rolin, *In Russia* (1987)
translated by Erica King

✵ ✵ ✵

*Some more on Vasilievsky Island, this time from*
*Petersburger Yury Piryutko, curator of the State*
*Museum of City Sculpture (part of the Alexander*
*Nevsky Monastery).*

Vasilievsky Island was designed by Le Blond as an ideal
citadel town which would incorporate all life's essentials.
And although his concept was rejected, and Trezzini hastily
changed it into a land-based plan, for a long time Vasilievsky
still tried to remain the centre of the city. Eventually it became
our Sorbonne. First of all, the Cadet Corps moved here, then
the Academy of Arts, the Mining Institute, the University,
the Bestuzhev Courses for women … It became the realm of
student and artistic culture. The island has essentially always
been that little bit closer to Europe than the rest. At first it
was foreigners who lived here, especially the Germans, who
called it 'Basil Insel'; they built their own churches and baked
their own little vanilla pastries, whose scent floated in the air
above the island. There are still a great number of little cafés,
snack bars and bistros. There are 'sacred' cellars where coffee
is brewed at student prices, and other little nooks and cran-
nies. There is also the typical Petersburg network of intercon-
necting courtyards. In a strange way, Le Blond's plan has been
partially implemented. There really are all life's essentials on
Vasilievsky Island. You could be born in the Ott Clinic[1], and
be buried at the Smolenskoye Cemetery. There really is everything you'd ever need here. […]

The Smolenka is the only river in the centre of the city
whose banks have not been tamed. It is still possible to go
down the muddy bank right to the quiet, dark water. But now,
with Golodai Island being actively developed, the situation is

---

1  A leading, specialised clinic at the Russian Academy of Medical Sciences Research
Institute named after Dmitry Ott – one of the best places to give birth! (Ed.)

changing before our very eyes. Business centres are creeping up to the gates of the cemetery, and skyscrapers are going up right behind them.

Yury Piryutko, 'Vasilievsky Island' in *Petersburg as Cinema* (2011) (ed. Lubov Arkus) translated by Sergei Afonin and Alice Jondorf

✳ ✳ ✳

*And Rolin again, this time on the outlying reaches of the city's waters.*

To the north of the big islands, Vasilievsky and Petersburg Island, lie a whole network of smaller islands in the Neva delta. It's a land of mists and potholes, wet roads beneath black and white trees, former aristocratic residencies that have become clinics all mixed up with the awful houses inhabited by the privileged people of today: almost superfluous to say that the Kirov Islands, those 'marshy banks' described in the prologue to *The Bronze Horseman*[1], are a melancholy place. A tall zinc chimney, from which issues peat smoke with a penetrating odour, eats away the roofs of the Yelagin Palace; the columns of painted wood on a nineteenth-century theatre crumble away next to some piles of gravel, a rusty concrete mixer. Not one person out walking, not a movement, nothing but bare trees, clouds, and water… Not a sound, except for drips falling from branches, an occasional bird-call. More than anywhere else this place lends plausibility to de Custine's prediction of the inevitable disappearance of 'this creation of Peter I, like a soap bubble in a puff of wind'. Beyond the river, the smoke from the factories hangs over the suburbs along the Chernaya River. The river itself is a sort of sewer where petals of oil undulate, a film of the stuff that doesn't in the least bother the decadent ducks.

Olivier Rolin, *In Russia* (1987)
translated by Erica King

---

1    A brief outline of the poem appears in the footnote on page 113 (Ed.)

✳ ✳ ✳

*With this portrait of Kronstadt – the sea-port town on Kotlin Isalnd, thirty kilometres west of St Petersburg proper – artist Oleg Kotelnikov reminds us that St Petersburg's waters are not just the canals and the Neva but the open sea and all that goes with it.*

Kronstadt was a closed and inaccessible town. In the past it was impossible to gain access without a special pass. The pass regime has been revoked, but this sense of inaccessibility has remained to this day. There is an elusive element of shape-shifting, even when compared to St Petersburg's legendary transformative skills. Kronstadt is built above the water, but appears to be structured according to the principle of reflection. There must be a reason why the two most famous structures on the island – the enormous Kronstadt Naval Cathedral and the huge Petrovsky dry dock – are like pyramids in reverse. If you go for a walk on Kronstadt – and it is an absolute delight to stroll here – you start walking in circles without even noticing it. Here you are walking on cast iron, which is the material still covering many of the causeways in Kronstadt. In the old days, all of Kronstadt was paved in cast iron to make it easier to transport armaments. This being said, there is no atmosphere of gloom or threat: instead, like most port cities the town could be called an island of love. Even St John of Kronstadt[1], who was sent here to admonish, was powerless to overcome the lax attitudes. Kronstadt fits so perfectly into the surrounding landscape; it is impossible to change it. Old-fashioned, neglected, pure, unconventional and austere.

The neat, even houses that seem to be trimmed and lined up in ranks perfectly match the image of the boring, measured life

---

1   St John of Kronstadt (1829–1908) first canonised by the Russian Church Abroad in 1964, and in 1990 by the Russian Orthodox Church. Worked, from 1855, at the naval base cathedral of St Andrew's. (Ed.)

you would find in the provincial backwaters. This unsophisticated aspect of Kronstadt is also discernible in the fact that there seems to be a distillation of time from eras past. The fading texture of Soviet Kronstadt can be felt especially strongly. The town is not adorned with the 'costume jewellery' of advertising, and a certain Soviet poverty can be felt, although not in an oppressive way. Sometimes it appears that life has completely abandoned the town, and that all the townsfolk have left and crossed over to the mainland. The impression of a territory that has been neglected and left without heirs is particularly acute as you come onto the Kronstadt Bypass Canal, whose quiet waters reflect the brick fortifications of the arsenal. Enormous stocks of ammunition from World War II are still stored within its walls to this day. The memories of other wars seem still to be drifting through the streets and squares that are now quiet for evermore.

The front door to Kronstadt and its seafront is the Merchant Harbour. There is a long pier leading to the lighthouse, with a great many wharfs that picturesquely divide the gulf into separate segments. The quiet cosiness and emptiness of the streets is suddenly transformed into a cheerful noisy crowd, with tourists, sailors, girls and fishermen. The grey hulls of ships and submarines from the Baltic Fleet lie in their moorings. The ferry to Oranienbaum leaves from here and large ships can be seen unhurriedly gliding through the Marine Channel to Petersburg, or sailing out into the Baltic.

Oleg Kotelnikov, 'Kronstadt' in *St Petersburg as Cinema* (2011) (ed. Lubov Arkus) translated by Sergei Afonin and Alice Jondorf

# Excellent prospekts

*St Petersburg is justly famous for its elegant architecture and broad thoroughfares or 'prospekts' – of which Nevsky Prospekt is the best known and most frequently written about. (Booklovers should visit the famous 'Dom Knigi'[1] bookshop at number 28. A detail from its frontage is shown above.) In this section we enjoy some of the city's wonderful buildings and sights. First, we arrive with enthusiastic visitor Duncan Fallowell.*

In a glare of sunshine St Petersburg begins to zoom towards us, its manifold façades sliding back on right and left in two endless strips of architectural plates. This is a city not of houses but of palatial blocks built on wide streets and canals; and

---

1  Literally 'House of Books'. Open continuously since 1911 – even during the Siege, it occupies the former headquarters of the Singer sewing machine company. Well worth a visit – and it has an English language section. (Ed.)

because height was always restricted, and the terrain is flat, they are under a huge sky. Despite ubiquitous dust, the confectionary colours of the stucco come through. Golden domes and spires break the pitching, chimneyed roofline with an opulent energy. Occasionally there are green trees and everywhere fanciful bridges over curving streaks of water. For a Londoner each view has an unearthly emptiness and integrated beauty that is spell-binding.

Leonid swerves to avoid a heap of rubble which rises up on our side of the road (there's plenty of rubble around but no rubbish – they must recycle everything), bounces into and out of a pothole, and we hit Nevsky Prospekt. Crowds! Traffic! But almost at once we veer out of it and round to the right, round to the left – a jostle of cadets in white caps skip between cars and bubble off across Palace Square, the Winter Palace shimmers past in an electrifying dazzle and is gone ... Leonid sweats at the wheel.

'Such a beautiful day.'

'I hate the heat,' he replies. 'I like winter. In winter you can cross-country ski.'

'My God, that's a beach in the centre of town!'

And it is – the genuine article, a long golden strand running beneath the bastions of the Peter and Paul Fortress on the bank of the Neva, chock-a-block with sun-worshippers, a few of whom venture into the oily brown slurrups of water. The Neva is very wide and so the heart of the city is an enormous expanse of water, majestic and irregular; closer examination reveals its majesty to be riven with dangerous currents and eddies.

Up at the Kirov Park, where riders and keep-fit enthusiasts strike heroic attitudes, Leonid points out Sosnovy Bor, the local nuclear power station trembling sixty kilometres away across the Gulf of Finland. It spat out some quite nasty stuff just before I arrived. Back down Kirovsky Prospekt with its mountainous apartment blocks, designed by and for laudanum-swilling neurotics circa 1900 – over Kirovsky Bridge – another park, and a technicolor prodigy! What in heaven's name is it? (My solemn cicerone offers information only upon request.)

'Church of Blood.'

'Why?'

'On site of Alexander II's assassination.' [...]

Nevsky Prospekt incidentally is the only thoroughfare in St Petersburg which is busy – and it's *always* busy. The pavements are lined with market stalls, and alongside them chorus lines of individuals stand motionlessly, each holding up a single object for sale – a book, a bottle, a jumper, anything. The heterogeneous crowd surges past them – office workers, shoppers, families, students, tourists, old men with a row of military medals pinned to frayed jackets, gypsy beggars barefoot and filthy. The young people are strikingly sexy, with a dash of bravura or fierceness in them and something spaced-out too. Slavs often have remarkable eyes and mouths. The weakest feature is the putty nose but this often confers charm to a face which would otherwise be too superb. The racial mix is very apparent and their bodies are well-made, thanks to work, exercise, national service: straight backs, firm limbs, a natural physical confidence in the walk. Girls show their legs in very short skirts, and boys their muscles in tight coloured singlets. It is quite believable that these people have been Europe's most resolute twentieth-century empire builders. But the hard life tells. Evidence of physical damage is widespread among all categories, often carried off with flair; scars, bandages, arms in slings or plaster, bashed noses, black eyes, purple bruises. Yes, damage can be colourful – uncovered lesions are marked with medicated paint in red, orange or green.

And uniforms can be colourful. These are no longer the uniforms of cavalry officers of the Imperial Guard who wore white elkskin breeches, nor those of the Circassian Guard who wore white kaftans with gold belts and high white lambskin caps; but they are nonetheless very colourful by non-royal standards. Black, grey, white, blue, green, khaki, decorated with gold and red; caps forward over eyes or level or on backs of heads, belts round trousers or round the waist of jackets Cossack-style, trousers over boots or tucked into boots; uniforms singly or collectively wherever you look. This prevalence is not threatening because the men inside them do not strut. They are part of the normal human round, picturesque, often at ease, chatting, smoking, sometimes relaxed to the point of loucheness. [...]

We take off past the Moscow Station, rattle down to the Alexander Nevsky Monastery (where the quintessence of damage is lined up on the Avenue of Cripples: bundles with missing parts, whole missing sections, each with its grimy upturned hat on the pathway), sweep up abreast the river to the blue and white, gold-tipped ensemble of the Smolny Convent. Observing a few silent minutes in front of it, while Leonid mops his deliquescence, the question which forms itself is: is this the prettiest arrangement that was ever put up anywhere in the world? [...]

My head is a jangle of snapshots but it is now clear that I am living in a unique habitat, a great eighteenth- and nineteenth-century city that is *absolutely complete*. This is the only thing which is clear, and the joy of it makes one afraid, that its completeness will not survive, because from a maintenance point of view we are in a disaster zone. What makes the historic centre complete is not simply that all the buildings are present — though for a major city of five million inhabitants that is unique enough — but that there is none of the commercial clutter which overlays every other city of comparable size. Also, Soviet architects were here enlightened on the subject of context. At the few infill sights created by the war, they produced (during the height of the Modern Movement) buildings in a vigorous classical style. Even Stalin respected the skyline.

Duncan Fallowell, *One Hot Summer in St Petersburg* (1994)

*Poet Joseph Brodsky celebrates the city's European look.*

In the epochs following Peter's, they started to build, not separate buildings but whole architectural ensembles, or, more precisely, architectural landscapes. Untouched till then by European architectural styles, Russia opened the sluices and the baroque and classicism gushed into and inundated the streets and embankments of St Petersburg. Organ-like forests of columns sprang high and lined up on the palatial façades ad infinitum in their miles-long Euclidian triumph. For the last half of the eighteenth and the first quarter of the nineteenth century, this city became a real safari for the best Italian and French architects, sculptors, and decorators. In acquiring its imperial look, this city was scrupulous to the very last detail: the granite revetment of the rivers and canals, the elaborate character of every curl on their cast-iron grilles, speak for themselves. So does the décor of the inner chambers in the palaces and country residences of the Tsar's family and the nobility, the décor whose variety and exquisiteness verge on obscenity.

Joseph Brodsky, 'A Guide to a Renamed City' (1979)
in *Less Than One: Selected Essays*

* * *

*Having already docked (in the 'Neva-land' section)
with the party of Enlightenment pilgrims in Malcolm
Bradbury's* To the Hermitage, *we are now going to
join them for the start of their conducted tour of the
city with Francophile Russian tour guide Galina.*

The bus sets off through the dockyard, past the various floating hotels, and passes out into the streets of the city. The view is not utopian. We're bouncing violently up and down over crane-tracks, potholes, tramlines, the wear and tear of a hard winter.

None of this deters Galina who, in her soft clinging Poiret, stands at the front addressing us all as the driver stares up at her dubiously. 'I will tell you a story of very good luck. Maybe you know, Petersburg is not always a lucky city. It has suffered everything. Flood, fire, earthquake, whirlwind, plague, all kinds of diseases. It has had repressions, rebellions, purges, revolutions. Everyone has tried to attack us, the Swedes, the Danes, the French, the Germans. We still remember the 900-day siege, when the Germans were on every side of the city, bombing us every night, and parents dragged the bodies of their children through the streets to the cemeteries. How can I say luck?'

'Tell us,' says Bo.

'It was only this,' says Galina. 'The city, you know, was named again after Lenin, but he hated it, and the capital was moved back to Moscow. And that is why you don't see those dreadful pointed ministries, the silly towers, the great Marxist steeples. And even when it was bombed and we rebuilt it, we rebuilt it as it was, a French city in the north. That is our luck, and soon you will see it through the window.'

'Where are we now, Galina?' asks Verso.

'Oh, this is Grand Avenue, also called Bolshoi Prospekt.' To tell the truth, the prospect is not impressive. We're bouncing down the dullest of avenues. People walk everywhere doing nothing very much. Children play between the tramlines, babushkas carry wrapped bundles along rough sidewalks. The aroma of dead smoke and wet oil does not fade. The apartment blocks have that battered and peeling look, the air of eternal neglect, that is the truest note of East European gloom. [...]

While we've talked, our bus has switched streets, moved over a block. The scene has changed, our views have completely altered. Now we ride along a splendid waterside embankment, looking across the width of a river at another splendid waterside embankment. Near us, on the edge of fast-flowing waters, two huge and top-hatted Egyptian sphinxes sit gazing enigmatically at each other, while at the same time framing up our own view of the scene. Beyond runs the wide Neva, where white tourboats probably already filled with our own Japanese tourists are shuttling back and forth. On the further embankment rise up large towers, bulbous onion domes, fine golden flèches.

'Now you ride on University Embankment,' says Galina. 'Here on Vasilievsky Island Peter built all his academies. Here is the Petersburg University, which I hope you will visit. Gogol went to teach world history there, you remember. His problem was only he didn't know any. There is the Kunstkammer, over here is the great Academical Clock. Now look across the river over there. Do you notice a green square? In it, something like a missile pointing at the sky? Do you know it?'

'Isn't it the Bronze Horseman?' asks Lars Person.

'*Oui, mon petit,* the statue of Falconet. Even this was by a Frenchman, you see. And now, *mes amis*, I will say nothing at all, even though you understand this is very difficult for me. But in one moment you will understand why.'

Eight Enlightenment Pilgrims, we look around, staring from bank to bank. Only one or two of us have been to the city before, and yet everything we see is more than half-familiar, spoken of by old repute. The Kunstkammer: that was where Peter kept all his waxworks and his odd curiosities, even down to the teeth he pulled. The flèche on this side is surely the Peter and Paul Fortress, where an ancestor of Vladimir Nabokov was the governor who imprisoned Dostoyevsky. There are other flèches, other domes: the high one on the further bank, beyond the English Embankment, must surely be Saint Isaac's Cathedral. The fine façades on each of the two banks look out at each other, just like the two solemn sphinxes, shaping and enclosing a distinctive space.

At the heart of this space is the water, into which all the buildings and both embankments seem to stare. The afternoon air is feeling cold now, and the sky seems to have purified itself to a clear lucid blue. The red afternoon sun is just beginning to dip. Ahead of us a stone bridge spans the Neva, joining the facing embankments to each other. Beyond, where several rivers seem to meet together, something strange seems to have happened to the light. In the clear bright air, the river itself seems to dissolve here: turn into luminous matter, become an encrimsoned shimmer, sky, sunlight and river all disintegrating into each other. Above this floating mirror or luminescent lake stands a row of splendid buildings, linked together, and suspended there as if by the forces of a mirage. The buildings, painted in green and white, are in the classical style, simple at heart and yet highly embellished, their walls caked with baroque pilasters and elaborate window frames. The roofs are verdigrised copper, and the façades run on and on, a Turneresque battery of Venetian palaces overlooking the waterless water.

'Notice, I say nothing at all,' says Galina. 'But I think you know what it is.' Indeed we do, Galina. Though most of us haven't seen these façades before, we've also known them for ever. They're the Winter Palace. They're the Hermitage ...

Malcolm Bradbury, To the Hermitage (2000)

✤ ✤ ✤

*One of St Petersburg's most eminent scholars and cultural figures of the twentieth century, Dmitry Likhachev (1906–1999), made some interesting observations about the city's characteristic architectural lines ... as well as its colours.*

Perhaps the most salient characteristic of town planning in Leningrad's appearance is the pre-eminence of horizontals over verticals. Horizontals form the foundation on which all other lines are drawn. The pre-eminence of horizontals is dictated by the presence of numerous waterways: Bolshaya Neva, Malaya Neva, Bolshaya Nevka, Malaya Nevka, Fontanka, Moyka, the

Griboedov and Kryukov canals and so forth. The contiguity of water and land creates ideal horizontal lines, especially if the land is framed by a dense array of embankments. The embankments constitute the second line, which is perhaps somewhat irregular, but just as resolute. It is as if Leningrad is doubly underlined. At the same time, we must take into account that the Neva generally remains at a constant level within its banks (except during rare autumn flooding); this level is, however, very high. Water in Leningrad fills up the city as if to the very brim. This always surprises visitors, who are used to cities on rivers with 'normal' cycles (higher water levels during spring flooding and in the autumn, with lower ones in the summer). [...]

'Low, marshy banks' are perhaps the only material feature of Petersburg to be found in either Pushkin or Dostoyevsky.

But even if we move away from the bodies of water, we find the same horizontal lines, determined by the almost perfectly flat ground on which the city is built. Continuous rows of houses are an extremely typical feature of Petersburg-Leningrad.

Due to the absence of rises and descents, the streets become the city's interior. Dostoyevsky treats the life of streets and squares precisely as an interior (especially in *Crime and Punishment*). Gardens and boulevards are fitted in among these densely built-up streets, which serves as yet another expression of the city's horizontality. Especially typical in this sense is Vasilievsky Island, where the very term 'street' disappears from street names. There are only three 'prospekts' and 'lines', the lines of houses.

The city's defining elements are the three spires: at the Peter and Paul Fortress, at the Admiralty and at the Mikhailovsky Castle. They appear to constitute perpendiculars to the horizontal lines and do not contradict them, but rather emphasize their existence. The spires are echoed by tall bell towers – the one designed by Chevakinsky on the Kryukov Canal and the other at the church in Sennaya Square (now demolished).

The mighty mass of St Isaac's Cathedral with the golden (and thus 'unarchitectural') dome was supposed to create a second centre for Leningrad, a centre constructed to mimic the role St. Peter's Cathedral plays in Rome. [...]

Among Leningrad's other traits, I consider the following two as most significant: the city's palette and its harmonious conjunction of great styles.

The colour of the houses plays a very important role in Leningrad. Few large European cities can compare to Leningrad in this respect. Leningrad needs colour: fog and rain obscure it more than they do any other city. That is why brick was never left unplastered, and the plaster required colour.

Dmitry Likhachev, 'The Skyline of the City on the Neva'
*Our Heritage. 1989. N° 1* translated by Maya Vinokour

❊ ❊ ❊

*At one of the darkest points of the Second World War, Sacheverell Sitwell – brother of Edith Sitwell (the poet probably best remembered for* Façade*) – decided to defy the mood of the moment and recreate a day in the life of St Petersburg in the year 1868. He concentrates on the city's beauty and the life of the wealthy, and may be accused by some of a fanciful romanticism about the city (which he had not visited) – and yet he does capture some of the truth of the place. And it's an utterly charming little book. Here, his focus is the Winter Palace.*

The Winter Palace, with its half-mile of great apartments on three floors, along the Neva, could have been built in no city but St Petersburg. Even the fact that nearly the whole of its interior was destroyed by fire in 1837, and rebuilt within a year, has made little difference to the original intention. Inter-

nally, it is largely a series of great halls, of no particular importance in themselves, decorated chiefly in the style of Nicholas
I, and forming a suitable background for the pomp of Court
ceremonies. At the same time, and owing to the scale of these,
it is more interesting than the generality of Royal palaces in
their ugliness and monotony. It compares, in ordinary, with the
palaces of Caserta and Madrid. But the Russian extravagance
puts it by itself. [...]

As we get nearer, driving through the great arch of the Etat
Major,[1] the entire Winter Palace comes into view blazing with
lights from every window. The horses' hooves sound loud in
the archway, and more and more of the endless palace unrolls
in perspective, in front across the square. Carriages and sledges
come in from every direction and make for different entrances,
the stream of all that silent traffic being broken by the Alexander Column, a huge monolith of granite with a statue of
an archangel a hundred and fifty feet into the air, and great
braziers burning at its foot. The polished granite looks so cold;
but, turning back, the great archway, behind, and the advancing
wings of the Etat Major, so immense in scale, enclose the square
and seem to shelter the coachmen and footmen who warm
themselves at the braziers, and watch more sleighs arriving and
the glittering lights. We are half-way across the square, passing
other sledges that have their harness covered with blue netting
in order that the snow shall not blow back upon the dresses
for the ball. At this moment the whole bulk of the palace, with
its three storeys, rises up like a ship before a rowing boat. The
further windows, at both ends, lose their separate illumination
and flatten out into one great whole that lies to either side,
and high above. There is an advancing portion, with a porch
in which we wait for the sledge in front to drop its passengers,
and drive away. This is the Ambassadors' entrance. There are

---

1   The great, curved General Staff building of the army, on Palace Square. (Ed.)

four other entrances. Grand Dukes come in by the Saltykov: Court officials by the Imperial: Civil officials by the Jurdan: military officers by the Commanders'. Court servants come forward and take the coats and furs. We are at the foot of the great staircase, the Escalier des Ambassadeurs, with wide and shallow steps of marble, thickly carpeted, and climbing in two flights. Upon the four other staircases, at different ends of the palace, it is the same. Every step is crowded, and the guests climb slowly into the golden halls above.

Sacheverell Sitwell, *Valse des Fleurs* (1941)

✳ ✳ ✳

*The Winter Palace forms part of the Hermitage. A visit with Duncan Fallowell ...*

Not everyone knows that the Hermitage is a chain of linked buildings of which the Winter Palace, though by far the largest, is only one. The smaller buildings make a kind of sense but the Winter Palace itself, though uniformly rococo without (its fronts are painted aquamarine but before the Revolution the exterior was red), is spectacularly incoherent within. Indeed the whole linkage is a centreless constellation of corridors, landings, staircases, rooms great and small, in disparate styles of sumptuous, sometimes mind-boggling embellishment, with no aggregate effect except that of disorientation among copious treasure and untold marvels: it is for getting lost in.

One of the most breathtaking interiors I couldn't locate the entrance to, or identify on the floor plan, and only discovered it by crossing a gallery at one end – a powderblue and white plaster hall with clustered pillars and four white petalled domes like the thousand-petalled lotuses of Brahma, Strawberry Hill meets the Arabian Nights, yet so light-hearted and unstrenuously itself. Absolutely enormous too, but – I couldn't find it again. [...]

43

Through this galaxy of worlds called the Hermitage shuffle parties with guides in diverse tongues, and curious tales may be overheard … In Tsarist days the doors of the Malachite Room were guarded by huge Negroes, Coptic Ethiopians. Pushkin's great-grandfather was the Ethiopian favourite of Peter the Great, who had been presented to the Tsar by the Sultan via Count Tolstoy, Russian ambassador to the Sublime Porte[1]. Peter loved his Ethiopian, granted him many privileges, and used his belly as a pillow …

Duncan Fallowell, One Hot Summer in St Petersburg (1994)

✳ ✳ ✳

*Back in the company of Sacheverell Sitwell, we pass from the Winter Palace to Nevsky Prospekt.*

The façade of the Winter Palace stretches for nearly half a mile along the Neva, that frozen river, till we reach the still vaster Admiralty, and passing under the tropheal arch of the Etat Major, third of these gigantic buildings, turn a corner, and are in a moment in the Nevsky Prospekt. […]

In the Nevsky Prospekt the spectacle is such as could not be imagined by those who have not seen it. A street three miles long and leading from the Champs Elysées to Whitechapel or Mile End Road. Down at the far end, which tails off as the crow flies, towards Moscow, the buildings, the people, and even the colour of the sky are already Asiatic, in the extent to which that word means wars and plagues and barbarian invasions. The first suburbs of another and an endless world, all plains and distance. Churches and synagogues, in plenty, help this illusion by their tawdry architecture. It could be thus all the way from Petersburg to Peking. In the other direction, towards the Neva, we begin to pass great porticos and palaces. And the colonnade of the Kazan cathedral, a semicircle of columns,

---

1   The government of the Ottoman Empire. (Ed.)

barbarian echo of the Roman travertine, but which, like the spire of the Admiralty, is in sign of St Petersburg. The painted shop signs, for those who cannot read, have given place to gilt lettering, dress-makers, jewellers, hairdressers. In one window the latest crinolines from Paris are displayed; or hung up in bunches like bright bird cages above the doors, all in the flaring gaslight as we glide past over the snows. Cakes and sweets in the confectioner's windows, especially at Elliseiv's, are like a childhood's dream. We pass by a confiserie of which the sign or emblem is a little shepherd girl. The windows are stacked with barley sugar, in stooks and pyramids of twisted pillars, while all the fantasy of a Gallic mind, in exile, shows itself in chocolates that are shaped like marennes or portugaises of the sandy flats, ranged upon green paper, ready for sale, in the wicker baskets of the oystermen; in white hens' eggs packed in miniature wooden crates, whole and unbroken, save for an invisible perforation through which liquid chocolate has been blown in to load and fill the shells; in chocolates flecked with gold leaf; sweets in infinity flavoured with all fruits; and dragées of as many colours as there are court ladies in *The Sleeping Beauty*.

Sacheverell Sitwell, *Valse des Fleurs* (1941)

❉ ❉ ❉

*One of the most famous portraits of Nevsky Prospekt was written by Nikolai Gogol (1809–1852) – best known for his novel* Dead Souls *and wonderful stories like 'The Nose' and 'The Overcoat'.*

There is nothing better than Nevsky Prospekt, at least not in Petersburg; for there it is everything. What does this street – the beauty of our capital – not shine with! I know that not one of its pale and clerical inhabitants would trade Nevsky Prospekt for anything in the world. Not only the one who is twenty-five years old, has an excellent moustache and a frock coat of an amazing cut, but even the one who has white hair sprouting on his chin and a head as smooth as a silver dish, he, too, is enchanted with Nevsky Prospekt. And the ladies! Oh, the ladies find Nevsky Prospekt still more pleasing. And who does not find it pleasing? The moment you enter Nevsky Prospekt, it already smells of nothing but festivity. Though you may have some sort of necessary, indispensable business, once you enter it you are sure to forget all business. Here is the only place where people do not go out of necessity, where they are not driven by the need and mercantile interest that envelop the whole of Petersburg. A man met on Nevsky Prospekt seems less of an egoist than on Morskaya, Gorokhovaya, Liteiny, Meshchanskaya, and other streets, where greed, self-interest, and necessity show on those walking or flying by in carriages and drozhkies. Nevsky Prospekt is the universal communication of Petersburg. Here the inhabitant of the Petersburg or Vyborg side who has not visited his friend in Peski or the Moscow Gate for several years can be absolutely certain of meeting him. No directory or inquiry office will provide such reliable information as Nevsky Prospekt. All-powerful Nevsky Prospekt! The only entertainment for a poor man at the Petersburg feast! How clean-swept are its sidewalks, and, God, how many feet have left their traces on it! The clumsy, dirty boot of the retired soldier, under the weight of which the very granite seems to crack, and the miniature shoe, light as smoke, of a young lady, who turns her head to the glittering shop windows as a sunflower turns toward the sun, and the clanking sword of a hope-filled sub-lieutenant that leaves a sharp scratch on it – everything wreaks upon it the power of strength or the power of weakness. What a quick phantasmagoria is performed on it in the course of a single day! How many changes it undergoes in the course of a single day and night!

Let us begin from earliest morning, when the whole of Petersburg smells of hot, freshly baked bread and is filled with old women in tattered dresses and coats carrying out their raids on churches and compassionate passers-by. At that time Nevsky Prospekt is empty: the stout shop owners and their sales clerks are still asleep in their Holland nightshirts or are soaping their noble cheeks and drinking coffee; beggars gather near the pastry shops, where a sleepy Ganymede, who yesterday was flying about with chocolate like a fly, crawls out, tieless, broom in hand, and tosses them stale cakes and leftovers. Down the streets trudge useful folk: Russian muzhiks[1] pass by occasionally, hurrying to work, their boots crusted with lime that even the Ekaterininsky Canal, famous for its cleanness, would be unable to wash off. At that time it is usually unfitting for ladies to go about, because the Russian people like to express themselves in such sharp terms as they would probably not hear even in the theatre. An occasional sleepy clerk will plod by, briefcase under his arm, if he has to pass Nevsky Prospekt on his way to the office. One may say decidedly that at that time, that is, until twelve o'clock, Nevsky Prospekt does not constitute anyone's goal, it serves only as a means: it gradually fills with people who have their own occupations, their own cares, their own vexations, and do not think about it at all. The Russian muzhik talks about his ten coppers or seven groats, the old men and women wave their arms and talk to themselves, sometimes with quite expressive gestures, but no one listens to them or laughs at them, except perhaps some urchins in hempen blouses, with empty bottles or repaired shoes in their hands, racing along Nevsky Prospekt like lightning. At that time, however you may be dressed, even if you have a peaked cap on your head instead of a hat, even if your collar sticks out too far over your tie – no one will notice it.

At twelve o'clock Nevsky Prospekt is invaded by tutors of all nations with their charges in cambric collars. English Joneses and French Coques walk hand in hand with the charges

---

1   Peasants – usually poor, having been serfs before the 1861 emancipation. (Ed.)

entrusted to their parental care and, with proper gravity, explain to them that the signs over the shops are made so that by means of them one may learn what is to be found inside the shop. Governesses, pale misses and rosy Slavs, walk majestically behind their light, fidgety girls, telling them to raise their shoulders a bit higher and straighten their backs; in short, at this time Nevsky Prospekt is a pedagogical Nevsky Prospekt. But the closer it comes to two o'clock, the fewer in number are the tutors, pedagogues, and children: they are finally supplanted by their loving progenitors, who hold on their arms their bright, multicoloured, weak-nerved companions.

Nikolai Gogol, 'Nevsky Prospekt' (1835)
translated by Richard Pevear and Larissa Volokhonsky

✳ ✳ ✳

*Andrei Bely with an amusing take on the Petersburg 'prospekt' at the start of the twentieth century.*

The wet, slippery Prospekt was intersected by a wet Prospekt at a ninety-degree angle; at the point of the lines' intersection stood a policeman …

And houses of exactly the same kind towered up there, and grey streams of people of exactly the same kind towered up there, and exactly the same kind of yellow-green mist was hanging there. Faces ran by in deep concentration; the pavements whispered and clicked their heels; they were scraped by galoshes; the nose of a man-in-the-street floated solemnly by. Noses flowed in their multitudes[1]: aquiline noses, noses like ducks' or like cockerels', greenish ones, white ones; and a lack of nose flowed by here too. People on their own flowed by here, couples, groups of three or four; bowler hat after bowler hat; bowlers, feathers, caps; caps, caps, feathers; tricorn, top hat, cap; scarf, umbrella, feather.

---

1 A reference to Nikolai Gogol's story 'The Nose'. (Ed.)

But parallel to this receding Prospekt was another receding Prospekt with just the same series of boxes, the same numbering, the same clouds; and with the same civil servant.

There is an infinity in the infinity of receding Prospekts with the infinity of intersecting shadows receding into infinity. The whole of St Petersburg is the infinity of the Prospekt raised to the power of *n*.

Andrei Bely, *Petersburg* (1916)
translated by John Elsworth

✳  ✳  ✳

*The protagonist of Victor Serge's* Conquered City *returns to St Petersburg a couple of years after the Revolution and finds Nevsky Prospekt very much changed.*

The train from Moscow had been about six hours late. The afternoon was fading. Danil walked up Nevsky Prospekt, on which he hadn't set foot in a year – of course, since the day after his arrest.

Tsar Peter's city, he thought, a window opened on Europe. What grandeur is yours, and what misery, what misery …

Nobility and grandeur still showed through the rags and tatters. Laundry hanging from dirty windows right on the main boulevard. Windows broken to allow for the passage of the chimney pipes of little iron stoves, spitting out their puffs of dirty black smoke against the façades of buildings. Mud-spattered shop fronts, crumbling façades, shop windows full of bullet holes and held together with tape, splintered shutters; watchmakers' shop windows displaying three watches, an old alarm clock, and one fancy pendulum clock; unspeakable grocery stores; herb teas packaged to look like real tea, as if there were still fools so stupid as to be taken in by these labels, tubes of saccharine, dubious vinegar, tooth powder – brush your teeth carefully, citizens, since you have nothing to use them on! – A nasty joyful feeling awakened within Danil.

Ah, what have they done to you, Tsar Peter's city, and in such a short time!

Here had stood the Café Italien, the Salzetti quartet; to the right of the entrance, on the mirrored corner, the prettiest prostitutes had sat smiling out with painted eyes from under their gorgeous hats; some of them spoke French with a funny accent and played the *Parisienne* even in bed ... Half the metal shutters were lowered, the pretty white door smudged with black under the press of dirty hands. HEADQUARTERS, 2ND SPECIAL BATTALION, TRANSFERRED TO KARL LIEBKNECHT STREET. CONSUMERS' COOPERATIVE, 4TH CHILDREN'S DINING HALL.

Danil pushed open the door, but all he could see through the herring fumes and the darkness were some broken mirrors. Farther along was the street of women's hat shops: MARIE-LOUISE, ELAINE, MADAME SYLVIA, SÉLYSETTE, aristocratic names taken from novels or the noms de guerre of courtesans. It had been a charming street, inhabited morning and evening by pretty errand girls and elegant ladies. Now sinister, piled high with snow banks.

Victor Serge, *Conquered City* (1932)
translated by Richard Greeman

✳ ✳ ✳

*German writer and traveller Wolfgang Koeppen
visited Russia in 1958. He shares some of his Petersburg experiences with us in a passage specially translated for this volume.*

We drove along Nevsky Prospekt, Petersburg's renowned long main street: well-maintained buildings – and I was struck by the stores, the many businesses, even restaurants and coffee houses, pastry cafés; colourful, cheerful awnings above the shop windows. And even though it might have been the same merchandise on offer here, the standard products of the Soviet Union, the streetscape was full of life compared with Moscow – was friendlier, more cheerful, more sophisticated and therefore more tolerant as well. People didn't rush around, either; in Leningrad you stroll. The Europa Hotel retained the splendour of the nobility who used to frequent it. Comfortable lounges, genuine carpets, bedrooms in alcoves furnished like the Lupanare brothel[1], enormous tiled ovens and huge old-fashioned bathtubs in the washrooms. The restaurant was a winter garden, potted palms and all kinds of greenery under a greenhouse roof. In the evening (this was during the White Nights) the view over the roofs was a beautiful and melancholy dream. Sometimes it made you think of Holland. You promenade along canals and under trees. Then you feel you could be in Hamburg, Lübeck, Copenhagen: tiled oyster cellars, the salt wind from the sea, the bright horizons, beauty and with it always a presentiment of death, an elating melancholy. A lot of history. Historic sites were respectfully preserved. Peter the Great rode a wave, he led Russia to the sea. His Summer Palace – a country house in the Summer Garden. Mythological figures along the avenues: Rococo Dianas and Minervas; the sailors of the Red Fleet are walking boldly over the gravel paths. The Winter Palace, greenish white and still regal, always. Here the Revolution began. Here the Revolution was victorious. The tsars' kingdom stretching to the sea capitulated before the crew of the *Red Dawn*. The cruiser *Aurora* raised the red flag and pointed its guns at the palace. The *Aurora* lies in the harbour, an ungainly box, a veteran of the Russo-Japanese War, completely motionless, entirely devoid of heroism; its fame seems implausible but you believe in the bad food, worm-ridden as on the *Potemkin*. A simple villa. The tsar gave it to his favourite dancer. A small latticed balcony. Here Lenin called forth the Revolution.

---

1   The official brothel of Pompeii. (Ed.)

The masses stormed around the house. Today it is quiet once again around the villa; a pleasant, quiet façade, but the dancer never returned. Lenin's last illegal residence in Petersburg. One room. An iron bed, a bookshelf, a petroleum lamp. Frugality. It makes you think of Calvin. Philosophers are dangerous. The most peculiar memorial to the Revolution is a cabin in Razliv. Lenin hid himself in this shack. Now it stands, shabby-looking, covered with straw, walled in by granite blocks of memory. But the last monument of the Revolution is the underground rail system of Leningrad: newer than that of Moscow, even deeper, even more magnificently built into the earth. Round temples cover the entrances. The escalators, conveyor belts for human freight, must take five minutes to ascend or descend. The Leningraders make use of the time. They read. They read thick books on the escalators. The shafts are temperature-controlled, filled with cold or warm air, the stations are like the marble galleries of a castle. Even in this hall of splendour he does not look up from his book. He is a young man. He is shabbily dressed. Is he reading the story of Raskolnikov?

Wolfgang Koeppen, *To Russia and Elsewhere: Sentimental Journeys* (1958) translated by Susan Thorne

❊ ❊ ❊

*We go with guide Galina (we've met her before) to St Isaac's Cathedral.*

'Now this enormous building in front, with the golden dome, don't you think we really must go in?'

'Why must we go in?'

'It's Saint Isaac's Cathedral. It's the highest place. From the top you can have the very best view of Petersburg. Let's take a look. Or maybe you don't like it?'

'It's just I prefer the churches with the onion domes.'

'The Orthodox styles, of course. But this one is designed by another Frenchman. And oh, by the way, for a little fact. Didro[1] lived at the Narishkin Palace over there.'

I look across the square, but Galina is already steering me toward the church ahead.

'What other Frenchman? Was he a friend of Didro?'

'Not a bit, he lived much later. His name was Auguste Mont-ferrand. He rebuilt the cathedral for our Tsars. He wanted to be buried here, but Tsar Alexander refused him. He died as soon as the cathedral was finished, but his body went back to Paris.'

'Why did the Tsar refuse him?'

'Because the cathedral finally took forty years to finish. The plans were wrong. Nothing fitted. He wasn't a true architect, but even so he built the greatest dome in all the north of Europe. You can see him still, he is carved up there on the façade.'

On the huge marble steps leading up to the cathedral there stands a long line of wrapped beggars, their hands outstretched: old men on homemade crutches, babushkas in black dresses and headscarves. Galina halts and opens up her handbag.

'I always give five kopecks, it brings us good luck,' she says.

We walked inside, hand over an entrance fee to someone, and find ourselves in a vast cathedral that feels much too big for itself. It's a great dark monster of rational baroque, a place of huge sculptures and mosaics, less a place of true worship than an opulent museum. High in the centre, above the crossing, there rises up Montferrand's vast open dome, the third largest after St Peter's and St Paul's. [...]

So we go up and up, by the spiral staircase through the layers of the cold rational cathedral, across the iron ladder to the balconies of the roof. I look out onto the endless rooftops of copper and tin, the broken chimney stacks, the domes of the Smolny Convent, the fingers of big buildings; then, beyond that, spreading out to the wide horizon and the still wider world,

---

1   i.e. Diderot (Ed.)

the factory chimney stacks, the grim slabs of endless apartment blocks, the thick dirty smoke-plumes rising from distant power stations, the hint of far palaces and fortresses, the grey glint of the Baltic sea.

This is what I see. It's somehow not quite what Galina sees. She sees a great city made of form and symmetry. For, as she carefully tries to show me, each part of this cunning and intricate city exactly balances some other. So two golden flèches, carefully matching each other on either bank of the Neva: one the Admiralty, the other the Peter and Paul Fortress. Two Tsars on horseback, one on either side of the cathedral. One of them is Big Peter, pointing like a projectile out to sea on the surge of his great pedestal; the other is Tsar Nicholas, who slaughtered the Decembrists just on the other side of this building, a stiff straight autocrat set erectile on his highly high horse. In front of the Admiralty, a full-length Nikolai Gogol stares across at his stone opposite, Mikhail Lermontov. Down there in front of the Smolny Convent, where Tsarina Catherine Veliko took care of her noble girls, the figure of Karl Marx is exchanging glances with his old collaborator Friedrich Engels. There, glittering upside down and mirrored in the luminous water of the Neva, is a second Admiralty, a second Hermitage.

Malcolm Bradbury, *To the Hermitage* (2000)

✳ ✳ ✳

*A different experience of the same place with Duncan Fallowell.*

St Isaac's balloons ahead, the cross mounted on an anchor at its apex (anchors and tritons are everywhere in St Petersburg). This is the almightiest cathedral in the city, with Samsonic columns to prove it outside, and within an opulence of malachite and lapis lazuli and harlequinades of coloured glass. The building is less forbidding than Kazan Cathedral in Nevsky

Prospekt, but both concoctions of rock weigh heavily on the ground and the down-pressure has been exacerbated by the Soviets having taken out any spiritual uplift. There are plans to return these prodigies to liturgical use and their interiors, at present dead ballrooms belonging to no one, would benefit from a mirage-like complexity of icons, candlelight and incense smoke.

'Let's go up,' says Dima. We buy another ticket and climb the spiral staircase to the drum [...]

We emerge at the great tourist view, available in 360 degrees. How galvanising to be above it all again, but this time at the centre, removed yet not estranged, able to read it, to relate one part to another. The city below is settled in a great stillness. I dash from point to point, grasping vast blocks of stillness which can be fitted together for the first time into an image of the whole, detached, tranquillised, susceptible to more than provisional or partial examination. There is a complementary ease across my back and shoulders and air moves naturally into the lungs, my whole being permeable to oxygen. While we stand up here, St Petersburg comes softly to a stop.

The city was premeditated and is often said to have a rational lay-out. There are rational elements of course but, given that they were in a position to command everything, the surprise is how irrational it is, how organic and unforced. From our vantage the city becomes an abstract, without relinquishing its humanity which is transformed into the frivolities of toytown. Childhood associations of play are invoked alongside the adult gratification of being in control: its grandeur shrinks to delight and all grandeur is transferred to ourselves, emperors of space. Now we and the sky are companions, smiling down at the town.

Duncan Fallowell, *One Hot Summer in St Petersburg* (1994)

*Now for an extraordinary visit made by American writer Truman Capote and described in* The Muses Are Heard[1]. *In 1957 he travelled with an opera company on a cultural exchange visit to Russia where they were to perform Gershwin's* Porgy *and* Bess. *Once installed in their hotel, a few of the company decide, despite the cold, to go for a stroll around the city.*

St Isaac's Square is hemmed on one side by a canal stemming from the Neva, a river that in winter threads through the city like a frozen Seine, and on the other by St Isaac's Cathedral, which is now an anti-religious museum. We walked toward the canal. The sky was sunless grey, and there was snow in the air, buoyant motes, playthings that seethed and floated like the toy flakes inside a crystal. It was noon, but there was no modern traffic on the square except for a car or two and a bus with its headlights burning. Now and then, though, horse-drawn sleds slithered across the snowy pavement. Along the embankments of the Neva, men on skis silently passed, and mothers aired their babies, dragging them in small sleds. Everywhere, like darting blackbirds, black-furred school children ice-skated on the pavements. Two of these children stopped to inspect us. They were twins, girls of nine or ten, and they wore grey rabbit coats and blue velvet bonnets. They had divided a pair of skates between them, but by holding hands and pushing together, they managed very well on one skate apiece. They looked at us with pretty brown puzzled eyes, as though wondering what made us different. Our clothes? Miss Ryan's lipstick? The soft waves in her loose blonde hair? Most foreigners in Russia soon become accustomed to this: the slight frown of the passer-by who is disturbed by something about you that he can't at once put his finger on, and who stops, stares, keeps glancing back, even

---

1   The title refers to the saying 'When the guns are silent, the Muses are heard' – appropriate to the Cold War period in which it took place. (Ed.)

quite often feels compelled to follow you. The twins followed us on to a footbridge that crossed the Neva, and watched while we paused to look at the view.

The canal, no more than a snowy ditch, was a sporting ground for children whose laughing shrillness combined with a ringing of bells, both sounds carrying on the strong, shivery winds that blow from the Bay of Finland. Skeleton trees, sheathed in ice, glittered against the austere fronts of palaces that lined the embankments and stretched to the distant Nevsky Prospekt. Leningrad, now a city of four million, the Soviet Union's second largest and nothernmost metropolis, was built to the taste of the Tsars, and Tsarist taste ran to French and Italian architecture, which accounts not only for the style but also for the colouring of the palaces along the Neva and in other old quarters. Parisian blacks and greys predominate, but suddenly, here and there, the hot Italian palette intervenes: a palace of bitter green, of brilliant ochre, pale blue, orange. A few of the palaces have been converted into apartments, most are used for offices. Peter the Great, who is given high marks by the current régime because he introduced the sciences to Russia, would probably approve the myriad television aerials that have settled like a swarm of metal insects on the roofs of this once Imperial city.

We crossed the bridge and wandered through opened iron gates into the deserted courtyard of a blue palace. It was the beginning of a labyrinth, an arctic Casbah, where one court-yard led into another via arcades and tunnels and across narrow streets snow-hushed and silent except for sleigh horses stamping their hooves, a drifting sound of bells, an occasional giggle from the twins, still trailing behind us.

The cold was like an anæsthetic; gradually, I felt numb enough to undergo major surgery. But Miss Ryan refused to turn back. 'This is St Petersburg, for God's sake. We're not just walking anywhere. I want to see as much as I can. And I'd better. From now on, you know where *I'll* be? Locked in a room typing a lot of nonsense for the Breens.' But I saw that she couldn't last much longer, her face was drunkard-red, a frost-bite spot whitened the tip of her nose. Minutes later, feeling its first sting, she was ready to seek the Astoria.

Truman Capote, The Muses Are Heard (1957)

✻ ✻ ✻

*Some more architectural delights with Sacheverell Sitwell. The second section of the extract takes us to the magnificent summer residence of the Imperial family (fifteen miles south from the centre of St Petersburg), Tsarskoe Selo, now a World Heritage Site.*

There had been Russian classical architects before Rossi: Zakharov, who built the Admiralty: and Voronikhin, architect of the Kazan Cathedral. The masterpiece of Rossi was the Michel Palace[1], built by Alexander I for his younger brother, and which elicited prodigies of admiration in its day. The front has a Corinthian portico of eight pillars; but it is more especially the interior that represents all that the Russian classical manner could accomplish. Floors inlaid with Carelian woods, and with rosewood, ebony, and mahogany; walls of scagliola, imitating the yellow Siena, shining mirrors, candelabra of Siberian jasper, pier tables of which the slabs are of opaque blue glass. Other rooms have walls of polished scagliola of a pure and dazzling white, with sky blue hangings; or imitation marble walls of a pigeon egg blue, highly polished, with eight columns at each end, of blue scagliola with gilt capitals. The curtains and their pelmets are designed by a master hand. They hang from light airy cornices, or in festoons and massive draperies which, drawn aside, display the marble walls painted with gilt arabesques, or, more simply, with cupids and wreaths of roses. This method of painting in oil

---

1 The Mikhailovsky (or Michael) Palace, which now houses the Russian Museum. (Ed.)

and gold upon scagliola, and fixing the colours, was the invention of Italian craftsmen working under Rossi. [...]

In St Petersburg, this style of the Regency, as we would call it, reaches to its zenith. In no other city was it used upon so lavish a scale; and, of this, the Michel Palace is the conspicuous example. An exotic air breathes upon those apartments of sky blue or dazzling white, their mirrors multiplying without end and their gilded ceilings, when it is considered that this is Russia, that the snow makes brighter the plumage in the bird cages that hang in the windows, that the servants enter in long caftans and with slippered feet, that there are caviar and vodka on the zakuski table. Classical building has never been so artificial as in this city of the Tsars.

The Marble Palace was not less exotic in its day. This is of earlier date and one who saw it in its prime, in 1799, remarks of it: 'The prodigies of enchantment which we read of in the Tales of the Genii are here called forth into reality, and the temples raised by the luxuriant fancy of our poets may be considered as a picture of the marble palace which Jupiter, when the burden of cares drives him from heaven, might make his delightful abode.' This palace was built by Catherine for her favourite, Orlov, and was lived in by another of her lovers, Stanislaus Poniatowski, last king of Poland, in his exile. Grigori Orlov was the Jupiter of this Marble Palace, but he died too soon and his place was taken by the elegant and ineffectual Poniatowski. [...]

Now we are at Tsarskoe Selo we should, at least, come up to the empty palace, for it is winter, and look through the gilded windows. An earlier traveller, whom we may envy, left the capital at sunrise and came here by sledge. All round, in every direction, there are pavilions and little palaces by Charles Cameron, Quarenghi, Menelas and Rossi; but come nearer! A façade, twelve hundred feet in length, and stained green and white and yellow, climbs out of the snow. [...]

Rastrelli was architect of this fantastic building. Its peculiar note is struck at the outset by the colouring of the external walls, a concession to barbarian taste, which was not content with brick or stone. The special purpose was against the monotony of snow, but it is as Russian in invention as the cathedral of St Basil and its coloured domes. From this are descended the painted façades of the Admiralty and of so many buildings in St Petersburg of the time of Nicholas I. This hybrid Italian has become as typical of Russia as the Russian cuisine or the classical ballets of Petipa.

The builder of Tsarskoe Selo was the Empress Elizabeth. Many of the rooms are in the rococo of her period, with the Russian flavour. A profusion of gilding, barbarian in its extravagance, doors and ceilings that are beautiful and splendid. A room of which the entire panelling is formed of amber, in homage to the Baltic and its sandy shores; and a hall of lapis lazuli with a parquet of ebony inlaid with wreaths of mother-of-pearl. A change in taste came with the arrival of Charles Cameron, an architect who was recommended to Catherine by his publication of a book of measured drawings of classical remains, another Adam, or James Wyatt, a reputed Jacobite, but little or nothing is yet known of him. At his first coming he was set to work by Catherine with the simplest materials. The bedroom of the Empress is often quoted because of its walls of porcelain and pilasters of violet glass. The latter are no more than panels of glass laid over velvet of that colour, due, probably, to a sketch or a mere suggestion from Cameron and appealing to Catherine because of its cleverness and as a joke or comment upon the extravagance of her other schemes. Later, he was allowed more expensive materials and, in addition to building, designed furniture of all descriptions and details that were as fine as jewellers' or goldsmiths' work. [...]

In the snow, and, indeed, in summer too, something even in the elegance and grace of the building, perhaps the fact that it is raised on its high terrace, recalls the prints and pictures of Russian fairs. Montagnes russes, the first mountain railways of the fairs, had to have a raised building at each end, a tower from which the slide or switchback took its start, and these were often given pillars and porticoes, with carved figures of dancers of the fair upon their side walls. By some transformation or metamorphosis, for it has no real structural resemblance, and may be due more to the colours in the sky or to some quite extraneous reason, the Colonnade of Tsarskoe Selo is not a hanging garden but a montagne russe — in imitation — for it has no action, no switchback, it is the summer dining room of Semiramis, yet, like all things Russian, it is Russian in total and in detail, and could be nothing else. We are to imagine Catherine dining in this Colonnade, her Russian elkhounds round her, her ambitions pointing her towards the Hellespont, with so much that is Oriental or Asiatic in the contradiction of these classic columns and the Tartar soil or substratum of her revenues. Syllables of the Russian tongue sound odd in this landscape of an Arcadian park, seen through the pillars. Today, on this winter afternoon, the flying colonnade of Tsarskoe Selo is like the Rialto of the Grand Canal run dry. Seen from below, it looks stranded in a pale green sky: a bridge, a colonnade, a pleasure barge, left empty in a long winter. We come back to the palace, as snow begins to fall again.

Sacheverell Sitwell, *Valse des Fleurs* (1941)

✻ ✻ ✻

*In the course of her novel on the Siege of Leningrad[1], Ice Road, Gillian Slovo introduces us to the district of Smolny and the famous Smolny Institute whose function has changed several times during its history.*

---

1   September 1941–January 1944 (Ed.)

To cater to their tsar's whim, the men whose job it was to build this new city of bridges and islands, this St Petersburg, first had to reclaim most of the land from marshes. Not so, however, in the district of Smolny, for Smolny, formerly the site of the tar yards for Peter's warships and then the favourite choice of residence for the Russian nobility, stands four metres above sea level from where it can look down on the mist and damp and fog that persecute the rest of Leningrad.

At the Smolny's apex, overlooking the Bolshaya Neva, sits the Smolny Institute. In this complex of buildings is history writ large: what started life as an orphan's convent championed by an empress was turned first into a school for the daughters of the nobility, then into the headquarters of the Petrograd Soviet, and finally it became the site of the second all-Russian Congress of Socialists and Workers and Soldiers Deputies. It is here that, in 1917, Lenin and Trotsky and Zinoviev and Kamenev stood, under the chandeliers and swirling cigarette smoke, to announce the birth of the Bolshevik state. And nowadays, as befits a building of this stature, the Smolny is Party headquarters and the busy, bustling centre of local government. [...]

Soon it will be dark but for the moment the sky, viewed through a feathery lattice of velvet brown branches, looks almost white. If it were summer there'd be stretches of clipped green and sparkling fountains but now the fountains are boxed in against the cold, and the lawns and flower beds are covered by uninterrupted beds of snow. [...]

To the left, rising above a screen of trees, she can see the exquisite cupolas of the white cathedral and, standing in the Smolny grounds and screened from the cathedral by those same trees, the bust of a man, with its bullish head, long beard, sweeping moustache and ferocious eyebrows. It's Friedrich Engels and opposite him, on the other side of the path, his match, his friend, the much more benign-looking, bushy-bearded Karl Marx. Natasha knows the statues well. She throws each a casual nod.

Quickening her step, she goes past the statue of Vladimir Ilyich Lenin and his pointing arm. In summer, he will be ringed by flowers – red tulips – but now he has only snow for his carpet, and a sprinkling of powdery snow on the back of his head and inside the folds of his cap.

Gillian Slovo, *Ice Road* (2004)

✻ ✻ ✻

*There have always been less grand areas of the city – and not just in the Petersburg of* Crime and Punishment. *Duncan Fallowell, usually a great enthusiast of the city, has to admit that all is not well for many of its residents. (He is describing St Petersburg as he found it in the early 1990s.)*

Walk along any street. Every fifty feet or so you will encounter an opening, large enough to take a lorry, into an inner courtyard. These are rarely ceremonial entrances. Most seem to have been crudely punched through the ground floor, a television-screen-shaped access into the heart of the tough life behind the delectable façade, a succession of private video clips at your shoulder as you walk along – man playing with cat, girl calling upwards, woman in rags hobbling with a stick to a bench. And sometimes children playing – but not as often as you'd expect. These are not spaces of boisterous expression. The clip is always specific, the courtyard possessed by a preponderating reserve, an underlying quiet and stillness into which the specific event is re-absorbed. City of 100,000 courtyards, none of them pretty – their accursed or ominous or defaced beauty is almost never compromised by a tree or a window box – usually it's debris and dustbins. Many are masterpieces of a nostalgia infinitely subtle in its gradations of decay. And all are brim-full of stories.

As often as you pass one of these openings, you will pass a telephone kiosk or hooded wall apparatus, probably inoperative, certainly with glass smashed. Cracked and broken glass is everywhere. Green glass, brown glass, white glass. The streets, yards and staircases are glass-splashed, urine-splashed, vomit-splashed. Unidentifiable vapours hang among rusty pipes. Electric wires snake up outside walls, up lamp-posts, across streets, swing aimlessly, exposing the population to rude awakenings. You are in a place of physical danger – loose steps, holes, things sticking out. You will be grazed, slapped, stabbed by inanimate objects. Plants push through pavements from the soggy earth below, making volcanoes of asphalt over which you stumble, or they dangle green arms from mouldering cornices and attics, pieces of which fall on you. Cobbles tumble askew among tramlines, railings are buckled, fences twisted, walls cracked or stained or pitted or dripping, sometimes no more than vertical rubble. Brickwork flushes red beneath a rout of stucco.

Mrs Podnak sighs 'It was not like this before.' But to wreck the physical tissues of a metropolis to their very pith takes a long period of time. Most of the last hundred years. And here we are at the end of the twentieth century in an arena of anachronisms, both of past and future, which render the place timeless. [...]

O seething and sleazy necrosis shot with paranoia! So magnificently, heart-rendingly beautiful and full of dread! Derelict from end to end, from top to bottom — I emphasise: you cannot imagine the splendour of this. It has to be witnessed. Everything broken. Not only cars, clocks, taps, windows. Also hearts, minds, memories, insides. Everyone has to make it up as they go along, day by day. We are living in a giant do-it-yourself kit. Therefore the mystery, the spirit, the drama are not broken. On the contrary, they are invigorated and flow as fluid pigments in coils, spasms and fitful lines through the days and nights of the city.

Duncan Fallowell, *One Hot Summer in St Petersburg* (1994)

\* \* \*

*Contemporary Petersburger Andrei Astvatsaturov –*
*well-known philologist, columnist and literary critic*
*– recalls a childhood and youth spent in one of the*
*less attractive residential areas of the city.*

'Windows to the East! A wonderful view! Sun in the morning!
Fresh air! A green neighbourhood!' declared a white-collar
worker, a rotund lady with mauve hair and a massive brooch on
a formidable bosom. My mother was sitting on a chair placed
side-on to a frail yellow table, holding me, a three-year-old, by
the hand. I didn't understand why the mauve lady wanted us to
move to the green neighbourhood. I'd always dreamt of living
in the red one. Leftist ideals must have been stirring inside me
even at that age. Life in a green neighbourhood, and I was
pretty certain of this already, would be pretty boring. [...]

A wonderful view ...

This wonderful view, which might absorb the most curious
person for all of two minutes, was something I had to enjoy for
my entire childhood and youth.

Across the road a hefty grey building towered above us, a
bulky, inelegant box – living proof that the big imperial style
was dying out – with a triangular roof from which short, toy-
like chimneys stuck out, resembling gappy teeth; this was the
halls of residence for students from developing countries. [...]
To the right of the student dorms, architects' ideas, lazily but
systematically continuing to clog up the barren scrubland with
typical five-storey apartment blocks, had suddenly gone and
plonked a metro station there, for no reason at all, in the mid-
seventies. It reminded me of the mausoleum on Red Square.
Only the mausoleum is red, and this was grey, like everything
around it had been from the start.

From above, looking down from the ninth floor, the metro
seemed far too short and squat to have anything to do with

the mighty Lenin. But then why not like Lenin? After all, a short building has everything to do with Lenin, especially considering the not exactly gigantic stature of the leader. But in essence it was definitely not Lenin-like. The metro station was subsequently hidden from view in the new millennium by an urban housing development. The authorities must have finally decided that local people didn't need to look at buildings like this everywhere they went. To the left of our window we could see the squat swimming pool building, hugging the ground, half covering the green oval of the stadium. And behind it, towering above the unkempt Polytechnic Institute park that surrounded it, an old, almost gothic-looking water tower, with two gigantic factory chimneys frozen alongside it, as if standing guard.

If you believe what the guidebooks say, in the 1960s the curved space of Muzhestva[1] Square – slightly to the right of my window – used to be surrounded by two-storey detached residences, cosy and comfortable, almost like dolls' houses, with crenellated turrets. But then the city authorities took them down, leaving just the one to edify future generations. Red brick hulks grew up in their place, and kiosks selling beer immediately attached themselves to the foot of them; neat, fragile, just like match boxes, only with roofs and canopies. A little further away was a massive regular cube – the Vyborgsky cinema, with a foyer, restaurant, and a huge auditorium with comfortable seats, a wide stage, and an old piano in its right-hand corner, a relic from the golden days of silent film.

And then there was Muzhestva Square, once no more than a patch of green grass with tram rails across it – when I was a child I thought the tram ran right on the grass – Muzhestva Square which could only really boast ramshackle constructions from the old regime, doomed by fate and time to rusty oblivion,

---

1   Square of Valour: the square was given its name in 1965 to commemorate the heroism of Leningraders during the Great Patriotic War of 1941–45. (Ed.)

and a puck-shaped public bathhouse behind which you could
see gloomy factory buildings. That same semi-residential
square eventually took on a dignified and civilised appearance,
the self-conscious pomp of a multi-stage theatre, an imperial
greatness and scale.

Andrei Astvatsaturov, *Skunskamera* (2010)
translated by Eve Harris

✳ ✳ ✳

*Art historian Ivan Chechot finds a certain charm in
newer districts, made up of blocks of flats. Below is
his account of Kupchino – a large residential area in
the south of the city.*

Kupchino was developed at the end of the Soviet period. Until
recently it was *de rigueur* to highlight the vulgarity and inhu-
manity of the architecture of that period. Today, however, many
people have spotted the wonderful professional expertise in
the architecture of the apartment blocks: the proportions, the
play of light and shade across the façades, and the monumental
scale of the buildings. Austerity is miles better than kitsch,
with the sort of fiddly pretentious tawdriness that architects
are producing nowadays. The countenance and disposition of
Kupchino is unified. It is indeed removed from the centre –
thank goodness! Residents of Kupchino feel confident and at
ease. It cuts itself off from Petersburg, because Petersburg looks
down its nose at Kupchino, while the view of the city from
Kupchino (or from any of the outlying districts) is of the city
as a whole, as a great metropolis lying on the Neva Lowlands.
This leads some of the more knowing residents of Kupchino
to indulge in lofty cogitations on matters of world history and
geography. Because of the space and unity of Kupchino, there
is a sense of a metaphysical relationship with the sky. This is
not the cramped 'communal flat' of the centre, hemmed in on
every side with palaces that produce in any thinking Peters-

burger a rush of pride, but also the awareness of just how alien these palaces are, owned by someone else. In Kupchino at least everything belongs here, there is no ambiguity or nostalgia for some grand, irretrievable past.

Ivan Chechot, 'Kupchino' in *St Petersburg as Cinema* (2011) (ed. Lubov Arkus) translated by Sergei Afonin and Alice Jondorf

❊ ❊ ❊

*Nikita Eliseev – essayist, columnist and expert on Russian film – adds to the portrait of the area.*

St Petersburg differs from western cities in never having engulfed little towns as it grew. It colonised empty spaces. In Petersburg, this sense of empty space, and the steamroller that went over it, destroying history, is concentrated in Kupchino. This is a spirit that is hostile to the little man, who defends himself with laughter and bits of metal from crumbling façades. There is no monument to this spirit of freedom, except in the form of Kafka's everlasting, accursed questions and the laughter of the Good Soldier Švejk. It is no accident that a monument to Hašek's hero[1] now stands among the modern tower blocks of Kupchino.

In 1716–1718, in the Finnish village of Kupsino, stood the estate of the most miserable and lonely hero in Russian history and Petersburg, Tsarevich Alexei[2]. Here is a Kafkaesque story if ever there was one. Peter the Great's son could feel himself changing from the king's son into a nasty little insect transfixed under the mercilessly poised iron heel of his father's boot.

---

1  Jaroslav Hašek's novel *The Good Soldier Švejk* in which the 'everyman' hero exposes the incompetences of military authority by means of passive resistance masked by apparent stupidity. (Ed.)

2  Peter the Great's son by a woman he did not love, the tsarevich was neglected and bullied all his life by his ambitious and visionary father, and finally condemned to death for treason. (Ed.)

The soul of the poor wretched tsarevich took up residence in the modular panel-built tower blocks of Kupchino that Nikita Khrushchev launched with a wave of the hand. That was in 1961. And thus the housing problem in the USSR was solved. The eccentric Khrushchev, who actually looked not unlike Švejk, rehabilitated the politically repressed, and issued passports to the workers on collective farms.

The cardboard-box houses could be thrown together quickly and cheaply. Kupchino encapsulates some of the same characteristics as Khrushchev. A desire to take the leap; the aspiration to clear the abyss in a single bound that Churchill spoke of in amazement when summing up the political style of the new Soviet leader. Petersburg is a cramped city. Kupchino bursts out of it with the space of wastelands, which can be sinister.

A pedestrian can find the identical boxes of the houses overwhelming. It would make a good setting for a film about a person lost and swallowed by expanse.

Nikita Eliseev, 'The Leap' in *St Petersburg as Cinema* (2011)
(ed. Lubov Arkus) translated by Sergei Afonin and Alice Jondorf

❋ ❋ ❋

*Historic districts not on the usual tourist itinerary have plenty to offer those with a taste for exquisite architecture and an interest in history. First, from essayist and journalist, Lev Lurie; then from the scholar Stanislav Savitsky.*

The Petrograd Side is unusual in having been constructed almost entirely in the space of ten years, from 1903 when the permanent Troitsky Bridge across to the left bank was opened, until 1914 when World War I started and all building activities stopped at once. This ragged and incomplete quality is still a central feature of the Petrograd Side, with its protective firewalls that never had another house built adjoining. But even over the course of those ten years, land prices rose forty-fold.

The district became a unique collection of architecture from the turn of the twentieth century. The buildings may be of different quality and varying styles, but they all trace the transition from Art Deco to Art Nouveau. This is not an aristocratic area; large mansions were only built nearer the islands and there are no official institutions here. It is a district of rented accommodation, with lifts, steam heating and garages. There is a trite view that Petersburg is 'not built for people', that it rejects their needs. That it is a city of 'dumb squares where they executed people before dawn'. But that is not the case. Vasilievsky Island and the Petrograd Side in particular were created specifically for people – more accurately for the middle classes. Even now the Petrograd Side seems to me the best area in Petersburg to live in.[…]

St Petersburg didn't particularly take to the Russian Revival style. It wasn't until the early twentieth century that a native, organic architecture appeared: Northern Art Nouveau. This was also imported, but only from Scandinavia, where it was very fashionable. Nevertheless, Northern Art Nouveau was entirely suited to the place: it worked best with granite, and Petersburg was definitely the 'granite city' by that time. Because the principal building boom was on the Petrograd Side during this period, there is more Northern Art Nouveau here than anywhere else: a hundred and seven buildings!

Lev Lurie, 'The Petrograd Side' in *St Petersburg as Cinema* (2011)
(ed. Lubov Arkus) translated by Sergei Afonin and Alice Jondorf

Kolomna is essentially the backyard of the centre. Life here is unpretentious and suited to pensioners, the literati and non-conformists of all shapes and colours. It has always housed scruffy little shops and establishments that are truly vernacular. As long ago as the nineteenth century, the place was teeming with people who were constantly mislaying their noses or losing their overcoats[1]. Kolomna is the most artistic district in Petersburg. It served as home to Pushkin, Gogol, Dostoyevsky, the great composers known as The Five, members of the World of Art movement, Blok, Vaginov and artists of the Arefyev Circle. It is the archetypal sidelines, a world of the marginalized and fantasists. The gateway to this world is Sennaya Square. Much as Les Halles are the 'belly of Paris' in Zola's novel, so Sennaya is the 'belly of Petersburg'. There has always been an intoxicated and barbarous marketplace here. It was here, near Moskovsky Prospekt, that Sonechka Marmeladova[2] stood. In the 1990s you could buy absolutely anything at this filthy trading post, from peaches to Kalashnikovs.

> Stanislav Savitsky, 'Kolomna' in *St Petersburg as Cinema* (2011) (ed. Lubov Arkus) translated by Sergei Afonin and Alice Jondorf

*But back to the celebrated centre of this beautiful city. Anthony Cross considers England's long-standing links with St Petersburg, enshrined in the very name of one of its most impressive parts – the English Embankment.*

In the reigns of the empresses, particularly in that of the great Catherine, the British consolidated their position as perhaps the most eminent and certainly most visible foreign community, their most affluent members acquiring impressive three-storeyed houses, 'with balconies large enough to drink tea in', along the embankment to the west of the Admiralty. Although it was only in the reign of Alexander I that this embankment officially received the name of the English Embankment, it had for at least two decades previously been widely known as the English Line or Quay. A prime position along the embankment was occupied by the English Church, which opened for divine

---

1   A reference to Nikolai Gogol's famous stories 'The Nose' and 'The Overcoat' (Ed.)

2   Character in Dostoyevsky's novel *Crime and Punishment*. (Ed.)

service for the first time in 1754 and continued until the British community was dispersed following the October Revolution of 1917. The British connection was lost or hidden during the Soviet period, but the Embankment of the Red Fleet reverted to the English Embankment, following the visit to the city of Queen Elizabeth II in 1994, and the city tourist administration vacated the English Church, which, however, now houses, uncomfortably, a souvenir store. The fortunate British occupants of houses along the embankment and their visitors looked out on one of the world's great views, across the wide Neva towards a run of magnificent buildings from the Academy of Arts to the west, passing the Menshikov Palace, the University, the Academy of Sciences, the Kunstkamera, towards the Strelka or eastern tip of Vasilievsky Island, and beyond, to the Peter and Paul Fortress, while those who walked along the University Embankment (as it was called subsequent to the University of St Petersburg occupying the buildings of Trezzini's Twelve Colleges in 1819) could admire the panorama of the left bank, its granite embankment sweeping from the end of the English Embankment in the west, unbroken past the Admiralty, once it had been finally closed as a shipyard in the 1870s, and the Winter Palace, down to the Marble Palace and the Summer Garden, the beauty of whose railings was sufficient to send home completely happy an Englishman who had journeyed to the city specifically to see them.

Anthony Cross, 'Homes by the Neva', in *Rossica* 10/11 (2003)

*More than once, St Petersburg has recovered from devastation – from floods, war, revolution, and civic incompetence – and managed to rebuild and renovate the best of itself. One of the most impressive examples was the remaking of the Winter Palace after the terrible fire of 1837.*

The next day the Emperor (Nicholas I) returned to the scene of destruction. Within the walls the fire still raged. It had been allowed to burn on, whilst all efforts were directed to saving the Hermitage, fortunately with complete success.

Long gazed Nicholas in deep sorrow at the grave of one of the prime ornaments of his beautiful city. At last he raised his head, passed his hand over his brow, and said, quite cheerfully, 'This day year will I again sleep in my room in the Winter Palace. Who undertakes the building?'

All present recoiled from the challenge. There stood around the Emperor many competent judges in such matters, but not one had the courage to undertake that which seemed impossible. There was a brief pause, and then General Kleinmichael, an aide-de-camp of the Emperor's, stepped forward and said, like the Duke of Alba to Don Philip, 'I will!'

'And the building is to be complete in a year?' asked the Emperor.

'Yes, Sire!'

''Tis good! Set to work!'

An hour later the still burning ruins were being cleared away. The destruction of the building had occurred in December 1837; by December, 1838, it was rebuilt. Three months later it was occupied by the court.

Kleinmichael had kept his word: the building was completed, completed in the time specified! But – at what a price! Only in Russia was such a wonderful work possible; only in Russia, where the will of the 'Master' is a decree of Providence; only in Russia, where they spare nothing, recoil from nothing, to fulfil his commands.

Under the Empress Elizabeth the palace had taken eight years to build; Kleinmichael completed it in one. True it is that almost the whole of the masonry resisted the fire, but the whole of the interior had to be reconstructed, and what a task that was! The work went on literally day and night; there was no pause for meals; the gangs of workmen relieved each other. Festivals were unheeded; the seasons themselves were overcome. To accelerate the work, the building was kept, the winter through, artificially heated to the excessive temperature of twenty-four to twenty-six degrees Réaumur. Many workmen sank under the heat, and were carried out dead or dying; a painter, who was decorating a ceiling, fell from his ladder struck with apoplexy. Neither money, health, nor life, was spared. The Emperor, who, at the time of the conflagration, had risked his own life by penetrating into the innermost apartments to save the lives of others, knew nothing of the means employed to carry out his will. In the December of the following year, and in proud consciousness of his power, he entered the resuscitated palace and rejoiced over his work. The whole was constructed on the previous plan, but with some improvements and many embellishments. With the Empress on his arm, and followed by his whole family, he traversed the apartments of this immense building, completed, in one year's time, by the labour of thousands of men. He reached the saloon of St George, the largest and most beautiful of all, and the royal family remained there longer than anywhere else, examining the costly gold mouldings of the ceiling, the five colossal bronze chandeliers, and the beautiful relieve over the throne, which represents St George slaying the dragon. The Empress was tired, and would have sat down; the patron spirit of Russia prevented her: as yet there was no furniture in the hall, so she leaned upon the Emperor's arm and walked into the next room, followed by the entire retinue. The last of these had scarcely passed through the door when a thundering crash resounded through the palace, which trembled to its very foundations, and the air was darkened by clouds of dust. The timbers of the ceiling of the saloon of St George had yielded to the weight of the chandeliers; and the whole had fallen in, crushing everything beneath its enormous mass. The saloon, a moment before so brilliant, was a heap of ruins. The splendid palace was again partly destroyed, but the genius of Russia had watched over her destiny – the imperial family were saved.

Edward Jerrmann, *Pictures of St Petersburg* (1852)

❈ ❈ ❈

*Alexander Solzhenitsyn meditates on both the beauty and the great cost in human lives that define the amazing creation which is the 'City on the Neva'.*

Genuflecting angels with lamps surround the Byzantine dome of St. Isaac's. Three faceted golden spires converse across the Neva and Moika. Lions, griffins and sphinxes, placed here and there, guard treasures or doze. The six-horse Victory team gallops above Rossi's cunning arch. Hundreds of porticos, thousands of columns, rearing horses, balking bulls. Foreign to us, and at the same time our most glorious magnificence.

What joy, that nothing more can be built here! – no squeezing a wedding-cake skyscraper into Nevsky, no slapping together a five-storey box by the Griboyedov Canal. […]

What a delight to wander down these avenues today! But it was with clenched teeth, cursing, rotting in murky swamps, that the Russians built this beauty. The bones of our ancestors packed and melted together, hardened into palaces – yellowish, greyish-brown, chocolate, green.

Terrifying to contemplate: our unwieldy, perishing lives, all the eruptions of our discord, the moans of those shot dead and the tears of wives – will all this, too, be entirely forgotten? Will all this, too, give rise to such finalized, eternal beauty?

Alexander Solzhenitsyn, 'City on the Neva' from *Littlest Pieces (1958–1960)* translated by Maya Vinokour

# White nights and dark days

*St Petersburg is a city with an awful lot of weather: read just about any book on the place and you'll find it cropping up again and again. And there are the seasonal extremes of light and dark, too, as this very northern city moves between long days when the sun scarcely sets – the famous 'White Nights' of midsummer – and the short days and long, long nights of winter. In this section we explore the seasons in St Petersburg and the weather you can expect to experience there. First, a general observation by Joseph Brodsky, then some advice from composer Sergei Prokofiev on how to avoid frost-bite starts a collection of pieces on winter.*

Everything can change in Petersburg except its weather. And its light. It's the northern light, pale and diffused, one in which both memory and eye operate with unusual sharpness. In this light, and thanks to the directness and length of the streets, a walker's thoughts travel farther than his destination, and a man with normal eyesight can make out at a distance of a mile the number of the approaching bus.

Joseph Brodsky, 'A Guide to a Renamed City' (1979)
in *Less Than One: Selected Essays*

✻ ✻ ✻

Saturday 19 February

During our musical evening the frost outside had become heavier and reached, I think, the coldest point since we came to the USSR. Whether or not this was so, the thermometer was showing below 20 degrees Réamur, which in the absence of a fur hat and fur collar starts to be a threat. While we dragged our way back to the hotel on sledges I kept my fingers and toes moving and pulled at my brow, lips and cheeks: keeping everything in motion warms the parts of the body liable to get frost-bitten. On the other hand the shock-cold of the frost helped cleanse my mind of all the sounds I'd been exposed to during the day.

Sergei Prokofiev, *Soviet Diary 1927 and Other Writings* (1991)
translated by Oleg Prokofiev

✻ ✻ ✻

It is nearly noon. He cannot bear the thought of returning to his room. He walks eastward along Sadovaya Street. The sky is low and grey, a cold wind blows; there is ice on the ground and the footing is slippery. A gloomy day, a day for trudging with the head lowered.

J. M. Coetzee, *The Master of Petersburg* (1994)

✻ ✻ ✻

Cold was crawling now through the city like an invisible fog, crawling into every cranny, into every cubbyhole, across the slums, up through the tower blocks, down along the Neva, elbowing aside all other concerns, crawling up the fat legs of its familiar winter throne. In three days, the tyranny would be established anew. And those in the converted palaces and executive apartments would be forever on the threshold of their homes and offices and restaurants, forever putting on or taking off their heavy cloaks and furs and gloves and brightly-coloured department-store scarves; those on broken chairs watching TV in their subdivided rooms had already donned their re-darned sweaters, their shawls, their ancient coats for the duration; and those lying in the lean-tos beneath the shadow of the power station now rose swaying to their feet and came out like sickened jackals scavenging for new cardboard, rags, rubbish to burn in their oil drums.

Henry lingered, shivering in the swelter of the super-heated bank. He kept patting himself – hand to knee, hand to cheekbone, one hand on the knuckles of the other. The first snow was falling on the Nevsky outside and a filthy quagmire of evil greys was already caking the ground. [...]

The pavement had turned into a thickening medley of slush and mottled grey ice. Pedestrians squelching, sliding, sloshing along. Hard to believe that from the moment the snow left heaven until the moment it touched the Earth, it was virgin white.

Edward Docx, *Self Help* (2007)

❊ ❊ ❊

To protect them from the frost, the statues along the paths of the Summer Garden have been enclosed in tall boxes made of wooden planks – beneath the sharp black pattern of branches, one could almost say they resemble sentry boxes for giant soldiers. People taking tentative steps, fur heads wreathed in breathy vapours. Behind the famous railings, the sky and the

Neva blend into a sort of grey plasma, a background to the arching of bridges, the arrow of a flight of birds. At the start of Voïnova Street stands a building with tall iron doors and bristling with aerials: it's the *Bolshoi Dom*, the Big House, the headquarters of the KGB. Behind the dirty, pleated curtains, one sees electric lights burning in broad daylight. Further on, at the edge of the Tauride garden, a greenhouse shelters a flower show. There's something a bit sad about seeing the admiring crowd jostling around the rather ordinary roses, cyclamen, carnations, and dahlias from a Moscow state farm, and which, in the window of a decent Parisian florist, would attract no attention whatsoever. But perhaps most people are there to wallow for a moment in the warmish air.

Olivier Rolin, *In Russia* (1987)
translated by Erica King

✳ ✳ ✳

She gazes down the straight section of the Neva just before it winds itself round the bend. Winter has taken hold, the ice forming a thick crust along the river banks while in its centre tiny, grey ice floes dot the syrupy water. For the moment the floes are still on the move, granulated waves heading, slowly, out towards the Gulf of Finland, but it's so cold that soon, Natasha knows, they will multiply and pile up, and form an ice garden of preposterous, needle-pointed shapes.

Like every child of Leningrad, she loves midsummer with its glorious white nights. How could anyone not fall then for the viscous Neva, a contrast to the glistening of the bayonets of Admiralty and the burnished dome of St Isaac's across the water? But for Natasha winter is also precious, for in winter there's an added bonus: mystery and delight. She loves the way this season changes texture, and great snowflakes keep floating down and, falling, mute sound. She loves the lie of them, as well, one flake upon the other until they form an interlocking series of undulating beds of dazzling white that, after a particularly vivid sunset, will turn an almost electric blue. And she never ceases to be entranced by the way that the combination of alabaster snow and the blue light of a full moon somehow combine to cover the earth in an unworldly glow.

Gillian Slovo, *Ice Road* (2004)

✳ ✳ ✳

Outside, it's bitterly cold; darkness sets in around three o'clock in the afternoon. My athletic grandmother Ada, my beautiful mother Laura's mother, curses as she drags me on the sledge through the streets of St Petersburg, barely recognisable in the driving snow and massive drifts covering the roofs and pavements. Over our winter shoes, we wear additional boots of black boiled wool, and over that rubber slippers, the northern version of rubber boots, called *valenki*.

Julya Rabinowich, *Splithead* (2009)
translated by Tess Lewis

✳ ✳ ✳

The sun rides low in a pale, clear sky. Emerging from the warren of alleys on to Voznesensky Prospekt, he has to close his eyes.

J. M. Coetzee, *The Master of Petersburg* (1994)

✳ ✳ ✳

The city was no less wondrous than in the summer. The temperature outside moved between minus twenty-five centigrade and plus five. With cracking and hissing noises the Neva and canals froze, thawed, refroze, their surfaces jagged with natural ice sculptures. The nights were long, from 4 pm to 10 am, and the snow fell like white fur. But there were many sunny days when the sky was blue and the snow city dazzled.

Duncan Fallowell, *One Hot Summer in St Petersburg* (1994)

\* \* \*

The sepia gloom of an arctic afternoon in midwinter invaded the rooms and was deepening to an oppressive black. A bronze angle, a surface of glass or polished mahogany here and there in the darkness, reflected the odds and ends of light from the street, where the globes of tall street lamps along its middle line were already diffusing their lunar glow. Gauzy shadows moved on the ceiling. In the stillness, the dry sound of a chrysanthemum petal falling upon the marble of a table made one's nerves twang.

My mother's boudoir had a convenient oriel for looking out on the Morskaya in the direction of the Maria Square. With lips pressed against the thin fabric that veiled the windowpane I would gradually taste the cold of the glass through the gauze. From that oriel, some years later, at the outbreak of the Revolution, I watched various engagements and saw my first dead man: he was being carried away on a stretcher, and from one dangling leg an ill-shod comrade kept trying to pull off the boot despite pushes and punches from the stretchermen – all this at a goodish trot. But in the days of Mr Burness' lessons there was nothing to watch save the dark, muffled street and its receding line of loftily suspended lamps, around which the snowflakes passed and repassed with a graceful, almost deliberately slackened motion, as if to show how the trick was done and how simple it was. From another angle, one might see a more generous stream of snow in a brighter, violet-tinged nimbus of gaslight, and then the jutting enclosure where I stood would seem to drift slowly up and up, like a balloon. At last one of the phantom sleighs gliding along the street would come to a stop, and with gawky haste Mr Burness in his fox-furred *shapka* would make for our door.

Vladimir Nabokov, Speak Memory (1967)

\* \* \*

In the dead of winter, when the palaces and mansions loom over the frozen river in their heavy snow trimmings and shawls like old imperial dignitaries, sunk up to their eyebrows in massive fur coats. When the crimson ball of the setting January sun paints their tall Venetian windows with liquid gold, a freezing man crossing the bridge on foot suddenly sees what Peter had in mind when he erected these walls: a giant mirror for a lonely planet. And, exhaling steam, he feels almost pity for those naked columns with their Doric hairdos, captured as though driven into this merciless cold, into this knee-high snow.

The lower the thermometer falls, the more abstract the city looks. Minus twenty-five centigrade is cold enough, but the temperature keeps falling as though, having done away with people, river, and buildings, it aims for ideas, for abstract concepts. With the white smoke floating above the roofs, the buildings along the embankments more and more resemble a stalled train bound for eternity. Trees in parks and public gardens look like school diagrams of human lungs with black caverns of crows' nests. And always in the distance, the golden needle of the Admiralty's spire tries, like a reversed ray, to anaesthetise the content of the clouds.

Joseph Brodsky, 'A Guide to a Renamed City' (1979)
in *Less Than One: Selected Essays*

\* \* \*

*But the city always had pleasures to offer, even in the harshest depths of winter – like the traditional New Year's Day party described by Lady Londonderry in 1836–7.*

The whole of the Hermitage and Winter Palace are thrown open and lighted up and crowds of the commonest and dirtiest people admitted. Above forty thousand tickets are issued and coachmen, servants, muzhiks, etc. are all allowed to enter, walk about and take refreshment.

The crowd, the heat, the smell, the squeeze are not to be imagined and nothing can penetrate the solid mass except when the Emperor appears, and holding up a finger requests his children to let him pass and the crowd falls back. It is spoken of as the most beautiful and touching sight to see the Sovereign in the midst of his subjects, the love and veneration shown, and the propriety of conduct of all these people high and low, rich and poor – not a case of drunkenness or dishonesty. Though all the treasures of the Palace are left open, not a bit of plate is ever missed.

Lady Londonderry, *The Russian Journal of Lady Londonderry,*
*1836–7*

✣ ✣ ✣

*One of the pleasures of a St Petersburg winter is the*
*sheer beauty created by the snow – as described by*
*nineteenth-century French writer Théophile Gautier.*

I was delighted to see Nevsky Prospekt powdered with snow and in its full winter dress. It's astonishing how much the place is improved by this. An endless silver ribbon unrolled as far as the eye could see, between the double line of palaces, mansions, and churches; every building highlighted by touches of white created a truly wonderful effect. The colours of the houses – rose, yellow, buff, mouse-grey – which are apt to look rather odd under normal circumstances, take on a harmony of tone when relieved by dazzling lines and sparkling snow-crystals. The Cathedral of Our Lady of Kazan, which we passed, was transformed to its great advantage: on its cupola now sat a Russian snow-cap; the cornices and Corinthian capitals were outlined in pure white; on the terrace of its semicircular colon-nade was a balustrade of bulky silver, like that adorning the *ikonostasis*; the steps leading to the portico were covered with a carpet of ermine, fine soft and splendid enough for a tsarina to set her foot upon.

Théophile Gautier, *Travels in Russia* (1867)
translated by Erica King

* * *

*The snow can be beautiful but deadly – a friend or an enemy. Which will it prove to be at the time of the Siege of Leningrad? An extract from Helen Dunmore's moving and evocative novel,* The Siege.

Anna has always loved the first snowfall of winter. She knows as soon as dawn comes that it'll be today. The sky remains dark, with a yellow tinge to the clouds. The light has a sharp, raw edge. Everything is waiting, silent and expectant.

Snow will come. The shrivelled leaves of autumn, the dying grasses, the chilly, dun-coloured earth, will all be covered. The snow will wipe away all mistakes. Light will stream upwards from the immaculate white of the ground.

When the first snow falls, Anna always goes to the Summer Garden. There, the noise of the city is muffled, and the park is eerily luminous. Small, naked-looking sparrows hop from twig to twig, dislodging a powder of snow. The trees are lit up like candelabra by the whiteness they hold in their arms. Underfoot, she hears for the first time the squeak of snow packing into the treads of her boots. She bends down, scoops up a handful of the new snow, throws it up into the air and watches it scatter into powdery fragments as it falls for the second time. And although she's cold and she ought to get home, she always stays much longer than she means to, because she knows that this feeling won't come again for another year. The snow will continue to fall, thaw, freeze, turn grey with use, be covered again and again by fresh blizzards. But nothing again will have the freshness, exhilaration and loneliness of the first snowfall. She's the one thing still warm and alive in a world which is going to sleep.

She looks up, into the snow which spirals down the steep funnels of the sky, whirls into her face, lands on her eyelashes and melts into tears. And then she goes back to the apartment, along streets where trams are already thrashing the new, soft snow into slush. Children skid around street-corners, yelling, their faces blazing crimson. Soon it'll be time for skis and sledges. And tomorrow, when she wakes, the snow will be thick and crusted with ice. The sun will be out, and all the shadows will be blue. This is how she has welcomed the snow every year of her life.

But not this year. The first snow falls on the fourteenth of October, drifting down through the sky and settling on the ruins of shelled houses, on to tank-traps, machine-gun nests and heaps of rubble. The snow is silent, but ominous. No one knows, this year, whether it will be an enemy or a friend. The Russian winter defeated Napoleon, people say to one another. Perhaps it will defeat Hitler, too.

Helen Dunmore, *The Siege* (2001)

❊ ❊ ❊

*A final evocation of the St Petersburg winter before the long dark nights begin to shorten.*

The long nights seemed reluctant to abandon the city. For a few hours each day a grey light of dawn or dusk filtered through the dirty white cloud ceiling and spread over things like the dim reflection of a distant glacier. Even the snow, which continued to fall, lacked brightness. This white, silent, weightless shroud stretched out to infinity in time and space. By three in the afternoon it was already necessary to light the lamps. Evening darkened the snow with hues of ash, deep blue, and the stubborn grey of old stones. Night took over, inexorable and calm: unreal. In the darkness the delta reverted to its geographical configurations. Dark cliffs of stone cut at right angles lined the frozen canals. A kind of dark phosphorescence emanated from the broad river of ice.

Sometimes the north winds blowing in from Spitsbergen and farther still – from Greenland, perhaps, perhaps from the pole by way of the Arctic Ocean, Norway, and the White Sea – gusted across the bleak estuary of the Neva. All at once the cold bit into the granite; the heavy fogs which had come up from the south across the Baltic vanished, and the denuded stones, earth, and trees were instantly covered with crystals of frost, each of which was a barely visible marvel composed of numbers, lines of force, and whiteness. The night changed its aspect, shedding its veils of unreality. The North Star appeared, the constellations opened the immensity of the world. The next day the bronze horsemen, covered with silver powder on their stone pedestals, seemed to step out of a strange festival; from the tall granite columns of St Isaac's cathedral to its pediment peopled with saints and even to its massive gilded cupola – all was covered with frost. The red granite façades and embankments took on a tint of pink and white ash under this magnificent cloak. The gardens, with their delicate filigree of branches, appeared enchanted.

Victor Serge, *Conquered City* (1932)
translated by Richard Greeman

*And, at last, the first signs of spring …*

A singular sight in St Petersburg is a train of little carts each loaded with one enormous, thick, square block of ice, all as if turned out of one mould of the clearest, transparent sea green, and when the sun plays on them as brilliant as aquamarines.

Sometimes these huge blocks are set up like a sort of Stonehenge or miniature Giant's Causeway on the Neva. I asked Madame Stroganov one day what they were for. '*Mais je les appelle les violettes de Petersburg,*' was her reply because it is a sort of hope of spring when people begin to fill their icehouses.

Lady Londonderry, The Russian Journal of Lady Londonderry,<br>1836–7

✶ ✶ ✶

They reached Liteiny Avenue at last. It was still thawing. A warm, damp, oppressive wind went whistling up and down the streets, carriages splashed through the mud, the horses' hoofs struck the cobbles in the road with a ringing sound. The people on the pavement slouched along in wet and dejected crowds with here and there a drunken man among them.

Fyodor Dostoyevsky The Idiot (1868/9)<br>translated by David Magarshack

✶ ✶ ✶

*The official start of spring is announced in the traditional St Petersburg way.*

His dreams were disturbed, but not broken, by the pounding rumble of cannon fire. He knew in the depths of his sleeping Russian soul that they were the cannons of the Peter and Paul fortress, signalling the breaking of the ice and the start of spring. And so the commander of that fortress entered his dream, in all his finery, offering him a crystal glass of pure Neva water, as if he, Kozodavlev, were the Tsar. But it was his hunger that finally woke him.

By the time he put on his coat to go out, a bright spring day was well under way.

There was still snow underfoot, hard-packed and obdurate after the long winter. Lattices of frost clung defiantly to the

87

bases of walls and parapets. But the sun was crisp and business-like in a clear sky. He felt its warmth on his face, the rays of the new season burning down destructively on the remnants of the old. As he walked, he was aware of the thin layer of greasy slush forming.

He came to the Moika river, heart quickening. The proximity of any large body of water did this to him now. Instinctively, before looking down at the surface of the river, Kozodavlev checked behind him, as if he believed that whoever was spying on him would have noticed this change in his physiology.

Which of these harmless-looking citizens, apparently going about their business without paying him any heed, was the Third Section spy assigned to watch him? He avoided looking too inquiringly into any of the faces that passed him by. But none of them jumped out. He was almost reassured.

At last he peered down, over the balustrade. He knew that he had been delaying this moment, and knew precisely why. It was as he had feared. The surface of the river was mottled with grey slabs of ice, edged in frothy white. Around the slabs, the black water seethed and lapped.

The thaw had begun.

R. N. Morris, *The Cleansing Flames* (2011)

❊ ❊ ❊

*But spring has brought its own problems to the city at certain times in its history. Victor Serge's* Conquered City *is set during the period of the Civil War, after the 1917 Revolution.*

The thaw was approaching. Piles of filth hardened by the cold filled the courtyards of buildings and the floors of whole rooms which would be transformed into cesspools with the first warm days. The water conduits had broken in many areas: they would soon be infested with disease. Typhus was already present; it was necessary to head off cholera, to clean up a huge enfeebled city within a few weeks. Kirk proposed to the Executive the formation of an extraordinary Committee of three with unlimited powers. Kirk telephoned the Urban Transportation Committee: 'I need four hundred trams …' At the other end of the wire Rubin answered: 'I'll give you thirty and you'll feed the horses yourself.' Kirk requisitioned the old retired tramway cars and posted notices declaring that 'persons belonging to the wealthy classes, aged 18-60,' were drafted into sanitation duty. Formed into teams supervised by the Poor People's Committees, this workforce would clean up the city. Only three hundred disinherited ex-rich people were to be found among the 750,000 inhabitants. Kirk, swearing in English into his stained moustache, ordered round-ups in the centre of the city and had the trams stopped in the streets to pull off well-dressed people who were adjudged ex-bourgeois by their appearance and sent off to sanitation duty with no further discussion.

Victor Serge, *Conquered City* (1932)
translated by Richard Greeman

✻ ✻ ✻

*The sense of energy and movement in the new season
is captured in this fragment by Nabokov.*

It was one of those rough, gusty, and lustrous mornings in St Petersburg, when the last transparent piece of Lagoda ice has been carried away to the gulf by the Neva, and her indigo waves heave and lap the granite of the embankment, and the tugboats and huge barges, moored along the quay, creak and scrape rhythmically, and the mahogany and brass of anchored steam yachts shine in the skittish sun.

Vladimir Nabokov, *Pnin* (1957)

✻ ✻ ✻

*The traditional celebration of spring's arrival in a novel set in the nineteenth century.*

The gilt dome of St Isaac's Cathedral caught fire in a blaze of easy splendour. A roar of approval greeted the effect, although the stone angels on the cathedral roof seemed about to take wing in panic. The sudden flare gave them a weightless, flighty vivacity.

Porfiry[1] imagined the boundless blue around the cathedral filled with the celestial beings, swooping and flapping as they sought a safe alighting place in the godless city, like seagulls swarming a fishing boat. Of course, the appearance of combustion had been caused by a shift in the sun's position in relation to the one, wispy cloud in the sky. The angels remained attached to the roof, steadfastly static.

Below, under the gaze of the stone angels, crowds of people were streaming around the cathedral on every side, all heading in one direction: north, drawn by the noise and bustle that possessed Admiralty Square. One corner of the fair was visible from where Porfiry and Virginsky were standing, at the end of Malaya Morskaya Street where it joined St Isaac's Square. The carnival colours and teeming movement held their gaze.

There was an undeniably savage edge to the rumble of the crowd, a ferocious hunger for something other than the simple pleasures of the fairground. No doubt many of them were already drunk. The mood seemed fractious, rather than celebratory, bordering on nasty. The grating whine of the barrel organs, incessantly churning out fragments of melody, repeated and overlapping, unmusical, meaningless and quite unpleasant, did nothing to lighten it.

'Yarilo,' murmured Porfiry.

'I beg your pardon?'

---

1 R. N. Morris bases his detective on the character Porfiry Petrovich, taken from Dostoyevsky's *Crime and Punishment*. It is Porfiry Petrovich who is in charge of solving the murders committed by Raskolnikov and who, along with Sonya, guides him towards confession. (Ed.)

'They greet the ancient deity of spring. Yarilo. Sometimes I wonder if we are a Christian nation at all.'

Virginsky offered no reply.

R. N. Morris, The Cleansing Flames (2011)

❋ ❋ ❋

*And those incredible 'White Nights' finally arrive …*

The school year usually is over by the end of May, when the White Nights arrive in this city, to stay throughout the whole month of June. A white night is a night when the sun leaves the sky for barely a couple of hours – a phenomenon quite familiar in the northern latitudes. It's the most magic time in the city, when you can write or read without a lamp at two o'clock in the morning, and when the buildings, deprived of shadows and their roofs rimmed with gold, look like a set of fragile china. It's so quiet around that you can almost hear the clink of a spoon falling in Finland. The transparent pink tint of the sky is so light that the pale-blue watercolour of the river almost fails to reflect it. And the bridges are drawn up as though the islands of the delta have unclasped their hands and slowly begun to drift, turning in the mainstream, toward the Baltic. On such nights, it's hard to fall asleep, because it's too light and because any dream will be inferior to this reality.

Joseph Brodsky, 'A Guide to a Renamed City' (1979)<br>in Less Than One: Selected Essays

❋ ❋ ❋

*A wonderful evocation of summer in St Petersburg from the opening of Helen Dunmore's* The Siege.

*June, 1941*

It's half past ten in the evening, but the light of day still glows through the lime leaves. They are so green that they look like an hallucination of the summer everyone had almost given up expecting. When you touch them, they are fresh and tender. It's like touching a baby's skin.

Such a late spring, murky and doubtful, clinging to winter's skirts. But this is how it happens here in Leningrad. Under the trees around the Admiralty, lakes of spongy ice turned grey. There was slush everywhere, and a raw, dirty wind off the Neva. There was a frost, a thaw, another frost.

Month after month ice-fishermen crouched by the holes they'd drilled in the ice, sitting out the winter, heads hunched into shoulders. And then, just when it seemed as if summer would forget about Leningrad this year, everything changed. Ice broke loose from the compacted mass around the Strelka. Seagulls preened on the floes as the current swept them under bridges, and down the widening Neva to the sea. The river ran full and fast, with a fresh wind tossing up waves so bright they stung your eyes. Everything that was rigid was crumbling, breaking away, floating.

People leaned on the parapets of the Dvortsovy bridge, watching the ice-floes rock as they passed under the arch. Their winter world was being destroyed. They wanted spring, of course they wanted it, more than anything. They longed for sun with every pore of their skin. [...]

Spring stripped everything bare. It showed the grey and weary skin of everyone over thirty. It lit up lips set in suffering, with wrinkles pulling sharply at the corners of the mouth.

But the lime trees' bare branches were spiked by the glitter of sunlight and birdsong. The birds had no doubts at all. They sang out loudly and certainly into the still-frozen world. They knew that winter was on the move.

Now it's June, and the night is brief as the brush of a wing, only an hour of yellow stars in a sky that never darkens beyond deep, tender blue.

No one sleeps. Crowds surge out of cafés and wander the streets, not caring where they go as long as they can lift their faces and drink the light. It's been dark for so many months.

A line of young men, arm in arm, stern with the effort of keeping on their feet, sways on the corner of Universitetskaya Embankment and Lieutenant Schmidt's bridge. They won't go home. They can't bear to part from one another. They'll walk, that's what they'll do, from one end of the city to another, from island to island, across stone bridges and shining water.

These are the nights that seal each generation of Leningraders to their city. These nights are their baptism. The summer light will flood every grain of Leningrad stone, as it floods every cell of their own bodies. At three o'clock in the morning, in full sun, they'll find themselves in some backstreet of little wooden houses, miles from anywhere. There'll be a cat licking its paws in a doorway, a lime tree with electric-green leaves hanging over a high wooden fence, and an old woman slowly making her way down the street with a little bunch of jasmine pinned to her jacket. Each flower will be as white and distinct as a star against the shabby grey. And she'll smile at the young men as if she's their grandmother. She won't disapprove of their drunkenness, their shouting and singing. She'll understand exactly how they feel.

However old you are, you can't stay indoors on a night like this. It stirs again, the promise and recklessness of white nights. Peter's icy, blood-sodden marshes bear up the city like a swan. The swan's wings are still folded, but they are trembling in the summer light, stirring, and getting ready to fly. Darkness scarcely touches them.

The wind breathes softly. Water laps under the midnight bridges. And suddenly you know there's no greater possible happiness than to be here, even when you're so old you're beyond walking. You lean out of your apartment window, with stiff joints and fading strength, over the city that will outlive you.

Helen Dunmore *The Siege* (2001)

✳ ✳ ✳

*But, of course, even in summer the skies can suddenly*
*turn dark …*

The nights are light in St Petersburg's summer but darkness
can come in the afternoon. The sky is boiling lead, pregnant
and pendulous. Its swollen teats seem to brush the steeples and
domes of the city in a rolling horizontal slide. The imminence is
uncanny, physically felt, one's brain a conduit between the sky
and the stomach. […]

At this point a roar breaks across the city, very loud and
increasing in volume. Hail is pouring from above, hitting us,
rattling spitefully round our feet – sudden lawns of white
combustion extend everywhere. We dash to a grand portico
assembled from caryatids and gryphons and rusticated pillars,
bulges of soft stucco flesh and splays of gripping claws. It
is enclosed by sheets of falling ice, deafening, bouncing like
smashed marble, cracking against the city's windowpanes.
Across the darkness lightning makes violent modulations of
light, and thunder augments the din.

'Funny weather for the time of year …'

'No,' he says, half smiling, but understanding too my use of
the word. 'Weather always funny in St Petersburg. Do you have
yellow rain in London?'

'No.'

'We do. And when the …' – he means 'puddles' – 'dry up,
there is yellow powder. Not always. But often. You must use
an umbrella or hat when it rains here. People who do not lose
their hair.' […]

When we step outside again it is as if Nature herself had
acquired the priestly glower. Overhead is a mass of dark clouds
tinged with greenish putrefaction. A wind hums. Individuals
quicken their pace, trying to gain a destination before the
waters break, but we are indecisive. Lightning flashes, the air

cracks, large drops descend, hitting the pavement like transparent tomatoes. The populace scatters into doorways and under arches as the low hot sky sobs against the upturned face of the city and Petersburg goes entirely out of focus, becomes a rough sketch of itself. The broken surfaces of roads are lakes and streams all in splashing commotion, while the grain and speed of the rain make the buildings appear to ascend – but ascend not into the sky, rather to lift up into the depths of a waveless sea, into a possible future when the barrage has given way and palaces are submerged, when ornate rooms enclose giant blocks of silent water, when chandeliers are strung with green weed, and fishes with flicking tails cruise slowly up pillared staircases …

Duncan Fallowell, *One Hot Summer in St Petersburg* (1994)

❉  ❉  ❉

*But all too soon the brief northern summer is over …*

The last dabs of sunlight on the great dome of St Isaac's vanished and the summer ended. The beautiful broad river – along whose granite banks the rotting hulks were fast being stripped bare – carried the bacilli of cholera, dysentery, and typhus down to the sea. The river was deserted. The absence of boats created great voids between the bridges. The golden spires rising above the Fortress, the Admiralty, the Old Castle, like old-fashioned court swords, turned pale in the whitening sky. In the Summer Garden the statues grieved over dead leaves; the grill at the gate imprisoned exiled goddesses.

Victor Serge, *Conquered City* (1932)
translated by Richard Greeman

❉  ❉  ❉

*Rain, wind and high tides bring back memories of disastrous floods.*

The sentiment about nature returning someday to reclaim its usurped property, yielded once under human assault, has its logic here. It derives from the long history of floods that have ravaged this city, from the city's palpable, physical proximity to the sea. Even though the trouble never goes beyond the Neva's jumping out of her granite straitjacket, the very sight of those massive leaden wads of clouds rushing in on the city from the Baltic makes the inhabitants weary with anxieties that are always there anyway. Sometimes, especially in the late fall, this kind of weather with its gushing winds, pouring rain, and the Neva tipping over the embankments lasts for weeks. Even though nothing changes, the mere time factor makes you think that it's getting worse. On such days, you recall that there are no dikes around the city and that you are literally surrounded by this fifth column of canals and tributaries; that you are practically living on an island, one of the hundred and one of them; that you saw in that movie – or was it in your dream? – that gigantic wave which et cetera, et cetera; and then you turn on the radio for the next forecast. Which usually sounds affirmative and optimistic.

Joseph Brodsky, 'A Guide to a Renamed City' (1979)
in *Less Than One: Selected Essays*

✳ ✳ ✳

*As well as rain and snow, the onset of winter in St Petersburg brings fog – as at the beginning of Dostoyevsky's novel,* The Idiot.

At about nine o'clock in the morning at the end of November, during a thaw, the Warsaw train was approaching St Petersburg at full speed. It was so damp and foggy that it was a long time before it grew light, and even then it was difficult to distinguish out of the carriage windows anything a few yards to the right and left of the railway track. Among the passengers were some who were returning from abroad; but it was the third-class compartments that were crowded most of all, chiefly with small business men who had boarded the train at the last stop. As usual, everyone was tired, everyone looked weary after a night's journey, everyone was chilled to the marrow, and everyone's face was pale and yellow, the colour of the fog.

Fyodor Dostoyevsky *The Idiot* (1868/9)
translated by David Magarshack

✳ ✳ ✳

*Then everything starts to turn slippery as winter sets in once more ...*

The last days of November, when the final crisp sunshine has gone, the days have grown short, the statues in the Summer Garden have all been shuttered, and the snow, bitter and hard, has already begun to fall. The skies at that time will be as dark as lead. The streets will be an ice-rink or a skid-pan, and on the Nevsky Prospekt, outside my guard-protected hotel, it will be almost too dangerous to walk out.

Malcolm Bradbury, *To the Hermitage* (2000)

✳ ✳ ✳

*And a final trip through St Petersburg's seasons – from a 1942 diary recording the Siege of Leningrad.*

MAY

Anyone who had seen Leningrad in January and February would hardly recognise the city now. Snowdrifts lay in the streets in those days, lumps of ice were slipping from the roofs, the pavements were hidden under layers of frozen snow, dirt was piled up in mounds, the yards were choked up with refuse, the debris of shattered walls lay scattered over the streets. There were bricks, broken barrels frozen into the snow, twisted, broken pipes, shattered window frames, piles of broken glass. This was the scene that met your eyes everywhere.

But now you walk along clean broad streets and splendid embankments that look just as though they had been swept with a gigantic broom. It was by no means easy to achieve this result. Three hundred thousand Leningraders worked day after day to clean up the city. [...]

The rails appeared from underneath the yard-deep snow, and the first tram went along them accompanied with the applause of thousands of people. It was not a swallow but a tram that brought the Spring to Leningrad in 1942. ...

JUNE

There is a glorious blue sky, and the clouds sailing up from the bay are white and fleecy. There are bunches of bird-cherry blossom in women's hands. In the tram-cars coming from the suburbs the women have sprays of wild cherry blossom in their laps, and spades in their hands. But those sun-burnt hands have not been digging only trenches; they are now working on the production front – the whole city is busy with its gardens. ...

JULY

This July heavy downpours drench the thick-grown, luxuriant foliage, the innumerable allotments, the metal domes of civic buildings and the spotted barrels of the anti-aircraft guns peering watchfully aloft.

Undisturbed by gardeners, the grass is growing rampantly in the parks. ...

AUGUST

August is nearly over. A man with the sunburnt, ordinary face of a Soviet civil servant is sitting on a bench in the square, where the yellow dahlias droop their heads in the flower-beds.

SEPTEMBER

It's Leningrad's second autumn of siege. Dark nights, foggy days, and heavy, grey waves on the Neva. ...

OCTOBER

The whole sky is overcast with heavy woolly clouds. In the autumn twilight the slanting rain pours down while a warm west wind drives the waters of the Neva back from the sea. Lit up by the lamps of the passing cars, the water in the canals seems swollen; here and there on the outskirts it swirls on a level with the banks. The dull sound of gun-fire comes from beyond this misty, sodden dusk. The wind from the Baltic tears at the shutters, rattles the broken window-panes, and drives before it the wet leaves in the parks, sweeping them into heaps. ...

NOVEMBER

The roofs and streets are covered with snow, and the ice floes on the Neva have frozen solid. The river has been halted and now forms a scaly grey field. The way is barred to the tugs and steamers. The trees seem to have been etched in black ink. This is the second winter of the blockade. The Leningraders are carting home their firewood on sledges. Women with their heads wrapped in shawls clear away the snow in the mornings. There are thin patterns of ice on the window-panes. At the least hint of warmth in the breeze the pavements are covered with a sticky mud and the Neva thaws – the gaps in the ice shine with a leaden glint. ...

DECEMBER

Gloom and fog. At one moment one's feet splash into puddles, the next they slip on the icy pavement. The yellow lights of the cars shine dimly in the fog. Water drips from the roofs, just as in April. The muffled bass note of a tug comes from the river. A warm wind from the sea bends the bare black branches of trees. It is December in Leningrad. [...]

It is already the seventeenth month of the blockade. The days are the darkest and shortest of the year. The evening comes so soon that the stars seem never to disappear from the sky and only hide for a while behind the low-hanging clouds. This makes the city even more gloomy and fantastic. One is reminded of the poetry of Alexander Blok which was inspired by mists of this sort, when the city suddenly vanishes or appears in the fantastic light of an occasional headlamp.

Nikolai Tikhonov, 'Leningrad Calendar, 1942'
(translator unknown)

# The great and the good, the not so good ... and everybody else

*The section starts with some 'greats': whether or not these particular greats were also good, or not so good, depends on your point of view. There has always been a certain tension between St Petersberg and Moscow, and if you were a dedicated Muscovite, you might not rate dedicated pro-Petersburgers, such as Peter I and Catherine II, as 'great' – though you probably wouldn't be able to deny their huge impact on Russia's history and culture ... and on present-day tourism to the former capital. Other rulers also made vital contributions to the city's development, but the best writing tends to be on these two iconic figures.*

101

> The French 'philosophe' Denis Diderot (1713-
> 84), a key figure of the Enlightenment, was much
> admired by Catherine the Great who had been trying
> to tempt him to visit St Petersburg. Eventually, in
> 1773, Diderot made the perilous journey to Cathe-
> rine's court and this event forms the central theme of
> Malcolm Bradbury's novel To the Hermitage, *which*
> *alternates between the St Petersburg of the eighteenth*
> *and late twentieth century. It was Diderot who had*
> *recommended the French sculptor Falconet to create*
> *the statue of Peter the Great that Catherine wanted*
> *to commission – the statue which became the subject*
> *of Pushkin's famous poem, 'The Bronze Horseman'.*
>
> In the extract below we meet Peter the Great in the
> form of Falconet's statue

Senate Square is a very fine square. It's a noble square, the very
square where – one day still very far ahead, when it is faced
and completed – the Imperial Mother[1], in homage to her great
predecessor, will raise up the huge bronze statue our man had
such a hand in. [...] From the great podium underneath the
cloth-covered statue, the Imperial Mother will bless her people,
declare a general amnesty for criminals and debtors.

Across the Neva, over there in the Peter and Paul Cathedral-
Fortress, the Great Metropolitan will strike Peter's tomb hard
with his staff. 'Arise, great monarch,' he'll say, 'and look out over
your pleasing and noble invention. For nothing you did has ever
faded, nor has its glory dimmed.' Back over the sunlit water, the
Empress will gesture, and the curtains hung round the statue
will drop. There will be Big Peter, incredibly raised up on the
back of his rearing horse, serpent between his legs, all tied to
the ground only by two little hooves and the sheet-anchor of the
horse's tail. His grand face, still with toolmarks on it, will come

---

1  Catherine the Great (Ed.)

into view. He'll be looking out possessively, first across the river, toward his own bones over there in the Peter and Paul, then, more grandly, out at the Baltic and the still un-Russianized world that lies temptingly out there to the West.

[...]

'And now you can see him. There he is.'

I look upward. There he is indeed. Big Peter, high-hatted, trapped on his rock-pedestal, rises up high above us on his horse. He's a flowing figure, as big as can be, big as bronze and Falconet can make him, dwarfing the square Intourist buses parked all around him, and shrinking to nothing all these dressed-up Russian wedding parties that have gathered round his pediment, to have their photos taken, somehow hoping to link their Posterity with his.

'You remember the poem of Pushkin, we all learn it at school?' asks Galina. '"Where lonely waters strive to reach the sea, he stood / And gazed before him, mind filled with the greatest thoughts."'

He's not what I've expected; in fact he looks perfectly pleasant as he sits up there, staring out at the Baltic as if he's expecting a fresh load of pictures, rising up out of his flowing rock pedestal, more civilized in looks than I imagined, more gallant, more – how can I put it? – French. The whole ensemble is so flowing and mobile it's not hard to see why Pushkin imagined the horse leaping down from the pedestal, and Peter and his mount thundering through the streets and squares of the city, chasing the guilty, the unhappy, the anxious to their dooms.

Malcolm Bradbury, *To the Hermitage* (2000)

✻ ✻ ✻

*As we have already seen, St Petersburg was founded upon the principles of European Enlightenment which Peter the Great (reigned 1682–1725) had encountered during his travels in Europe and through socialising*

> *with foreigners in Moscow's 'German Quarter' (where they were obliged to live). Both Peter and a number of his successors (though not all) pursued Enlightenment values in the priorities they gave to such things as science, education, architecture and the arts – all of which have helped to define St Petersburg throughout its history. Here's a piece about some of Peter's important innovations.*

Peter strove to make Petersburg safe, habitable, and pleasant. To this end he organised the police, establishing the general Policemeister's Chancellery in 1718. Peter's conception of the police was not simply that of crime prevention, law enforcement, or surveillance. In fact the city's police force numbered no more than a hundred men. Drawing on rationalist Western European concepts of the well-ordered police state, the police were given broad responsibilities designed to rationalise and civilise society. The first general Policemeister was the Portuguese-born Anton Devier, a former ship's cabin boy whom Peter met while in Holland during a mock naval battle. Impressed by Devier's abilities, Peter invited him to Petersburg, initially as one of his orderlies. Devier served Peter loyally and zealously, and continued as Policemeister after Peter's death. […]

Peter issued Devier with a detailed thirteen-part instruction outlining the Policemeister's obligations, which reflect police science's concept of the broad social role of the institution. Devier's duties included not only enforcement of criminal laws, but publication of all Peter's decrees, organising refuse collection, setting up guards and patrols to keep beggars and vagrants off the streets (it was illegal to give alms to them; charitable donations were to be made to charitable organisations such as hospitals), suppressing street fighting, organising fire-fighting measures, exercising quality control and imposing hygienic measures at markets, cleaning up the slaughterhouses, enforcing construction requirements, maintaining canals and docks, ensuring compliance by residents with their obligations to pave and maintain streets and sidewalks and strengthen embankments, enforcing rules on traders (including their dress), and combating desertion by workers, soldiers, and sailors. The General Policemeister's Chancellery effectively became the general administrative body of the city. The Governor's Office made larger decisions in the city and administered lesser details only outside the city proper.

This vast effort was possible because the city's residents were drafted into supplementing Devier's small force to beautify and maintain the city, at their own expense. Citizens were subject to numerous burdensome requirements, and were fined or subject to corporal punishment if they did not comply. They had to keep the streets and pavements in front of their homes clean. When trees were planted, they were responsible for supplying the trees, and when paving was being done they had to supply sand and other materials and prepare the area by their homes. Residents living on the river and canals had to reinforce the embankments, and were forbidden from polluting the waterways. A decree of 3 September 1718 required that 'each resident shall, early each morning before people walk the streets … sweep all dirt from bridges and streets in front of their homes so that there will be no refuse, and maintain the paving stones'. Special taxes and duties were imposed on city residents in order to fund municipal improvements, maintenance and repair, city lighting, sanitation, and other measures.

However burdensome, these efforts made Petersburg unique in Russia, and indeed in Europe. Its main streets were wide and straight, and many were paved and lit at night. It featured canals, parks, and gardens. And it was relatively safe, orderly and clean. In these respects Petersburg was better than most Western European cities.

Arthur George with Elena George, *St Petersburg: A History* (2003)

✻ ✻ ✻

*Catherine the Great (reigned 1762–96) was devoted
to Peter the Great's vision and developed it during her
own reign. She was also devoted to Diderot and the
second part of the extract below covers the French
philosopher's visit to her court.*

She's a cunning clever queen, without any question. As she shops
and builds, she calculates and thinks. Like an earlier queen,
Christina, at the further end of the Baltic, she's an honest blue-
stocking: a splendid learned lady with a fine European education.
She's arrived in the winter snows from one of the back courts
of German Europe, a small-ranking Prussian princess who, still
only fat and fourteen, has married a prince: the mad little soldier
who will in time become Peter the Third. Once enthroned as his
tsarina in dirty old Moscow, it has taken her no time at all to
deal with this plodding marital encumbrance. Finding, as only
a clever and ambitious princess can, sponsors and conspira-
tors, guardsmen and lovers, she manages a grand palace coup,
displacing her unpopular husband to prison and becoming
sole mistress of the Russias. Not much later comes Tsar Peter's
strange and fortunate death, from a sudden attack of the haem-
orrhoids. Now she's Empress Autocratix of All the Russias,
Tsarina of Kazan, Astrakhan and Siberia, Princess of Estonia,
Livonia, Karelia. Dame of goodness knows where. When rival
Romanovs appear (as they do so often) they are perfectly likely
to suffer the same fate as her spouse, and probably in the same
prison. There is, for instance, the mysterious 'Prisoner Number
One', clearly a perfectly valid pretender, an entirely genuine
imposter, for whose strange maddened end she expresses deep
surprise and accepts no responsibility, none at all.

But in a woman of such huge charms and splendid talents
these little tricks and contrivances can always be excused.
True, she seems to have adapted quite easily to some of the
harsh Russian ways, but she still preserves the high European

graces. She's a popular princess, an enlightened empress, especially when seen from a distance. She has Enlightenment tastes, she listens to the messages of reason, she's in tune with the newest thought of the age. She's a creature of destiny, dreams and desire: a true queen of hearts. She takes lovers from everywhere, her Night-Emperors: burly brute-lovers for the body, more aesthetic lovers for the mind. Meantime, along the ever improving banks of the Neva, rotting Petrine wood turns magically into long-lasting stone, and once mean streets open out into the most inviting *prospekts*. Soon there's a university, an Academy of Arts, another of sciences; an Italian theatre, a great observatory, a Temple of Minerva, a library, even a mysterious astronomical clock whose interior can be entered to disclose the inner workings of the unmistakably rational universe. She more than reads; she thinks, studies, argues. She's drawn to grand ideas and learning; she looks to Paris and the great *Encyclopedia* itself. No sooner has she taken power than she writes warm letters to the makers and shakers: Voltaire and Rousseau, d'Holbach and d'Alembert, the people who think new thoughts not just for Paris – where court, church and censor are all too ready to burn their books or stack their authors in prison – but for the self-redeeming progressive cosmos itself.

And, truth to tell, in the course of her great Enlightenment shopping spree she has purchased our Thinker[1] himself. [...]

In the shining corridors of the Hermitage, simply everyone is asking to meet him. It's only the Empress herself who's detained. But weddings are like that: great and demanding occasions, even if it's the marriage of an obnoxious son she once thought to dispose of in much the way she had his supposed father, the last tsar. For weddings, at least this one, are state events, demanding so much attention to this, so much protocol about that. There must be balls, parties, fireworks, cannon-shots, church blessings, state receptions, each one of which she must be seen at. There are

---

1   Denis Diderot (Ed.)

faces to kiss; mother of the groom. There are foreign ambassadors everywhere, each to be entertained, courted, or threatened. There's a new daughter-in-law to induct into the ways of the Orthodox Church (just as happened to her, twenty years before), and whose duties as bearer of tsars and progenitrix of dynasties need to be very carefully spelled out. Treaties to sign first thing in the morning, relatives to see, new alliances to be forged in the Hermitage corridors, for in the wake of weddings all the treaties change. And to complicate matters there's the rumoured Cossack rebellion, a problem with Turkey, a fresh batch of royal impostors to jail, and a conspiracy and turmoil all round the court as, thanks to the wedding, allegiances shift. No, it's not always great, being Great.

But she's certainly not forgotten her French philosopher, a man whom she's been trying to tempt here for the past eleven years. […]

And suddenly there she is: a living statue in herself. Despite what the portraits tell you, she's definitely in her middle years, fiftyish or so. She's high-foreheaded, long-faced, pointy-chinned, rouge-cheeked. She's big, plump and round, but very stately and now wearing something very masculine and half-regimental; on her ripe shape it's the costume of a diva. Dashkova suddenly ushers him forward. The courtiers watch. The moment has come; he looks, looks down, bows low, reaches out, kisses the plump imperial hand that appears before him.

'I'm French,' he says. 'My name is Diderot.'

'And I am Catherine, Russia,' she says, 'the Hermit of the Hermitage. May I welcome my dear librarian to the place where one day his books will come to rest for all eternity.'

'Yes, Your Imperial Majesty, that was truly my most wonderful piece of fortune. My pension and my Posterity. How happy I felt when you promised me that. I knew I should be happy even when I was dead. I took my lute down from the wall and sang a love-song to you.'

'My good fortune too,' says the Empress Autocratrix of All the Russias, Tsarina of Kazan and Lady of Pskov. 'Never did I think by buying a man's dusty library and letting him continue to use it I'd win so many compliments. Tell me, how do you like it, my Palais d'Hiver?'

'It's exactly as I expected,' our man says. 'I do believe I dreamt it once.'

'But you only dreamt, I built,' she says. 'In truth I build like mad.'

'You know you're now considered the benefactress of the whole of Europe?'

She nods her diamonded head: 'So they do say.'

'No other person does more for art or humanity, or more generously spreads the fine new light of reason. No one more sees the wisdom of sense. In you we have perfect proof that the light flows from the north to the south.'

Malcolm Bradbury, *To the Hermitage* (2000)

✳ ✳ ✳

*Catherine the Great appears in many stories and memoirs of time – including Casanova's account of his life in which he recounts meeting the empress in the Summer Garden and striking up a friendship with her. Another garden meeting with the empress occurs in* The Captain's Daughter, *a story by Alexander Pushkin (1799–1837), the first great name in Russian literature and very much a 'Petersburg' writer. In this story a young woman goes to Tsarskoe Selo to petition Catherine the Great on behalf of her imprisoned father. While walking in the garden before seeking her audience, she encounters a woman – the empress herself (though the young woman doesn't, of course, realise this at the time). Here's a snippet.*

Early next morning, Marya Ivanovna woke, dressed and quietly went into the Palace grounds. It was an exquisite morning, with the sun lighting the tops of the linden trees, which were already turning yellow in the cool breath of autumn. The broad lake glittered, motionless. The swans, barely awake, came sailing majestically out from under the banks' overhanging bushes. Marya Ivanovna walked towards a lovely lawn where a monument had just been erected to the recent victories of Count Pyotr Alexandrovitch Rumyantsev. Suddenly a little white dog, an English breed, ran up to her, barking. Alarmed, Marya Ivanovna stopped in her tracks. At the same moment she heard a pleasant female voice saying:

'Don't be afraid; he doesn't bite.'

And Marya Ivanovna saw a lady sitting on the bench opposite the monument. Marya Ivanovna seated herself on the opposite end of the bench. The lady scrutinised her; Marya Ivanovna, in her turn, by several furtive glances, was able to examine her from head to toe. She was wearing a white morning-gown, a night-cap and jacket. She looked about forty. Her plump, rosy face gave off an aura of dignity and calm, and her blue eyes and reticent smile had indescribable charm. The lady was the first to break the silence.

'I suppose you are a stranger here?' she said.

'Yes, ma'am; I only arrived from the country yesterday.'

Alexander Pushkin, *The Captain's Daughter* (1836)
translated by I. Silver

❊ ❊ ❊

*Pushkin died tragically young in one of history's most famous duels. A contemporary account of the event.*

*January 29, 1837.*
An important and terribly sad event in our literature: Pushkin died today of a wound he received in a duel.

Last night I was at Pletnyov's: it was from him that I first heard of this tragedy. D'Anthès, a cavalry officer and Pushkin's opponent, was the first to fire, the bullet entered Pushkin's stomach. Nevertheless Pushkin managed a return shot which shattered d'Anthès's hand. Today, Pushkin is no longer in this world. [...]

*30 January.*
D'Anthès is a shallow man, but an adroit, friendly Frenchman who has sparkled in our salons as a star of the first magnitude. He would often visit the Pushkins. We all know that the poet's wife is beautiful. D'Anthès, as a Frenchman and a frequenter of salons, became too friendly with her, and she did not have enough tact to draw a line between herself and him, a line beyond which no man must pass in his relations with a woman who does not belong to him. In society there are always people who feed on the reputations of their friends: they welcomed this opportunity and spread rumours of a relationship between d'Anthès and Pushkin's wife. These reached Pushkin and, of course, troubled his already agitated soul. He forbade d'Anthès's visits. The latter was insulted and declared that he was visiting not Pushkin's wife but his sister-in-law, with whom he was in love. Thereupon Pushkin demanded that he marry the young girl, and the match was arranged.

In the meantime the poet received, on successive days, anonymous letters that congratulated him on being a cuckold. In one letter he was even sent a membership card in the society of cuckolds, with an imaginary signature of President Naryshkin. Moreover, Baron von Heckeren, who had adopted d'Anthès, was very dissatisfied with his marriage to Pushkin's sister-in-law, who, it was said, was older than her husband and without means. To von Heckeren are ascribed the following words: 'Pushkin thinks that with this marriage, he has split up d'Anthès and his wife. On the contrary he has merely brought them close together, thanks to a new family relationship.'

Pushkin flew into a rage and wrote von Heckeren a letter, full of insults. He demanded that the latter, as a father, curb his young man. The letter was of course read by d'Anthès — he demanded satisfaction and the affair ended beyond the city limits, at ten paces. D'Anthès was the first to fire. Pushkin fell. D'Anthès ran towards him, but the poet, gathering up his strength, ordered his adversary to return to his place, aimed at his heart but hit his hand which d'Anthès, either owing to an awkward movement or out of precaution, had placed over his chest.

Pushkin was wounded in the abdomen, the bullet entering his stomach. When he was brought home, he summoned his wife and children, blessed them and requested Dr Arendt to ask the emperor not to abandon them and to pardon Danzas, his second.

The emperor wrote him a letter in his own hand, promising to take care of his family and do all for Danzas that was possible. In addition he asked that before his death he do all that a Christian should. Pushkin demanded a priest. He died on the 29th, Friday, at 3pm. [...]

*1 February.*
Pushkin's funeral. It was a real 'people's' funeral. Anyone and everyone in St Petersburg who thinks or reads thronged to the church where the mass was being sung for the poet. This took place in the church on Konyushennaya Street. The square was covered with carriage and people, but not a single homespun or sheepskin coat was to be seen among them.

The church was filled with notables. The entire diplomatic corps was present. Only those in uniform or holding tickets were admitted. Every face expressed sadness – at least on the surface. Alongside me stood Baron Rosen, Karlhof, Kukolnik and

Pletnyov. I said my last farewell to Pushkin. His face had changed significantly, for decay had set in. I left the church with Kukolnik.

'At least we managed to move up ahead,' he said, pointing to the crowd coming to pay homage to the remains of one of its finest sons.

Platon Obodovsky fell on my breast, sobbing like a child.

Alexander Nikitenko, *The Diary of a Russian Censor* (1837)
[translator unknown]

❋ ❋ ❋

*Pushkin's name will always be linked with Falconet's statue of Peter the Great through his long poem 'The Bronze Horseman'. Nikita Eliseev reflects on the symbolic force of the horseman and the district associated with him – including its links with the infamous 'mad monk', Rasputin.*

Pushkin's *The Bronze Horseman*[1] was the first story of Petersburg that included the myth of the city, and it is tied to Kolomna and Vasilievsky Island. The hero lives in Kolomna, and he is emblematic of Petersburg. His name is Evgeny, and he is a minor clerk, an abject madman who becomes overburdened with the full weight of the state. It was no coincidence that Pushkin chose Kolomna. It is a district more than any other where fate's implacability can be sensed, along with the inevitability of mundane disaster. [...]

The symbol of misfortune, absurd and rational in equal measure, the symbol of Evgeny fleeing from the Bronze Horseman, is indelibly imprinted on this district. In the thunder of hooves from the Bronze Horseman there was always the

---

1 The poem begins with a mythologised history of St Petersburg, followed by an ode expressing the poet/narrator's love for the city, then, against a backdrop of a storm and the rising waters of the Neva, a poor young man, Yevgeny, discovers that his beloved, Parasha, has been drowned. For a year he roams as a madman before cursing the famous statue of Peter the Great. The statue comes to life and pursues Yevgeny, whose corpse is later found in a ruined hut floating on the water. (Ed.)

promise of historical retribution to be heard. It is no wonder that Nicholas I so feared the resonance of the lines. He knew that sinister law of fate that transforms the hunter, sooner or later, into prey.

Rasputin was killed here, in an attempt to cleanse the dynasty of disgrace. Although the story of his murder was more suited to pulp fiction, it became the source of inspiration for composers. In 2010 a Finnish staging of Rautavaara's[1] opera, *Rasputin*, was put on at the Mariinsky, not far from the scene of the crime. Up on stage Nicholas II, who hated Finland and dreamed of banning the language, sang in Finnish in a sad tenor. It was not the all-powerful autocrat, the ruler of half the world, but a sad little man who had been tossed onto the throne by a whim of fate; it was Evgeny, chased by the Bronze Horseman of history. Symbolic, unforeseen coincidences are par for the course in Petersburg.

Nikita Eliseev, 'Symbol of Misfortune' in
*St Petersburg as Cinema* (2011) (ed. Lubov Arkus)
translated by Sergei Afonin and Alice Jondorf

✳ ✳ ✳

*There are a number of famous literary characters associated with St Petersburg. In fact, our ideas about the city may well be partly formed by our acquaintance with such fictional people as Natasha from Tolstoy's* War and Peace, *Goncharov's eponymous Oblomov, and Raskolnikov from Dostoyevsky's* Crime and Punishment. *First, Natasha Rostov attending the famous New Year's ball – just a brief glimpse which comes with advice to look out the whole passage about the ball, in Part Three of the novel. (It's interesting to note that Tolstoy attributes part of her freshness and attractiveness to her not being the 'usual' St Petersburg type …)*

---

1   Einojuhani Rautavaara b.1928 – Finnish composer. (Ed.)

On December 31, the eve of the new year, 1810, for *le réveillon*[1], a ball was given by a grand dignitary of Catherine's time. The ball was to be attended by the diplomatic corps and the sovereign.

The dignitary's well-known house on the English Embankment shone with countless lights. Police stood by the brightly lit porch laid with red baize, and not merely gendarmes, but a mounted police chief and dozens of police officers. Carriages drove away and new ones drove up with red-liveried footmen and footmen with feathers in their hats. Men in uniform, stars and sashes emerged from the carriages; ladies in satin and ermine carefully descended the noisily flipped down footrests, and stepped hastily and soundlessly over the baize of the porch.

Almost every time a new carriage drove up, a whisper ran through the crowd and hats were doffed. [...]

Natasha had not had a free moment since the morning of that day and had never once had time to think about what lay ahead of her.

In the damp, cold air, in the incomplete darkness of the crowded, rocking carriage, she imagined vividly for the first time what awaited her at the ball, in the brightly lit rooms – music, flowers, dancing, the sovereign, all the brilliant youth of Petersburg. What awaited her was so beautiful that she did not even believe it could happen: so out of keeping it was with the impression of the cold, the crowdedness, the darkness of the carriage. She understood what awaited her only when, having stepped over the red baize of the porch, she entered the front hall, took off her fur coat, and walked beside Sonya in front of her mother between the flowers on the lighted stairway. Only then did she remember how one had to behave at a ball, and try to assume the majestic manner she considered necessary for a girl at a ball. But, luckily for her, she felt her eyes looking everywhere at once: she saw nothing clearly, her pulse beat a

---

1   The New Year's Eve Party (Ed.)

hundred times a minute, and the blood began to throb in her heart. She was unable to assume that manner which would have made her ridiculous, and walked on, faint with excitement and only trying as hard as she could to conceal it. And this was the manner that was most becoming to her. […]

The next day Prince Andrei remembered yesterday's ball but his thought did not dwell on it for long. 'Yes, it was a very brilliant ball. And then, too … yes, Miss Rostov is very sweet. There's something fresh in her, something special, something non-Petersburg, that makes her different.'

Leo Tolstoy, *War and Peace* (1869)
translated by Richard Pevear and Larissa Volokhonsky

❊ ❊ ❊

*Ivan Goncharov's eponymous tragi-comic 'hero', Oblomov, is famous for his lethargy, liking nothing so much as hanging around the house in his dressing-gown. He has become, however, one of St Petersburg's most renowned literary personages and quickly made his creator famous throughout Russia.*

Ilya Ilyich Oblomov was lying in bed one morning in his flat in Gorokhovaya Street in one of those large houses which have as many inhabitants as a country town.

He was a man of about thirty-two or three, of medium height and pleasant appearance, with dark grey eyes, but with a total absence of any definite idea, any concentration, in his features. Thoughts promenaded freely all over his face, fluttered about in his eyes, reposed on his half-parted lips, concealed themselves in the furrows of his brow, and then vanished completely – and it was at such moments that an expression of serene unconcern spread all over his face. This unconcern passed from his face to the contours of his body and even into the folds of his dressing-gown.

Occasionally a sombre look of something like fatigue or

boredom crept into his eyes; but neither fatigue nor boredom could banish for a moment the mildness which was the predominant and fundamental expression not only of his face but of his whole soul, so serenely and unashamedly reflected in his eyes, his smile and every movement of his head and hands. [...]

Oblomov's complexion was not ruddy, nor dark, nor particularly pale, but rather nondescript, or seemed to be so because he had grown so fat and flabby – which was unusual for a man of his age – whether because of lack of exercise, or fresh air, or both, it is difficult to say. Generally speaking, his body, if one were to judge by the dull and excessively white colour of his neck, his small, chubby hands, and his soft shoulders, seemed too effeminate for a man.

His hands, too, even when he was excited, were kept in check by a certain kind of mildness and laziness which was not without its own touch of gracefulness. If his mind was troubled, his eyes were clouded over, lines appeared on his forehead, and he was plunged into doubt, sadness, and fear; but his anxiety seldom took the form of any definite idea and still more seldom was it transformed into a decision. All his anxiety resolved itself into a sigh and dissolved into apathy or drowsiness.

Ivan Goncharov, *Oblomov* (1859)<br>translated by David Magarshak

✻ ✻ ✻

*After the 'light' of Natasha and the 'half-light' of Oblomov, we have the dark of Raskolnikov and what was, for some, the misery of poverty in nineteenth-century St Petersburg at times leading, as in this young man's case, to unspeakable crimes ...*

It was terribly hot in the street, and the stifling air, the crowds of people, the heaps of mortar everywhere, the scaffolding and the bricks, the dust and that peculiar summer stench which is so

117

familiar to everyone who lives in Petersburg and cannot afford to rent a cottage in the country – all that had a most unfortunate effect on the young man's already overwrought nerves. And the unendurable stench from the pubs, which are particularly numerous in that part of the town, and the drunks he came across every few yards although it was a weekday, provided the finishing touch to a picture already sufficiently dismal and horrible. For a brief moment, an expression of the profoundest disgust passed over the young man's refined face. He was, incidentally, quite an extraordinarily handsome young man, with beautiful dark eyes, dark brown hair, over medium height, slim, and well-built. But soon he sank into a sort of deep reverie, or perhaps he might even more truly be said to have fallen into a kind of coma, and he went on his way without paying any attention to his surroundings and without ever giving them a thought. From time to time he would mutter something to himself because of his habit of indulging in soliloquies, a habit to which he had just acknowledged himself to be addicted. At that moment he was fully aware that his thoughts were at times confused and that he was very weak: for two days now he had had hardly anything to eat.

He was so badly dressed that any other man in his place, even if he were accustomed to it, would have been ashamed to go out in the daytime into the streets in such rags. It was true, though, that in that particular part of the town it would be hard to astonish anyone by the clothes one wore. The proximity of the Hay Market[1], the great number of disorderly houses, and most of all, the working-class population which crammed these streets and alleyways in the centre of Petersburg, lent so bizarre an aspect to the whole place that it would indeed have been strange to be surprised at meeting any man, however curiously dressed. But so much bitter contempt had accumulated in the young man's heart that, notwithstanding his occasional youthful fastidiousness in dress, he was least of all ashamed of his rags in the street. […]

---

1   Also known as Sennoy Market, on Sennaya Square. (Ed.)

118

With a sinking heart and trembling nervously, he approached an enormous house which, on one side, looked out to the Yekaterinsky Canal and, on the other, on to Sadovaya Street. This house was divided up into small flats and inhabited by all sorts of tradespeople – tailors, locksmiths, cooks, Germans of every description, girls earning a living in all sorts of ways, low-grade civil servants, and so on. People entering or leaving the house seemed to be darting to and fro under its two gates and across its two courtyards. The young man was very pleased not to meet any of them and he at once slipped, without being seen, through the gates and up the flight of stairs to the right. The stairs were dark and narrow (it was the 'back' entrance), but he knew all that already, having made a careful study of it before, and the whole situation appealed to him: in such darkness even a pair of prying eyes were not dangerous. 'If I'm so frightened now,' the thought crossed his mind involuntarily as he mounted to the fourth floor, 'what would it be like if I were really going to do it?'

Fyodor Dostoyevsky, *Crime and Punishment* (1866)
translated by David Magarshack

❖ ❖ ❖

*Dostoyevsky himself becomes a character in J. M. Coetzee's novel,* The Master of Petersburg, *in which Coetzee imagines a particular period in the writer's life – the year 1869, just after the death of Dostoyevsky's stepson in St Petersburg.*

It is six o'clock and the streets are still thronged when he hastens out bearing his parcel. He follows Gorokhovaya Street to the Fontanka Canal, and joins the press of people crossing the bridge. Midway he stops and leans over the ledge.

The water is frozen over by now, all but a ragged channel in the centre. What a clutter there must be under the ice on the canal-bed! With the spring thaw one could trawl a veritable harvest of guilty secrets here: knives, axes, bloodstained clothing. Worse, too. Easy to kill the spirit, harder to dispose of what is left after that. The burial service and its incantations directed, if the truth be told, not at the soul but at the obstinate body, conjuring it not to rise and return.

Thus, gingerly, like a man probing his own wound, he readmits Pavel to his thoughts. Under his blanket of earth and snow on Yelagin Island, Pavel, unappeased, still stubbornly exists. Pavel tenses himself against the aeons he must outlast till the day of the resurrection when tombs shall be riven open and graves yawn, gritting his teeth as a bare skull does, enduring what he must endure till the sun will shine on him again and he can slacken his tensed limbs. Poor child!

A young couple have paused beside him, the man with his arm around the woman's shoulders. He edges away from them. Beneath the bridge the black water courses sluggishly, lapping around a broken crate festooned with icicles. On the ledge he cradles the canvas parcel, tied with string. The girl glances at him, glances away. At that instant he gives the parcel a nudge.

It falls on to the ice just to one side of the channel and lies there in full view of everyone.

He cannot believe what has happened. He is directly over the channel, yet he has got it wrong! Is it a trick of parallax? Do some objects not fall vertically?

'Now you're in trouble!' says a voice to his left, startling him. A man in a workman's cap, old, greybearded, winks broadly. What a devil's-face! 'Won't be safe to step on for another week at least, I'd say. What do you think you're going to do now?'

Time for a fit, he thinks. Then my cup will be full. He sees himself convulsing and foaming at the mouth, a crowd gathering around, and the greybeard pointing, for the benefit of all, to where the pistol lies on the ice. A fit, like a bolt from heaven to strike the sinner down. But the bolt does not come. 'Mind your own business!' he mutters, and hurries away.

J. M. Coetzee, *The Master of Petersburg* (1994)

✳ ✳ ✳

*Visiting the literary sights of St Petersburg is one of the many, many pleasures the city has to offer. Wolfgang Koeppen recounts 'the Dostoyevsky tour' as it was in 1958.*

A woman leads me, a little librarian; she has gone looking for the sites where events took place. Dostoyevsky liked to take rooms in corner houses. There must have been a view of a church out of his window. This is the house of Raskolnikov. A tenement building. Even today a tenement building. Gloomy. Grey, crumbling plaster. In the courtyard, stacked wood for the oven. The dilapidated shack of the manager. Here Raskolnikov fetched the axe, hung it in the loop under his coat. The axe is lying there. He could fetch it today. But what monsters are there to strike dead? A dirty gateway. A small, pretty girl is playing with a ball. Large, inscrutable eyes fixed on the visitor. This is Sonja's house. The canal. A bridge. Raskolnikov went along this route, hid his meagre plunder. There were wooden houses and taverns here. Now stone buildings stand here. The taverns have disappeared. Light shines down, remarkably pale, and the square is boring. A barracks is being torn down. A backhoe reaches down into the foundations. A children's theatre is being built here, one of the large, beautiful stage facilities for youth that you find in many Russian cities. Yet Dostoyevsky was supposed to have been executed in the courtyard of the barracks. Drums beat, they rumbled about death, about immortality. Dostoyevsky heard himself pardoned to the House of the Dead[1], heard the pardoning of his genius.

> Wolfgang Koeppen, *To Russia and Elsewhere:*
> *Sentimental Journeys* (1958)
> translated by Susan Thorne

---

1   i.e. prison – *The House of the Dead* is the title of Dostoyevsky's autobiographical book about his years in Siberia. (Ed.)

✽  ✽  ✽

*Among the most famous residents of St Petersburg are a host of dancers and musicians. The great ballerina Tamara Karsavina recalls her first sight of the even more famous Nijinsky.*

One morning I came up earlier than usual; the boys were just finishing their practice. I glanced casually, and could not believe my eyes; one boy in a leap rose far above the heads of the others and seemed to tarry in the air. 'Who is this?' I asked Mikhail Obukov, his master. 'It is Nijinksy; the little devil never comes down with the music.' He then called Nijinsky forward by himself and made him show me some steps. A prodigy was before my eyes. He stopped dancing, and I felt it was all unreal and could not have been; the boy looked quite unconscious of his achievement, prosy and even backward. 'Shut your mouth,' were his master's parting words. 'You fly-swallower.' 'Off with you all now.' Like peas falling out of a bag, the boys rushed off, their patter a hollow repercussion in the vaulted passage. In utter amazement I asked Mikhail why nobody spoke of this remarkable boy, and he about to finish[1]. 'They will soon,' chuckled Mikhail. 'Don't you worry.'

Recognition of Nijinsky's wonderful gifts could not fail to be unanimous from the moment he came on the stage; there was some reserve, however, in the appreciation of his personality. 'He is not much to look at, and will never be a first-rate mime.' The troupe as well as the audience misjudged the unique quality of his talent; had he tried to follow an approved pattern of male perfection, he would never have given the full measure of his genius. In later years, Diaghilev, with that clear perception of his that was almost uncanny, revealed to the world and to the artist himself the latter's true shape. At the expense of his better self, Nijinsky valiantly tried to answer the requirements

---

1  i.e. to graduate from the Imperial School of Dancing. (Ed.)

of the traditional type till Diaghilev the wizard touched him with his magic wand. The guise of a plain, unprepossessing boy fell off – a creature exotic, feline, elfin completely eclipsed the respectable comeliness, the dignified commonplace of conventional virility.

Tamara Karsavina, *Theatre Street* (1930)

✳ ✳ ✳

*More on St Petersburg's great dancers in the 'For Art's Sake' section. The city is also famed for its music and two twentieth-century composers in particular come to mind – Prokofiev and Shostakovich. Both have written music inspired by the city. A snippet from Prokofiev's* Autobiography *shows an unlikely source of inspiration for one piece.*

The February Revolution found me in Petrograd. I and those I associated with welcomed it with open arms. I was in the streets of Petrograd while the fighting was going on, hiding behind house corners when the shooting came too close. Number 19 of the *Visions Fugitives* written at this time partly reflected my impressions – the feeling of the crowd rather than the inner essence of the Revolution.

Sergei Prokofiev, 'Autobiography' in *Soviet Diary 1927 and Other writings* (1991) translated by Oleg Prokofiev

✳ ✳ ✳

*But it is Shostakovich above all who will always be associated with the city, if for no other reason than for his great Seventh Symphony, the 'Leningrad', so famously performed during the Siege. (Again, more on this later.)*

Dmitry Shostakovich was Leningrad's most eminent citizen. Already recognised, alongside Sergei Prokofiev and Igor Stravinsky, as one of his country's great contemporary composers, he had remained in the Soviet Union throughout the worst of Stalin's Terror. Subjected to lavish praise, interspersed with denunciation and intimidation, he survived by judiciously avoiding public criticism of Stalin. After the collapse of the Soviet-Nazi Non-Aggression Pact caused by Hitler's invasion of Russia in June 1941, Shostakovich applied to join the Red Army, but was twice turned down on account of his poor eyesight. He then applied successfully to join the People's Volunteer Brigades, writing that 'only by fighting can we save humanity from destruction'. Such was his international reputation that he appeared on the front cover of *Time* magazine in the uniform of a Soviet firefighter, waiting to defend Leningrad from the encircling Panzer divisions with which Hitler – who had likened the city to 'a viper' that had to be crushed – expected to accomplish his crazed urge to obliterate its very existence. But it was Shostakovich's extraordinary Seventh Symphony, which he dedicated to 'my native city', that was his greatest contribution to the morale of the nation.

Jonathan Dimbleby, *Russia: A Journey to the
Heart of a Land and its People* (2008)

✳  ✳  ✳

*Along with Shostakovich, Anna Akhmatova – one of
the greatest Russian poets of the twentieth century
– remained among the most 'dedicated' residents of
the city. In his memoirs, Shostakovich reflects on their
relationship.*

I was always put off by conversation with Akhmatova, because we were such different people. Yet we both lived in the same city and were equally devoted to it, we had the same world view, and common acquaintances, she seemed to respect my music, and I esteemed her work highly, both her early poems and her late ones, and of course, the *Requiem*. Particularly the

*Requiem.* I honour it as a memorial to all the victims of the years of terror. It's so simply written, without any melodrama. Melodrama would have ruined it.

I would greatly love to set it to music, but the music exists already. It was written by Boris Tishchenko, and I think that it's a marvellous work. Tishchenko brought to the *Requiem* what I think it lacked: protest. In Akhmatova, you feel a kind of submission to fate. Perhaps it's a matter of generations.

And so, despite our mutual likes, I had trouble talking with Akhmatova. I bring this up apropos 'historic meetings'. A special such meeting with Akhmatova was arranged for me in Komarovo, near Leningrad, and it turned out to be quite embarrassing. We were all tie-less out there – it's the country after all. They tried to talk me into dressing more appropriately for a meeting with the celebrated poetess, and I just said, 'Come off it. A fat old woman is coming, that's all.' I was very lighthearted about the whole thing. I didn't put on a good suit or a tie. When I saw Akhmatova, I felt nervous. She was a *grande dame*, quite real. The celebrated poetess, dressed with great thought. You could tell that she had paid attention to her clothes, prepared for the historic meeting, and behaved in a manner commensurate with the occasion. And there I was, tie-less. I felt naked.

We sat in silence. I was silent and Akhmatova was silent. We said nothing for a while and then parted.

Dmitry Shostakovich, *Testimony* (1979)
translated by Antonina W. Bouis

❉ ❉ ❉

*And what of the ordinary inhabitants of the city? One distinguished English visitor to the city has nothing but praise for its people.*

On Thursday 9th we left St Petersburg. Its climate is certainly as pernicious as the deadly upas tree; the severe cold, the damp exhalations attendant on its marshy position, and the sudden changes of temperature make it most trying to the strongest constitutions, but it is a wonderfully magnificent city and a most agreeable séjour. The colossal scale of everything – its palaces, institutions, buildings, fêtes, etc. strike the mind with wonder, while the kindness, cordiality and friendly hospitality of the people warm the heart. They are the most intelligent, agreeable, *distingués* clever persons imaginable.

Lady Londonderry, *The Russian Journal of Lady Londonderry,*
1836–7

✳ ✳ ✳

*Another English visitor pauses in his luscious description of the Imperial city in 1868 to give a thought to the poor.*

What happens to the poor in this enormous city? It is the town of Dives and Lazarus: of palaces and filthy cellars. Not a face, in those, that was not bleared and blotched and blurred by drink. The walls are slimy wet with breath. Men and women are huddled together on the wooden benches. There are degrees, descending steps of poverty, even here. If you would have a hideous vision, look lower, upon a hundred men and women dressed in rags, most of them with bruised faces, too sunk to speak, intent only to keep life in them and not be put into the ice-cold ground. The huge machine of government grinds round over their heads. That military pomp is the toy or plaything of an autocrat. St Petersburg is but for those who know this contrast, and can take pleasure in it. There are sixty, eighty, a hundred thousand, here, who live in cellars and have not enough to eat. There is equal poverty elsewhere but not such cold.

Sacheverell Sitwell, *Valse des Fleurs* (1941)

✳ ✳ ✳

126

*We join a congregation of Orthodox Petersburgers,
along with detective Porfiry Petrovitch, as they attend
the Easter service.*

Porfiry finished reading *What Is To Be Done?* on Sunday morning. He put the book down and left his apartment.

He headed straight for Haymarket Square, where he joined the traffic of worshippers flowing to and from the Church of the Assumption of the Virgin Mary. The cathedral stood like a bastion over the square, its minaret-like towers asserting the essential orientalism of the Orthodox religion. It both drew and repelled: it drew the faithful, the true believers, the true Russians, eastern- and inward-looking; and it repelled all those who would look to the west, outside Russia, for their ideas and influences.

Porfiry was drawn. He felt the simple need to be in an Orthodox church. Perhaps it was a reaction against the book he had just finished reading. He had never considered himself as a Slavophile; on the contrary, he had prided himself on being receptive to new ideas, from wherever they came. He knew that if Russia was to progress, as she must, she could not afford to isolate herself from the rest of Europe. It was simply that, increasingly as he grew older, he found himself comforted by the overwhelming scent of incense and the warm dazzle of the candle-lit icons. And the only God he could believe in was the Russian God.

Porfiry crossed himself as he entered.

The throng inside the church was lively, almost excitable. As always, there was a loose informality to the congregation. People came and went all the time, while the priests and monks continued to chant and drone. There was a soft murmur of chatter which echoed and overlapped, giving the impression that the multitude of saints and celestial beings depicted on the tiers of icons all around were joining in the conversations.

The priests took a dim view of all this talking in church, but there was little they could do to stop it. The Church invited its flock to be as children in their Father's house. It could hardly be surprised if some of them behaved like naughty children.

The three doors of the iconostasis stood open, as they had done since Midnight Mass on Good Friday. This towering screen, a full six tiers of icons in height, shielded the altar sanctuary from the congregation in the nave. Encrusted with a grid of thick gilt frames, populated with holy personages, it symbolised the division between Heaven and Earth. For most of the year the doors were kept closed, with only the clergy being allowed to pass through them. The doors would close again later that day, at the None, or Ninth Hour of prayer, that is to say, at about three o'clock that afternoon. Porfiry felt a surge of emotion as he considered the symbolism of the doors' opening. He felt a corresponding opening of his heart. It seemed to be a gesture of transcendent generosity on the part of the Church. Heaven stood open to him, and to all the miscreant congregation. He was possessed by hope.

R. N. Morris, *The Cleansing Flames* (2011)

✻ ✻ ✻

*Returning to the city of her childhood, the narrator of Julya Rabinowich's* Splithead *recalls times with her grandmother in the past.*

I am on the move with Grandma Ada. The scene is outside of time. I see myself with her in autumn as the enormous trees along the grey boulevards hurl their leaves at us on the salty wind that seems to come directly from the Gulf of Finland. I slide on the ice with her, dazzled by the glittering sunlight. The ice creaks and I bite into my frozen liverwurst, which sticks to my fingers, while she, wearing her light linen dress, leads me by the hand across the sun-warmed dust covering the boulevards of St Petersburg, her other hand holding her straw hat. And always, we're playing.

We play everything she has taught me: Russian fairy tales and classic literature, absurdly blended together and adapted by me into a predictable division of roles. I am the squirrel; she is Hercules. I am Margarita, the Master's lover; she is the big bad wolf. She is always the villain. For the sake of my education, she grits her teeth and plays along until I take it one step too far in a crowded Russian city bus – and when I say crowded, I mean it, my nose pressed into my neighbour's stomach from the pressure of all the bodies around me. Ada is playing Penelope, Odysseus' wife, while I am the loved one finally returned home, who hasn't yet identified himself, and I can't keep from asking the childish question of whether she, Penelope, hasn't completely worn herself out, what with all her suitors? My grandmother turns as red as the shining Kremlin star of ruby-coloured glass. Even the pickled war veteran across from us is curious. With forced cheerfulness, Ada declares, 'But please, it's all just child's play!'

I wander between the world of my childhood, the world of high culture and the proletarian world around me.

Julya Rabinowich, *Splithead* (2009)
translated by Tess Lewis

❊ ❊ ❊

*Andrei Astvatsaturov also reflects on growing up as a Petersburger.*

The grey building of the students' dormitory opposite our house, full of noisy shouts and laughter in my childhood years, was now submerged in gloomy lethargy. [...]

I remember the inscription 'LONG LIVE THE FRIENDSHIP OF NATIONS' on a huge panel, scrawled, as I wanted to believe back then, by the hand of some kind giant master by the pavement on Maurice Thorez Prospekt[1]. [...]

---

1  Named after the long-time leader of the French Communist Party. (Ed.)

All of us, as it seemed to me then, believed in our slogans. And the dormitory building was the stronghold of our belief, its living confirmation.

And it was, at the same time, a window into the big wide world. Though perhaps not into Europe. The window to Europe was the city itself. That was always drummed into me, first at kindergarten, then at school in literature lessons and in extra-curricular activities, that Peter, the Bronze Horseman, had built our city on a marsh not out of mischief and not on a whim. That he had cut a window through to Europe.

What I understood here was that we were all pretty much European. Or there were a lot of Europeans amongst us. Or, in the worst case scenario, we could regularly observe Europeans through the window he'd cut out. But I never observed anything like it myself. And all this talk about Peter, about the Swedes, about the window into Europe – it all made my head spin. I had never actually seen this Peter. Only in pictures and in films. And my grandmother would read me poetry about him, too. She used to take me to the Bronze Horseman and sing Peter's praises. At first I even thought he was a friend of hers.

Why did I need to know all this? I could never understand and it confused me. The world around me had nothing to do with Peter, nothing to do with the Swedes, and nothing at all to do with Europe. I sometimes think that the confusion in my head back then continues to have a grip on today's growing minds.

Andrei Astvatsaturov, *Skunskamera* (2010)
translated by Eve Harris

* * *

*We'll finish with a passing thought for some who might have become Petersburgers but who ended up as exhibits in the Museum of Anthropology[1] (the Kunskamera) instead. Ironically, they have inhabited the city far longer than those who have walked the city's streets. (The exhibits described here by Duncan Fallowell reflect the eighteenth-century interest in science and all kinds of natural 'curiosities'.)*

The Naval Museum, in one of the city's most famous buildings (the Old Stock Exchange), is closed to-day. He has another idea. We walk round the bend to the Museum of Anthropology which, among the artefact displays of Eskimos and maharajahs, situated by the entrance, make a frightful stink as overture. Dima insists on buying the tickets and heads straight for the Samurai warriors dressed to kill.

'You like this? I like this. Over here is the knife for hara-kiri.' But he's twisting about; this isn't what he's looking for; and he speaks to an attendant. 'It's that way.'

We descend into a circular space beneath the central lantern and confront a dumbfounding array of monstrosities. Pickled embryos of calf, lamb and dog; gadgets and samples of primitive dentistry; a calf with two heads, less attractively patterned than the one at the Hereford Museum, but more complete in body. Greatest interest however is excited by the cabinets of pickled human foetuses, whole babies, and baby parts, all of whose flesh has assumed the creamy texture of bleached chamois leather.

The whole babies, after gutting, have been sewn up with black thread like crazy cushions. Many are malformed – eye in forehead, Siamese twins side by side, Siamese twins back to back. One squat figure is embracing itself as if shivering, staring

---

1 Its full name is 'Peter the Great's Museum of Anthropology and Ethnography at the Russian Academy of Sciences.' Founded by Peter the Great himself, it was the first public museum in Russia. (Ed.)

out at the spectators (mostly enthralled and jostling schoolchildren) with a bewildered intensity in blind eyes. Others resemble infantile buddhas adrift in nirvana.

Of the parts, there are several tiny severed ears arranged in a bouquet; there is free-floating nose and mouth with teeth; babies' brain, hand, arm, foot cleverly combined; hand clutching an ear; or several legs and an ear just so; all suggestive of the Japanese tradition of flower arranging. Indeed Dima says these jars were often valued as ornaments, conversation pieces, in eighteenth-century drawing-rooms.

A number of the little loves' faces are distorted into expressions of distress by being squished painfully against the glass. Some are horrifically asleep. Others look happier – one says 'How do you do?' with bleary eyes; one gurgles up at us playfully, its features magnified by refraction through the preserving fluid.

Duncan Fallowell, *One Hot Summer in St Petersburg* (1994)

# For art's sake

*In his poem 'To Michael Frayn: a letter from Leningrad',
Clive James describes an April visit to the city. After
much walking and looking he can understand how
every kind of creative artist might consider the city to
have been designed exclusively with a view to inspiring
them to works of genius. Here we can only hint at the
great wealth of the artistic achievements to have come
from the city. Indeed, already by the nineteenth century
(remember, it was only founded in the eighteenth!), St
Petersburg had become almost a synonym for 'culture'.
The generous patronage and close personal involve-
ment of the Imperial family played a large part in this.
Most notably, the Imperial School of Dancing was the
main engine for creating what would become a world-
famous phenomenon – the Russian ballet.*

The Imperial School of Dancing produced the most famous dancers of the modern world. It was Paul I who established the Imperial School, for both sexes, in a palace between the Nevsky Prospekt and the Fontanka Canal, and engaged Didelot, the great choreographer, to teach the pupils. From 1801 until 1917 the Imperial School trained dancers for the Mariinsky Theatre. The regime was austere or military. The girl pupils were dressed as though at a convent school; the boys are described, in the life of Nijinsky, as receiving three uniforms; black for everyday, dark blue for the holidays, grey linen for the summer; a silver lyre was embroidered on their velvet collars; they were allowed two overcoats, one with a collar of astrakhan; and patent-leather boots. Eventually, after eight years of tuition, they would graduate to the Mariinsky Theatre and disappear into its corps de ballet of a hundred and eighty dancers. In addition to their special training they were given a good education. They visited the museums; they walked in a crocodile along the Nevsky Prospekt, after breakfast, and of course wearing their patent-leather boots and their military caps with the double-headed eagle, in gold, upon the front; in the evening they were driven to the theatre, boys and girls apart, in landaus from the Imperial Stables.

Upon occasion, in those same landaus, they were taken to the theatre in the Hermitage, where they performed before the Tsar and his family. This little theatre is a building by Quarenghi. It is not large and has no boxes. The stalls rise in the form of an amphitheatre, as in Palladio's theatre at Vicenza, and in front are armchairs for the Imperial Family. This theatre, which was added in 1780, connects with the rest of the Hermitage by a bridge thrown over a canal, the arch, itself, being occupied by a foyer or anteroom, lit on each side by lofty windows, and giving views over the Neva and the street of the Millionaia. The façade of this theatre, with its pilastered front and recesses filled with statues, is a masterpiece of Quarenghi and, after his portico to the manège of the Gardes à cheval, his best building in St Petersburg. As to the Mariinsky Theatre, that was designed by Rossi[1], last of the classical architects in Russia. It was here that the dancers of the Imperial Ballet gave their performances. The whole of the expenses both of the school and the theatre were borne by the Tsar's privy purse, and under Nicholas II, after the public had paid for their seats there was often an annual deficit of two hundred thousand pounds to be met. Such was the price paid by an autocrat for the art of Russian dancing. To the income of the Tsars it was the equivalent of no more than the upkeep of two yachts.

Sacheverell Sitwell, *Valse des Fleurs* (1941)

✿ ✿ ✿

*Among the pupils of the Imperial School was Anna Pavlova. Her status as an international star even led to her writing about the school, during a tour of the U.S.A., in* The Ladies' Home Journal.

I learned my art under as nearly perfect conditions as one ever found on this earth. The Russian ballet owes its subtle perfection of detail, its greatness, its rank to the fact that it is made up of dancers who from the day they went to live in the dormitories of the Imperial School saw nothing – were surrounded by nothing – but beauty – beauty! – and the highest standards physically, mentally, morally and spiritually.

From the very hour that my mother gave me into the keeping of the Imperial School to the time I began my world wanderings I never saw a badly painted, cheap or stupid picture; I never read an ill-written, tawdry or trashy book; I never saw acting that was not of the finest; I never attended an ill-made play or a badly-sung opera; I never ate a badly cooked or ill-

---

1   In fact it was designed Alberto Cavos. However, Rossi did design the Academy of the Russian Ballet on Architect Rossi Street – formerly Theatre Street. (Ed.)

chosen meal; I never slept in a poorly ventilated room; I neither worked nor played too long; I never witnessed gross manners […] My general education, from mathematics and languages to science, came to me from the finest teachers procurable. The special training in dancing was in the hands of Marius Petipa and his associates. […]

In truth, the Imperial School as it was founded […] was a French school housed in Russia. But French it did not remain. The Russian temperament quickly absorbed the Latin, nationalised it, coloured it with the Slavic emotionalism, until in the end […] the school was uniquely and completely Russian.

Anna Pavlova, 'Reflections',
in *The Ladies Home Journal* (Philadelphia) Sept 1924

✻ ✻ ✻

*American Gladys Malvern's story of the life of Anna Pavlova*, Dancing Star, *was written for children. Well researched, it introduces young readers to some of the greatest names in Russian culture. Near the beginning is a vivid picture of what life was like at the Imperial Ballet School.*

Girls who were first-year students wore plain brown cashmere dresses. Anna, pale and dark, knew that the colour was unbecoming, but it didn't matter – nothing mattered but just to learn to dance. Even if your hair was curly, you were not permitted to wear it that way. It had to be brushed back, straight and tight from your forehead, braided in a single braid, and tied at the end with a black ribbon.

Promptly at eight there reverberated through the long corridors and spacious dormitories the tolling of a great bell. Anna's dormitory held fifty beds, and scarcely had the echoes of the bell died away before fifty girls, eyes still heavy with sleep, rushed down the corridor to the washroom. After washing in cold water they formed a neat line and marched to the governesses, who were ready and waiting with combs and brushes. When their hair was combed, they returned to the dormitory and put on their dancing dresses, then they made their beds. When all beds were made, they fell into a single line and marched towards the door.

At the door sat another blue-robed governess, sober-faced, hawk-eyed. As they reached her, each girl stopped and curtsied.

Then, without being told, the girl turned all the way around. The governess looked the student over. If all was neat and tidy, she motioned the girl forward and turned her gaze to the next in line. If a governess was not liked, Anna soon learned that secretly she was called a 'toad'.

In winter, over the dancing dress, the girls wore a wide, dark woollen shawl with long fringe. During the second year the student received another dress, this time of blue serge with a tight waist and gathered skirt. There was a fichu of stiff white lawn which was worn crossed in front, a black apron, white cotton stockings, black slippers. The only change that was made was on Sundays, when a white apron was worn.

Every girl was given one new dress each year. The new one was worn on Sundays, the old one on week-days.

Once inspection was over, the line formed again, this time two by two. Religious training was considered highly important. The school had its own chapel, and into it now every pupil marched, girls and boys, juniors and seniors. The boys sat on one side, the girls on the other. After chapel, there was the line to be formed again — boys two by two, girls two by two — this time the march led to a great wide hall where breakfast was served.

Here, also, boys and girls were separated. The girls had their own tables, the boys had theirs. Each table was presided over by a governess who kept a strict, all-seeing eye over table manners.

After breakfast, the inevitable line had to be formed, and the boys went to a large, airy room on the third floor, while the girls went to one like it on the second floor. This was a vast, sunny room with tall windows. It was furnished simply with a grand piano, numerous small sofas against the walls, floor-length mirrors. On its walls were paintings of Russian rulers. [...]

At noon, with the sharp ringing of the midday bell, the dancing lessons ended. Again the children formed into line and returned to the dining-room for lunch. After lunch, they were taken for a walk in the care of the governess. Even now, however, they did not leave the school. In the courtyard was a small garden, and round and round they walked sedately for twenty minutes.

In winter the girls wore black coats lined with red fox, high boots, and bonnets of black silk. Returning from their walk, lessons began again. This time in fencing, languages, reading, writing, arithmetic, music and — what Anna loved best — make-up. The students entered the make-up room, which had lights around each mirror like a real dressing-room in the theatre, and little tables crowded with grease paint, rouge, brushes, powder.

At four o'clock another bell summoned them to dinner. After dinner they had a little interval of freedom, then more lessons. Sometimes some of the children were to appear in mob scenes at the theatre, sometimes there were pupils' performances. These occasions were times of jubilee, for the nightly lessons ended, and rehearsals took their place. Supper was at eight, and by nine the younger ones were in bed.

In a surprisingly short time Anna began to feel completely at home in the school. Discipline was strict, but she thrived on it. Every spare moment when she could get by herself, she practised. The place fairly buzzed with energy, ambition.

Gladys Malvern, *Dancing Star* (1946)

* * *

*Another famous graduate of the Imperial School was Tamara Karsavina. In her memoirs,* Theatre Street, *she recalls how pupils of the school were sometimes required to dance at the Court Theatre.*

Every year there were several performances given at the Court Theatre of the Hermitage, where the stage was spacious enough for the production of any ballet or opera. The pick of the cast was nominated to take part in these performances. On these occasions the *corps de ballet* would be suppressed, and solo dancers take the ranks. I remember especially the night of a fancy-dress ball, when the entire Court wore historical Russian dresses. That of the Empress Alexandra Fyodorovna was the genuine saraphan of the Tsaritsa Miloslavskaya. Being on that night only one of the *corps de ballet*, where comparatively little concentration was required, I was entirely taken up with the splendour of all that I could see in front of me. I strained my eyes trying to distinguish figures in the semi-obscurity of the audience. Those three in front, the Tsar and both Tsaritsas, one could see distinctly. The young Empress, in a heavy tiara, put on over a gauze kerchief entirely concealing her hair, looked like an icon of rigid beauty; she held her head very stiff, and I could not help feeling it would be difficult for her to bend over her plate at supper. I had a better view of her in the interval while peeping through the hole in the curtain, for which there was great competition; her dress of heavy brocade was sewn over with jewels.

In the dressing-room, where several of us were getting ready, I was reprimanded for putting on old shoes. 'Can't you produce better ones for the Imperial Family, you born ragamuffin?' The whole of the dressing-room supported the ironical remark, and I was made to wear a brand new pair.

As a pupil at school, I had danced at the Hermitage before. Then we were taken straight away at the end, and missed the best part of it – the supper. One or other member of the Imperial Family would come to have supper with the artists; most often, as on this occasion, it would be the Grand Duke Vladimir and his sons, who inherited their father's great love of the theatre.

Tamara Karsavina, Theatre Street (1930)

✻ ✻ ✻

*The name of Serge Diaghilev is associated in most people's minds with ballet, and with his world-famous company, the 'Ballets Russes', with which some of the greatest artists of the time, in all fields, were associated. But he was a great impresario in other fields, too.*

During 1905, many writers and artists, seeing either danger, hopelessness, or opportunity, left for long stays in Europe. [...] Diaghilev was always one to focus on opportunities, and he used this one to start exhibiting Russian art abroad and put together with other *miriskusniki*[1] his greatest creation, the *Ballets Russes*, which one specialist has called 'basically *Mir iskusstva*[2] transplanted from Petersburg to Paris.' [...] Diaghilev had the best possible base to draw on, for ballet in Petersburg had already developed into the world's best, thanks to lavish funding from the imperial treasury which had attracted the best Russian and foreign talent to train dancers and choreograph the ballets, especially Marius Petipa. Petipa's art was made possible by the scores of talented and well-trained dancers emerging from the Imperial Ballet School on Theatre Street behind Rossi's Alexandrinsky Theatre, where master instructors such as Lev Ivanov, the Italian Enrico Cecchetti, Ekaterina Vazem, and the Swede Christian Johannson produced such stars as Tamara Karsavina, Anna

---

1   Members of the 'World of Art' movement. (Ed.)
2   The 'World of Art' movement (Ed.)

Pavlova, Vaslav Nijinsky, Mikhail Fokin (soon Frenchified to Michel Fokine) and, of course, Kshessinskaya.

Diaghilev's leadership, organisational abilities, and contacts at *Mir iskusstva* led Prince Volkonsky, head of Imperial Theatres, in 1899 to employ him at the Mariinsky. Diaghilev in turn invited Bakst, Benois and other *miriskusniki* to create scenery and costumes for its ballet and opera productions. [...]

While at the Mariinsky, Diaghilev met the great bass, Fyodor Chaliapin, who first performed there on 20 December 1899, and thereafter always played to a full house. With his stunning voice, the skills of a tragic actor, and directorial talents, one contemporary called him 'a performer of genius, an artist of unsurpassed talent on the operatic stage! In his roles he was inimitable, original and grandiose!' Together with Diaghilev and the *miriskusniki*, he revived opera in Petersburg, which in recent decades had been outshone by the ballet. [...] Beginning in 1909, Chaliapin would team up with Diaghilev in the *Saison Russes* to showcase Russian opera to the world. [...]

Following his triumphal exhibition of portraits in 1905, in 1906 Diaghilev, uninspired by recent exhibitions in Paris, introduced Russian paintings to the West in a large exhibition at the Salon d'Automne in Paris, which was followed in 1907 with a series of 'historical concerts' at the Opéra. In 1908, he brought Russian opera to Paris with the western première of *Boris Godunov* in Rimsky-Korsakov's orchestration[1], which also launched the international career of Chaliapin. Finally, for the 1909 season, Diaghilev was ready to launch the *Ballets Russes*. [...]

In the *Ballets Russes*, the opening of Russia's Window to the West had come full circle. Petersburg had drawn from Europe an art form, transformed it into a more beautiful, powerful, and modern means of expression, and returned it to the West and all the world.

Arthur George with Elena George, *St Petersburg: A History* (2004)

---

1   The original version is by Mussorgsky. (Ed.)

For art's sake

❋ ❋ ❋

*Russian novelist Andrei Bitov (see also his* Pushkin
House, *translated by Susan Brownsberger) throws
some cold water on the pleasures of the ballet in his
native city.*

A person born in Petersburg is born in the ballet – how, then,
can he apprehend this dusty, clumsy convention, when he is
taken to the famous Kirovsky (formerly Mariinsky[1]) Theatre
for the first time? To this day, my mind retains that first, nause-
ating dizziness, caused by a convention within a convention, by
a convention imitating a convention …

In those times convention in set design was impermissible,
the sets were 'like the real thing'; the audience applauded set
changes with especial readiness (today I seem to discern in this
applause a sincerity of relief, a kind of release at encountering
the understandable and the accessible…): we saw the real Peter
and Paul Fortress, which we had already seen in real life that
day, real snow was falling … and into this snow a naked ballerina in a ballet skirt – also snow-white – would flit onstage
to our applause … She 'expressed' the sorrow of encountering
her beloved through her leaps across the stage, a sorrow we'd
all had the chance to read about during the intermission, in
the synopsis included in the programme; so we sat there with
bated breath, overlaying what we'd just read with what we'd
just seen, and at the right moment, we would know when to
applaud by the prima ballerina's facial expression … I never
managed to get rid of this burning and unconquerable childhood feeling of shame and awkwardness (which, moreover,
can never be admitted to anyone) at the given and mandatory
nature of this rapture, at our universal homage to this glory,
which predated us. […] Sure, maybe in some category we took
second or even third place, but in ballet we inarguably took

---

1    Bitov is writing before the original name – Mariinsky – was returned to the theatre. (Ed.)

first. Just like Petersburg's somehow more impeccable baroque, our ballet, beaten, later than the rest of Europe's, out of serf performers, was probably also more impeccable; but why, in a world that had shifted and exiled all other signs and significances of the old world, did ballet alone remain at its former, ineradicable level?

Andrei Bitov, 'Why I Don't Like Ballet At All' in
*Life in Windy Weather* (1991) translated by Maya Vinokour

✻  ✻  ✻

*But we'll return to the positive view of ballet. Here's Tamara Karsavina again, this time on the world-famous Mariinsky Theatre.*

The Mariinsky Theatre invariably began the season by *A Life for the Tsar*[1], a patriotic opera. The first Sunday of September the ballet opened. About a fortnight before the season the company assembled. The first day was more in the nature of a review of troops. We reported to the *régisseur* and went home till a notice of rehearsal summoned such as were wanted. The whole service of notifying the company was carried out by five couriers attached to the staff. They usually went on foot, each working his assigned district. A telephone was not installed at the rehearsal-room till much later.

My first part was in a group of solo dancers. I was put together with Pavlova, Sedova and Trefilova, then virtually ballerinas. [...]

There had been a period when, by the majority of the public, the ballet was regarded with scepticism and the lovers of it thought eccentric. Now, no longer the Cinderella of the stage, the ballet had become fashionable. A competition for seats, for the right to be a subscriber, well proved the interest it aroused. To obtain a seat, a petition to the Chancery of the Imperial Theatres had to be filed; the chance of success was so

---

1   By Mikhail Glinka, written in 1836. (Ed.)

small that big premiums were constantly offered by advertisement to the original holders of the stalls. The subscribers held tenaciously to their prerogative. No outsider could ever penetrate into the first row of stalls without a Sesame, a favour of a *balletomane* friend. Even then, a new face would be looked upon as an intrusion and eyed suspiciously by the neighbours. The seats were handed down from father to son, the name of *balletomane*, once given in derision, was becoming almost an hereditary dignity. Having picked up the gauntlet, the *balletomanes* bore their name proudly. Whatever there may have been of personal motives in the attachment of some of them to the ballet, the cult of this delicate art was always uppermost.

A very knowledgeable, exacting, somewhat dogmatic and conservative public, *balletomanes* were capable of high enthusiasm. They were conservative in the extreme. A new venture, the slightest variation from the old canons were heresy to them; an occasional modification of a step an irreverence as well as a disappointment. There were some favourite steps eagerly awaited. One could feel from the stage how the whole audience stiffened in breathless expectation of a favourite passage. The passage well executed, the whole theatre burst out clapping in measure to the music. Artistic reputations were made and undone by casual remarks of the leaders of the stalls. A foreign celebrity, in a series of performances, displayed a sound virtuosity. She was round-shouldered. 'A flying turkey,' drawled Skalkovsky. His remark had been caught and repeated all round. They were a tyrannical public, those *balletomanes*, and pig-headed to a degree; if once they pronounced a dancer lacking some quality, no amount of evidence to the contrary would dispel the prejudice. They classified and ticketed the dancers as graceful, dramatic, lyrical, and did not encourage any attempt to develop qualities beyond those originally assigned. But they were enthusiastic. On no account would they miss a performance. When Mathilde Kshessinskaya went to dance at Moscow, the first row of stalls at the Mariinsky emptied; her faithful had followed her.

Less pontifical, but hardly of smaller importance, were the lesser *balletomanes*, the pit and the gallery. They also crowned and dethroned. Erudition and the terminology of the ballet they may have lacked, but in spontaneity of admiration, in fanatical transports of young enthusiasm they far outstripped their colleagues of the stalls. While the stalls preserved a certain decorum, the gallery spared not their throats. Long after the stalls had emptied and the lights gone down in the auditorium, the gallery raved. The safety curtain crept down, dust sheets were brought in; the gallery still shouted. A last rite was to be performed yet – waiting at the stage door. Manifestations at the stage door varied in proportion to the popularity of each artist. They ranged from silence to delirious outbursts. Sometimes a group of young people would follow their idol, keeping at a distance, a silent escort. [...]

Only a certain number of seats in the gallery belonged to subscribers. The rest went on sale. The box office opened at eight o'clock in the morning. Even in the bitterest cold the queue round the theatre started overnight, though a ten hours' vigil by no means ensured a ticket.

Tamara Karsavina, *Theatre Street* (1930)

✳ ✳ ✳

*Another experience of the Mariinsky – this time jumping forward to 1957 when American writer Truman Capote travelled with an opera company to perform Gershwin's* Porgy *and* Bess *in Russia. It's the period of the Cold War and the contrast between the two societies encountering each other for the first time face to face makes for some very interesting situations!*

The ballet was at the Mariinsky theatre, which has been renamed, though no one calls it that, the Kirov, after the old revolutionary and friend of Stalin's whose assassination in 1934 is said to have initiated the first of the Moscow trials. Galina Ulanova, the Bolshoi's prima ballerina, made her début in this theatre, and the Leningrad Opera and Ballet Company, which is now installed there on a repertorial basis, is considered first class by Soviet critics. Except for the Fenice in Venice, a theatre it somewhat resembles in its eighteenth-century size and style and heating system, I think it the most beautiful theatre I've ever seen. Unfortunately, the old seats have been replaced by wooden ones, rather like those in a school auditorium, and their harsh, natural colour makes too raw a contrast against the subtle greys and silvers of the Mariinsky's simplified rococo interior.

Despite the chilliness of the theatre, everyone, ladies included, was required to leave their coats at the cloakroom; even Mrs Gershwin was forced to part with her mink, for in Russia it is thought uncultured, *nye kulturni* at its extremist, to enter a theatre, restaurant, museum, any such place, wearing a coat or wrap. At the moment, the principal sufferer from the ruling was Miss Ryan. A tall, striking blonde, Miss Ryan was wearing a low strapless dress that hugged her curves cleverly; and as she swayed down the aisle, masculine eyes swerved in her direction like flowers turning towards the sun. For that matter, the entrance of the entire company was creating a mass stir in the crowded audience. People were standing up to get a better view of the Americans and their black ties, silks and sparkles. Much attention was centred on Earl Bruce Jackson and his fiancée, Helen Thigpen. They were sitting in the Royal Box, where a hammer and sickle blotted out the Imperial crest. Jackson, lolling his hand over the edge of the box so that his jewellery, a ring on every finger, could be seen to advantage, was slowly inclining his head right and left, like Queen Victoria.

146

'I'd be freezing if I weren't so embarrassed,' said Miss Ryan, as an usher seated her. 'Just look, they think I'm *indecent*.' One couldn't deny there was a touch of criticism in the glances Miss Ryan's shoulders were receiving from surrounding Russian women. Mrs. Gershwin, who was wearing a becoming green cocktail dress, said, 'I *told* Wilva Breen we shouldn't get all dressed up. I knew we'd look ridiculous. Well, darling, never again. But really, what *should* we wear?' she asked, looking about as if hunting fashion hints among the audience's melancholy, shapeless attire. 'I didn't bring anything that wasn't pretty.' […]

Chandeliers dimmed and the orchestra conductor raised his baton. The ballet, in three acts with two intermissions, was called *Corsair*. The average Soviet ballet is far less concerned with dancing than with stupendous production, and *Corsair*, though a minor work in their repertory, involves as much change of scenery as the extravagant vaudevilles at Radio City Music Hall or the Folies Bergère, two theatres where *Corsair* would feel quite at home, except that the choreography and its execution are not up to the standards of the former, and the latter would never tolerate a scene of dancing slave girls swathed to the neck. The theme of *Corsair* is very similar to *The Fountains of the Bakhchisarai*, a poem of Pushkin's that the Bolshoi ballet has taken and swollen into one of its prize exhibits. In *Fountains*, an aristocratic girl is kidnapped by a barbaric Tartar chieftain and hauled off to his harem where, for three hours of playing time, many vile adventures befall her. In *Corsair*, this girl's twin sister undergoes somewhat the same ordeal; here she is the victim of a shipwreck (brilliantly simulated on stage with thunder, lightning, torrents of water crashing against the stricken vessel) who is captured by pirates, after which, for three hours, ditto. Both these tales, and countless like them, reflect a tendency in contemporary Soviet theatre to rely on fantasy and legend; it would seem that the modern author who wishes to roam beyond the propagandist garden finds that the only safe path is the one that leads him into the forest of fairy stories. But even fantasy needs realistic underpinning, reminders of the recognisable, the human; without them, the power of life is not there, nor is art, a dual absence that occurs too often in the Soviet theatre, whose practitioners appear to believe that trick effects and technical wizardry can be made to supplant them. The Ministry of Culture frequently boasts that Russia is the sole country to have produced an art-culture *en rapport* with its population. The reaction of the audience to *Corsair* was nothing to disprove the claim; every set, every solo brought chandelier-shaking rounds of applause.

Truman Capote, *The Muses Are Heard* (1957)

* * *

*While on the subject of the city's great theatrical tradition, here is a heart-breaking account of attempts to maintain a cultural life during the terrible time of the Siege of Leningrad, from the novel* The Life of an Unknown Man *by Andreï Makine.*

Turning towards the Neva they saw a long queue outside a building. Famished as they were, they instinctively made the link: a crowd, ration tickets, a piece of bread. But this queue had an unusual look about it. People were going in at the door but no one was coming out, as if they had decided to eat their rations on the spot, away from the icy blast coming off the Baltic Sea. As they drew closer Volsky and Mila discovered to their amazement that this was a theatre and people, rendered mute with exhaustion, were going to watch a performance. The poster for the Musical Comedy Theatre announced an operetta: *The Three Musketeers* ...

Without conferring, they moved towards the stage door. An old man, candle in hand, reminiscent of a lost character in a Chekhov play, greeted them, led them to the manager's office.

The latter was in the middle of breaking up wood and stoking an iron stove on which a saucepan was warming. He raised an emaciated face to them and his smile stretched the skin on his angular cheekbones. His eyes seemed fixed on a vision of horror. Volsky mentioned the Conservatoire, asked if they could be useful ...

Suddenly the man thrust him aside and, by moving adroitly, just had time to catch Mila as she passed out. When she came to he murmured, still with that smile which left the expression in his eyes unaltered: 'In the old days actors were trained to support heroines who fainted ...' He invited them to drink a bowl of soup, which was, in fact, hot water with a little meal floating in it.

Their offer was accepted with a remark Volsky would remember for the rest of his life: 'We need voices.' His eyes met Mila's. Voices ... In truth, that was all they had left.

Their lives merged with that of the theatre. They assisted in putting up scenery, gave a helping hand to wardrobe, cooked meals for the singers and musicians. And in the evening they went on stage. Volsky believed that by engaging an excess of walk-on actors, the director was seeking to encourage them. But after several performances he realised that this casting related to the frequency with which the actors died. By taking part in the show, the walk-ons were learning all the roles and could thus take over from anyone who, one day, did not return. [...]

Everyone strove for the performances to go on as before. But, of course, everything was different. They acted by candle-light in an auditorium where it was ten degrees below. Often the show was interrupted by an air-raid siren. The audience would go down into the basement, those who no longer had the strength to do so remaining huddled in their seats, staring at the stage emptied by the sound of bombing ... Applause was no longer heard. Too weak, their hands frozen in mittens, people would bow to thank the actors. This silent gratitude was more touching than any number of ovations.

Andreï Makine, *The Life of an Unknown Man* (2009)
translated by Geoffrey Strachan

❋ ❋ ❋

*St Petersburg is a city of writers. Indeed, many of our ideas about the city are likely to have been formed by reading some of the great Russian classics. Nobel laureate Joseph Brodsky (1940–96) was exiled by the Soviet regime, but always retained a love for his native city. In this section from his 'Guide to a Renamed City', he considers some of St Petersburg's astonishingly rich literary heritage.*

But perhaps more than by its canals and rivers, this extremely 'premeditated city' as Dostoyevsky termed it, has been reflected in the literature of Russia. For water can talk about surfaces only, and exposed ones at that. The depiction of both the actual and mental interior of the city, of its impact on the people and their inner world, became the main subject of Russian literature almost from the very day of this city's founding. Technically speaking, Russian literature was born here, on the shores of the Neva. If, as the saying goes, all Russian writers 'came out of Gogol's *Overcoat*,' it's worth remembering then that this overcoat was ripped off that poor civil servant's shoulders nowhere else but in St Petersburg, at the very beginning of the nineteenth century. The tone, however, was set by Pushkin's *The Bronze Horseman*, whose hero, a clerk in some department, upon losing his beloved to a flood, accuses the mounted statue of the Emperor of negligence (no dikes) and goes insane when he sees the enraged Peter on his horse jumping off the pedestal and rushing in pursuit to trample him, an offender, into the ground. (This could be, of course, a simple tale about a little man's rebellion against arbitrary power, or one about persecution mania, subconscious versus superego, and so forth, were it not for the magnificence of the verses themselves – the best ever written in praise of this city, with the exception of those by Osip Mandelstam, who was literally stamped into the ground of the empire a century after Pushkin was killed in a duel.)

At any rate, by the beginning of the nineteenth century, St Petersburg was already the capital of Russian letters, a fact that had very little to do with the actual presence of the court here. After all, the court sat in Moscow for centuries and yet almost nothing came out of there. The reason for this sudden outburst of creative power was again mostly geographical. In the context of the Russian life in those days, the emergence of St Petersburg was similar to the discovery of the New World: it gave pensive men of the time a chance to look upon themselves and the nation as though from outside. In other words, this city provided them with the possibility of objectifying the country. [...]

Coming from the nobility, gentry, or clergy, all these writers belonged, to use an economic stratification, to the middle class: the class which is almost solely responsible for the existence of literature everywhere. With two or three exceptions, all of them lived by the pen, i.e., meagerly enough to understand without exegesis or bewilderment the plight of those worse off as well as the splendour of those at the top. The second attracted their attention far less if only because the chances of moving up were far smaller. Consequently, we have a pretty thorough, almost stereoscopic picture of the inner, real St Petersburg, for it is the poor who constitute the main body of reality; the little man is always universal. Furthermore, the more perfect his immediate surroundings are, the more jarring and incongruous he looks. No wonder that all of them – the retired officers, impoverished widows, robbed civil servants, hungry journalists, humiliated clerks, tubercular students, and so forth – seen against the impeccable utopian background of classicistic porticoes, haunted the imagination of writers and flooded the very first chapters of Russian prose. [...]

Today when you think of St Petersburg you can't distinguish the fictional from the real. Which is rather odd for a place only two hundred and seventy-six years old. The guide will show you today the building of the Third Section of the police, where Dostoyevsky was tried, as well as the house where his character Raskolnikov killed that old money-lending woman with an axe.

Joseph Brodsky, 'A Guide to a Renamed City' (1979)
in *Less Than One: Selected Essays*

✻  ✻  ✻

*Brodsky wasn't the only writer to suffer persecution during the Soviet period. In fact, he escaped quite lightly compared with many.*

One of the most notable Leningraders to vanish at this time was the absurdist writer Daniil Yuvachov, better known by his pen-name Daniil Kharms. A relic of the avant-garde 1920s, he cultivated a range of eccentricities, studying the occult, drinking nothing but milk and parading the neighbourhood around his Mayakovsky Street flat in a deerstalker, shooting jacket, plus-fours, saucer-sized pocket watch and checked socks. His scraps of prose and dialogue – unpublished until the late 1980s – capture the drabness and mad bureaucratic violence of his times with nightmare black humour. In one, a man dreams again and again of a policeman hiding in the bushes, and gets thinner and thinner until a sanitary inspector orders him to be folded up and thrown out with the rubbish. In another, inquisitive old women lean out of a window, tumbling one after another to the ground. In a third, friends quarrel over whether or not the number seven comes before the number eight, until distracted by a child who 'fortunately' falls off a park bench and breaks its jaw. Kharms was arrested in August and sent to the psychiatric wing of the Kresty prison, where he died, of unknown causes, two months later. Why was he picked out? 'Perhaps,' as the siege historian Harrison Salisbury put it, just because he 'wore a funny hat.'

Anna Reid, *Leningrad: Tragedy of a City Under Siege, 1941–44* (2011)

\* \* \*

*Back to Brodsky for a look at the work of Osip Mandelstam (1891–1938), whose life was cut short by the brutality of Stalinist repression.*

In order to understand his poetry better, the English-speaking reader perhaps ought to realize that Mandelstam was a Jew who was living in the capital of Imperial Russia, whose dominant religion was Orthodoxy, whose political structure was inherently Byzantine, and whose alphabet had been devised by two Greek monks. Historically speaking, this organic blend was most strongly felt in Petersburg, which became Mandelstam's 'familiar as tears' eschatological niche for the rest of his not-that-long life.

It was long enough, however, to immortalize this place, and if his poetry was sometimes called 'Petersburgian', there is more than one reason to consider this definition both accurate and complimentary. Accurate because, apart from being the administrative capital of the empire, Petersburg was also the spiritual centre of it, and in the beginning of the century the strands of that current were merging there the way they do in Mandelstam's poems. Complimentary because both poet and the city profited in meaning by their confrontation. If the West was Athens, Petersburg in the teens of this century was Alexandria. This 'window on Europe', as Petersburg was called by some gentle souls of the Enlightenment, this 'most invented city', as it was defined later by Dostoyevsky, lying at the latitude of Vancouver, in the mouth of a river as wide as the Hudson between Manhattan and New Jersey, was and is beautiful with that kind of beauty which happens to be caused by madness – or which tries to conceal this madness. Classicism never had so much room, and the Italian architects who kept being invited by successive Russian monarchs understood this all too well. The giant, infinite, vertical rafts of white columns from the façades of the embankments' palaces belonging to the Tsar, his family, the aristocracy, embassies, and the *nouveaux riches* are carried by the reflecting river down to the Baltic. On the main avenue of the empire – Nevsky Prospekt – there are churches of all creeds. The endless, wide streets are filled with cabriolets, newly introduced automobiles, idle, well-dressed crowds, first-class boutiques, confectioneries, etc. Immensely wide squares with mounted statues of previous rulers and triumphal columns taller than Nelson's. Lots of publishing houses, magazines, newspapers, political parties (more than in contemporary America), theatres, restaurants, gypsies. All this is surrounded by the brick Birnam Wood of the factories' smoking chimneys and covered by the damp, grey, widespread blanket of the Northern Hemisphere's sky. One war is lost, another – a world war – is impending, and you are a little Jewish boy with a heart full of Russian iambic pentameters.

In this giant-scale embodiment of perfect order, iambic beat is as natural as cobblestones. Petersburg is a cradle of Russian poetry and, what is more, of its prosody. The idea of a noble structure, regardless of the quality of the content (sometimes precisely *against* its quality, which creates a terrific sense of disparity – indicating not so much the author's but the verse's own evaluation of the described phenomenon), is utterly local. The whole thing started a century ago, and Mandelstam's usage of strict meters in his first book, *Stone*, is clearly reminiscent of Pushkin, and of his pleiad. And yet, again, it is not a result of some conscious choice, nor is it a sign of Mandelstam's style being predetermined by the preceding or contemporary processes in Russian poetry.

Joseph Brodsky, 'The Child of Civilisation' (1977)<br>translated by Bernard Meares, in Less Than One: Selected Essays

✳ ✳ ✳

*Anna Akhmatova was a full participant in the life of the city. Although she described it as 'A dark city on a menacing river', as 'a city loved with bitter love', 'misty, calm, severe', she also described the city with great tenderness – rather as one might see the faults of a parent but love them greatly nevertheless.*

Together with Pushkin, Akhmatova stands as the quintessential poet of Petersburg who drew inspiration from it. [...] To her Petersburg was man's and nature's transcendent work of art, a deserving source of artistic and spiritual inspiration, and often of optimism, love, and even salvation. To capture its mystique, she utilized the city's concrete details and images: clouds, light, White Nights, mist, the Neva, enchained embankments, empty balconies, monuments in shadows, palaces, flowers. For someone who so deeply and perceptively felt the city's rhythms and integrated them into her own life, the images came naturally and she knew instinctively, like Pushkin, which word or expression to call up. In her poems the seemingly cold face of the city lit up and smiled. When war and revolution threatened, she never saw Petersburg as accursed or as Peter's misguided adventure. Instead, she portrayed pain intimately and vividly in the lives of its citizens.

Arthur George with Elena George, *St Petersburg: A History* (2004)

✳ ✳ ✳

*Moving on to the visual arts, Nikolai Gogol gives his opinion of 'a strange phenomenon' – the Petersburg artist of the nineteenth century ...*

This young man belonged to a class which represents quite a strange phenomenon among us and belongs as much to the citizens of Petersburg as a person who comes to us in a dream belongs to the real world. This exceptional group is highly unusual in a city in which everyone is either an official, a shopkeeper, or a German artisan. He was an artist. A strange phenomenon, is it not? A Petersburg artist! An artist in the land of snows, an artist in the land of Finns, where everything is wet, smooth, flat, pale, grey, misty. These artists do not in the least resemble Italian artists – proud, ardent, like Italy and its sky; on the contrary, they are for the most part kind and meek people, bashful, lighthearted, with a quiet love for their art, who drink tea with their two friends in a small room, who talk modestly about their favourite subject and are totally indifferent to all superfluity. He is forever inviting some old beggar woman to his place and making her sit for a good six hours, so as to transfer her pathetic, insensible expression to canvas. He paints his room in perspective, with all sorts of artistic clutter appearing in it: plaster arms and legs turned coffee-coloured with time and dust, broken easels, an overturned palette, a friend playing a guitar, paint-stained walls, and an open window through which comes a glimpse of the pale Neva and poor fishermen in red shirts. They paint almost everything in dull, greyish colours – the indelible imprint of the north.

Nikolai Gogol, 'Nevsky Prospekt' (1835)
translated by Richard Pevear and Larissa Volokhonsky

❊ ❊ ❊

*For most visitors to the city, the visual arts in St Petersburg are synonymous with the Hermitage. Although usually associated with art of the past, recent developments include a new space dedicated to modern and contemporary art (see Tim Stanley's article in the last section of the book). Three pieces which take us for a visit to what is probably the world's most famous museum. In the first, Malcolm Bradbury reminds us of one of the building's iconic moments – the so-called 'storming of the Winter Palace' at the time of the 1917 Revolution – and contrasts it with the modern scene.*

Odd, though, that the great inevitable machine called History should have gone on to produce what we witness here right now. For, where the people surged and the great gates tumbled, American backpackers knock back their cans of Coke, Japanese tourists photograph each other standing next to something or other, and weary-looking Russian army conscripts smoke on the steps and eye up the endless supplies of young foreign girls. Inside, in the great buildings, vast tour parties sweep past each other, going in all directions, up and down the staircases, along the thirteen miles of stone corridors, into the twelve hundred rooms of paintings, objects, every kind of treasure, two million different items from all over the world. And from all over the world the people come to see them. They swarm through the Little Hermitage, the Big Hermitage, the Old Hermitage, the Hermitage Theatre, steered about in sheep-flocks by those bossy Russian guides who once used to promote socialism, comradeship, peace and world friendship and now promote Constructivist posters and *Demoiselles d'Avignon* T-shirts.

Today the world seems to be one museum after another. And of course everyone wants to see this one. [...] World-famous paintings hang in an unbelievable profusion. Every age and stage of art is depicted, from primitive to the highest baroque and the richest romanticism and so, in the great cycle of being, back down to primitive abstraction again. Every material, precious or semi-precious, has been mined, chipped, shaped, forged, fashioned. Every kind of human skill, craft and art has been used. Every nation and people seems to be represented. Every image and icon is kept in stock. [...]

Tired travellers look at it all, in a kind of worried desperation. Painting after painting passes across the retina, signals to the brain-cells, passes into confusion, excess, redundancy. The tourists pause a while, hunt round for the tea rooms, the chairs and the couches (and why are there never enough?). They put down their cameras, they take off their shoes. Girls chitter and chatter in front of the huge Rembrandts. Boys chase them through the endless rooms of the building, from gallery to gallery.

'And all this is simply for myself and the mice to admire,' the great Empress is supposed to have said once, in quiet satisfaction, after the great boatloads sent north by Golitsyn and Diderot arrived, were uncrated, hung on new walls that had to be built to display them. Now the collections collect the tourists in their millions, coming from every part of the globe.

Malcolm Bradbury, To the Hermitage (2000)

✻ ✻ ✻

*The tired visitors mentioned by Bradbury are nothing new: composer Sergei Prokofiev's diary for 1927 records the utter exhaustion of trying to 'do' such a vast collection of art and artefacts.*

Thursday 10 February

We were led into the Hermitage by a special entrance, having come as privileged visitors. We were met by the director, Troynitsky, a very interesting and rather elegant-looking man, who, despite being a former pupil of the Lyceum and in no way a Bolshevik, has been in charge of the Hermitage for many years and has managed to administer it with great skill and ability, avoiding all the underwater obstacles which contact with the communist government are liable to place in one's way.

Troynitsky personally showed us the most precious part of the Hermitage – the jewellery collection. This section is not easily accessible even to the director, since it is necessary as a preliminary to sign a book, pass the guards and undergo a number of formalities. In the jewel-room many curious and beautiful objects had been assembled, although I'm not normally keen on things just because their value is incalculable. Among them were tiaras all covered with diamonds, snuff-boxes and swords belonging to the tsars, everything iridescent with multi-coloured stones. Troynitsky, with a kind of nonchalance which concealed a great deal of pride, showed us all these objects with short explanations and the odd joke.

From the jewel-room, where, by the way, we were locked in while we were there, we went on to the Scythian section. Instead of Troynitsky we were shown around by a specialist working there. Here the most interesting things were articles made out of beaten gold.

After the Scythian section the Persian, and a new specialist, but our visit by now had lasted for several hours and we had grown tired. It was getting dark and we almost ran without stopping through the picture gallery. We couldn't look at everything in detail, but couldn't fail to see what a large portion of the Winter Palace had been taken over by the Hermitage.

By the time we at last got out we were completely exhausted.

Sergei Prokofiev, Soviet Diary 1927 and Other Writings (1991)<br>translated by Oleg Prokofiev

✽ ✽ ✽

*And now with Truman Capote, whose account ends with a comic but touching example of how a work of art can bring together people from very different backgrounds.*

The Hermitage is part of the Winter Palace, which in recent years has been repainted the Imperial colour, a frosty char-treuse-*vert*. Its miles of silvery windows overlook a park and a wide expanse of the Neva River. 'The Winter Palace was started working 1764 and took seventy-eight years to finish,' said the guide, a mannish girl with a brisk, whip'-em-through attitude. 'It consists of four buildings and contains, as you see, the world's greatest museum. This where we are standing is the Ambassadorial Staircase, used by the ambassadors mounting to see the Tsar.'

In the ectoplasmic wake of those ambassadors our party followed her up marble stairs that curved under a filigree ceiling of white and gold. We passed through a splendid hall of green malachite, like a corridor under the sea, and here there were French windows where a few of us paused to look across the Neva at a misty-hazy view of that celebrated torture chamber, the Peter-Paul fortress. 'Come, come,' the guide urged. 'There is much to see and we will not accomplish our mission if we linger at useless spectacles.' [...]

Some six kilometres later, the group, its ranks thinned by fatigue cases, stumbled into the last exhibit hall, weak-legged after two hours of inspecting Egyptian mummies and Italian Madonnas, craning their necks at excellent old masters excruciatingly hung, poking about the sarcophagus of Alexander Nevsky, and marvelling over a pair of Peter the Great's Goliath-large boots, 'Made,' said the guide, 'by this progressive man with his own hands.' Now, in the last hall, the guide commanded us to 'go to the window and view the hanging garden.'

'But where,' bleated Miss Swann, 'where *is* the garden?'

'Under the snow,' said the guide. 'And over here,' she said, directing attention to the final item on the agenda, 'is our famous The Peacock.'

The Peacock, an exotic mechanical folly constructed by the eighteenth-century clockmaker, James Cox, was brought to Russia as a gift for Catherine II. It is housed in a glass cage the size of a garden gazebo. The focus of the piece is a peacock perched among the gilded leaves of a bronze tree. Balanced on other branches are an owl, a cock rooster, a squirrel nibbling a nut. At the base of the tree there is a scattering of mushrooms, one of which forms the face of a clock. 'When the hour strikes, we have here a forceful happening,' said the guide. 'The peacock spreads her tail, and the rooster cackles. The owl blinks her eyes, and the squirrel has a good munch.' [...]

A gang of soldiers, part of another tour, approached The Peacock just as the hour chimed, and the soldiers, country boys with their heads shaved bald, their drab uniforms sagging in the seat like diapers, had the double enchantment of gaping at foreigners and watching the golden-eyed winkings of an owl, a peacock flash its bronze feathers in the wan light of the Winter Palace. The Americans and the soldiers crowded close to hear the rooster crow.

Truman Capote, *The Muses Are Heard* (1957)

✳ ✳ ✳

*If art can bring people together, it can also highlight the fissures in society. This was particularly the case in twentieth-century Russia. Julya Rabinowich on one aspect of the contemporary art scene in St Petersburg, showing that the engagement of art with politics continues. (More on the contemporary art scene in 'A Sleeping Beauty wakes'.)*

Naïve, with long hair and bell-bottoms, small artists' groups with names that announce their agendas, like 'the Non-conformists', stumble from a heady mini-revolt into bigger troubles. The wide array of works, from the superb to the negligible, have a common denominator: the complete rejection of every precept of socialist realism. The first group exhibition offers a unique event that leads to inevitable disaster.

The public, bored with red-blooded peasant women and flag-waving heroes, pour into the show even before the opening. Sensationalist. The police officer, appointed guardian of public morals by the dithering city council, is overwhelmed by the bewildering number of viewers. In the hubbub, he loses the equanimity of a state apparatus representative and cracks down hard. Alarmed by his desperate whistles, a militia unit soon arrives on the scene to separate the onlookers from the artists. Contamination of the social body by the usual suspects must

161

be obviated. Their world-view is known to be as contagious as measles. Quarantine is barely maintained by forcing the spectators into that half of the room, which has a metre-high wall topped with a small wrought-iron fence. The militia sweat, scream, whistle and almost end up unintentionally triggering mass panic. Because of the room's particular interior design, their call to order rings out as 'Viewers behind the fence; artists up against the wall!'

Not long after this, the organization is banned. Outraged and agitated, the artists meet in secret in their studios. Since these are not official communal apartments, the artists have the advantage of being able to choose who can live there. I'm often taken along to one of the studios, a dusty, smoke-filled basement vault.

An old wagon wheel with dripping wax candles emerges from the darkness of the ceiling. Gnawed bones of various lengths and thicknesses hang on ribbons tied to the wheel. I often glance up warily to measure them against the length of my forearm.

After all, my father had explained, his face dead serious, that we would be visiting a cannibal. He answered my hopeful question if other children would be there with a meaningful silence.

The studio's owner is a fat, bearded man, blustering and coarse.

His thundering laughter echoes throughout the room, and he serves shashlik, grilled in the open fireplace, the fat sizzling in the flames. In counterbalance to his appearance he produces mannered fairy-tale illustrations filled with pastel-coloured landscapes. I don't trust his treacly pictures for an instant. He laughs and jokes incessantly. He is open to all guests and art lovers. With his intercession, my father gets his own nude model. Later, we find out he had informed on my father to the authorities. For the moment, however, the group frequents this studio less than others. Among the members' works you can find, in equal measure, the abstract and the absurd, kitsch and tedium.

They listen to the Beatles and try to tune in to American radio stations. The women paint their eyes as black as the abyss. They pass round banned samizdat literature. Samizdat is the Communist version of covert resistance. The free spirits stay up all night retyping page after page of works they will publish in this way. The banned books will be intricately smuggled over the border by revolutionaries and priests. And this is how the Bible ends up in the company of pornographic beatnik trash.

Julya Rabinowich, *Splithead* (2009),
translated by Tess Lewis

✳  ✳  ✳

*Film is another artistic medium firmly rooted in the city, the government supported 'Lenfilm' having been a key contributor to this. In fact some of us may have acquired our ideas of the Russian Revolution from the great film-maker, Sergei Eisenstein – who may have taken a little more than poetic license …*

What's rendered in the history books as the Great October Socialist Revolution was, in fact, a plain *coup d'état*, and a bloodless one at that. Following the signal – a blank-fire shot of the cruiser *Aurora*'s bow gun – a platoon of the newly formed Red Guards walked into the Winter Palace and arrested a bunch of ministers of the Provisional Government idling there, vainly trying to take care of Russia after the Tsar's abdication. The Red Guards didn't meet any resistance; they raped half of the female unit guarding the palace and looted its chambers. At that, two Red Guardsmen were shot and one drowned in the wine cellars. The only shooting that ever took place in the Palace Square, with bodies falling and the searchlight crossing the sky, was Sergei Eisenstein's.

Joseph Brodsky, 'A Guide to a Renamed City' (1979)
in *Less Than One: Selected Essays*

✻ ✻ ✻

*An expert on Russian cinema, Anna Kovalova explores the unique relationship between the city and the medium of film.*

St Petersburg is more than photogenic – it is cinemagenic. People started filming it long before cameras and film were invented. It is no accident that Eisenstein said of Pushkin's *The Bronze Horseman* that it was almost a camera-ready story board.

The famous monument would later appear again and again in films from Petersburg and Leningrad. Sometimes its presence on the screen would be motivated by the plot, but more often than not it would be entirely unnecessary, just an extra. *The Bronze Horseman* is of course the logo for Lenfilm studios. Most probably the impulse of movement that is inherent in the sculpture was recognized by Catherine the Great who commissioned the piece. She was dissatisfied with the monument, and wrote to Falconet about her impressions: 'If this horse of yours came to life in your studio, in the manner of Pygmalion's statue, then, judging by the expression on its face, it would wreak the most dreadful havoc.' This strange statue really does sometimes seem to be moving, and sometimes to be standing still. It is not only cinemagenic, it is in fact cinema, and has been watched for centuries, along with St Petersburg itself.

The city did not immediately find its way into feature films the moment cinema came to Russia. For a long time only newsreels were shot in the city. After all, any guardian of the law could put a stop to filming on location at any moment: 'Hello, hello, hello, what's all this then! There's no law on the books that permits cinematographising!' But that isn't the only problem – pre-revolutionary film felt more at ease in the studio. Even Yakov Protazanov's famous *Queen of Spades* (1916) was filmed in the studio, avoiding any contact with Petersburg's streets.

Even so, St Petersburg was later to become one of the central characters in Russian film. Not a set, or a stage or scenery, but the actual hero, with a destiny and a personality.

St Petersburg came into the world later than all the other world capitals and cultural centres. It is younger even than New York and Boston. Our city is embarrassed at being so young, and has a burning wish to look older than it is. Our favourite temporal framework is the pluperfect.

The past and history are sacred here.

St Petersburg appears universal precisely because of this histrionic habit of attempting to appear more ancient, and adding the same again or more to its three hundred years' history. Virtually any historical period can be filmed in the city.

Films about Petersburg's past are almost never shot in the studio: only interior shots might be set up in a studio, but not the city itself. Modern Petersburg has been turned into the Petersburg of the past dozens of times. Past and present collide and engage in uncompromising battle both in the city's streets and on the screens of cinema houses. If you compare films about the 'past' and the 'present' in Petersburg that have been shot within a decade of each other, you might come to some paradoxical and quite astonishing conclusions.

Anna Kovalova, 'Cinema in St Petersburg: St Petersburg in Cinema'
in *St Petersburg as Cinema* (2011) (ed. Lyubov Arkus)
translated by Sergei Afonin and Alice Jondorf

✳ ✳ ✳

*Art historian Mikhail German notes the tendency to*
*romanticise the city in films of the pre-war Soviet era.*

The world of cinema gradually poeticized and embellished the city: in the film *Musical Story* there was gleaming asphalt laid beneath the wheels of taxi-driver hero Petya Govorkov – a future great singer (played by Sergei Lemeshev) and the ZIS car of the stupid and arrogant Tarakanov (Erast Garin). The amusingly Americanised utopia was lit by iron lampposts and played out against patrician façades of Petersburg palaces; the city became a set for unctuously romantic (although talented in their own way) revolutionary cinema fairy tales. Its factories were prettified by the skill of brilliant cinematographers, becoming sets for the famous films about Maxim, with 'legends made in the world of prose' as Emile Verhaeren expressed it; and Leningrad became encased in a magical legend about itself. What now was Dostoyevsky's 'uncertain, fantastic light here in St Petersburg'?

The city returned to reality on 22 June 1941 with the start of war.

Mikhail German, 'City Chronotopes'
in *St Petersburg as Cinema* (2011)
(ed. Lubov Arkus) translated by Sergei Afonin and Alice Jondorf

❉ ❉ ❉

*Several years after emigrating from the USSR, the narrator of Serge Dovlatov's* The Suitcase *discovers a battered suitcase he'd brought with him gathering dust at the back of the wardrobe. Each item he finds inside provokes a humorous story that combines the closely observed realities of Soviet life with delightful satire and a kind of comic nostalgia. This is from the story of a pair of driving gloves. Sergei Dovlatov (1941-90), grew up in Leningrad but was eventually forced into exile as a result of his writings. Here, the attempt to make an 'underground' film is given Dovlatov's characteristic treatment, the narrator having been chosen to star in the film simply because, at six foot four inches, he is (nearly) tall enough to play Peter the Great (who was six foot seven).*

The canteen took up the northern part of the sixth floor. The windows opened onto the Fontanka River. The three rooms could hold over a hundred people. Schlippenbach dragged me into an alcove, to a table for two. Apparently we were going to have a highly confidential conversation.

We got beer and sandwiches. Schlippenbach lowered his voice a bit and began.

'I turned to you because I value cultured people. I'm a cultured person. There aren't many of us. To tell the truth, I'm surprised there are as many as there are – aristocrats are a dying breed, like prehistoric animals. But let's talk business. I've decided to do an underground film on my own. I'm tired of giving the best years of my life to run-of-the-mill journalism – I want to do real creative work. Anyhow, I start shooting tomorrow. It will be a ten-minute film, a satire. Here's the plot: a mysterious stranger appears in Leningrad. We see right off that he's Tsar Peter the Great, the man who founded the city two hundred and sixty years ago. Now the great sovereign finds himself smack in the middle of vulgar Soviet reality. A policeman threatens to run him in. Two winos ask him to chip in for a bottle. Whores take him for a rich foreigner. KGB agents think he's a spy, and so on. In short, it's a drunken whorehouse of a city. The Tsar cries, 'What have I done? ... Why ever did I build this whorish city?''

Schlippenbach laughed so hard that the paper napkins flew up in the air. Then he added, 'The film will be politically touchy, to put it mildly. It will have to be shown in private apartments. I'm hoping Western journalists will see it – that will guarantee worldwide resonance. The consequences may be most unexpected. So, you think it over, weigh the facts. Do you accept?'

'You said to think it over ...'

'How long can you think? Just agree!'

'Where will you get the equipment?'

'No need to worry about that. Don't forget, I work at Lenfilm studios. Everyone there is a friend, from the top directors down to the lighting crew. The equipment is mine to use. I've been running a camera since I was a child. So think about it and decide. You suit me. This is a role I can trust only to a like-minded individual. We'll go to the studios tomorrow, get the necessary props, talk to make-up. And we'll start.'

'I said I have to think about it …'

'I'll call you.' […]

So, we went down to Lenfilm. Schlippenbach called some guy named Chipa, in the props department, and got a pass.

The room we came to was jammed with cupboards and crates. I smelt mildew and mothballs. Fluorescent lights blinked and crackled overhead. A stuffed bear reared up in the corner. A cat strolled down the long table.

Chipa came out from behind a curtain. He was a middle-aged man in a striped T-shirt and top hat. […]

He said, 'Here you go, Chief!' and laid out a pile of junk on the table: tall black boots, a brocade waistcoat, a frock coat, a broad-brimmed hat and a sword. Then he got out a pair of gauntlets, like the ones early car enthusiasts used to wear.

'What about trousers?' Schlippenbach reminded him.

Chipa opened a crate and lifted out a pair of velvet breeches with gold braid. I pulled them on with great difficulty. They wouldn't fasten. 'They'll do,' Chipa said. 'Use twine.' As we were leaving he suddenly said, 'When I was inside I wanted out. But now, if I have a few drinks I start missing the camp. What people! Lefty, One-Eye, Diesel!'

We put the stuff in a suitcase and took the elevator down to make-up.

By the way, this was my first visit to Lenfilm. I thought I'd see lots of interesting things – creative bustle, famous actors, maybe Chursina trying on a French bikini and Tenyakova standing next to her, dying of envy. In reality, Lenfilm was like a gigantic government office: plain women carrying papers through the corridors, the rattle of typewriters from everywhere. We never did run into any colourful individuals, except maybe Chipa with his striped T-shirt and top hat.

The make-up woman, Lyudmila Alexandrovna, sat me down at a mirror and gazed into it from over my shoulder for a while.

'Well?' Schlippenbach demanded.

'The head's not great – C-plus – but the overall look is fantastic.'

Lyudmila Alexandrovna touched my lip, pulled at my nose, brushed her fingers over my ear. Then she put a black wig on me. She glued on a moustache. With light strokes of a pencil, she rounded my cheeks.

'Amazing!' Schlippenbach was delighted. 'A typical tsar!'

Then I suited up and we called for a taxi. I walked through the studios dressed as the great emperor. A couple of people turned to look – not many. Schlippenbach dropped by to see one other pal. This one gave us two black boxes of equipment – for money this time.

'How much?' Schlippenbach asked.

'Four roubles and twelve kopeks,' was the answer. The price of a bottle.

'I heard you switched to white wine.'

'And you believed that?'

In the taxi Schlippenbach explained: 'You don't need to read the script – everything will be built on improvisation, like in Antonioni. Tsar Peter finds himself in modern Leningrad. Everything is disgusting and alien. He goes into a grocery store. He starts shouting, "Where's the smoked venison, the mead, the anise vodka? Who bankrupted my domain, the barbarians?" That kind of thing. We're going to Vasilievsky Island now. Galina is waiting for us with the van.'

'Who's Galina?'

'From supplies at Lenfilm. She has a company van. Said she'd meet us after work. Incredibly cultured woman. We wrote the screenplay together. At a friend's apartment. Anyway, let's go to Vasilievsky Island. Do the first shots. The tsar heads from the Rostral Column towards Nevsky Prospekt. He's in shock. He keeps slowing down and looking around. Get it? You know – be scared of cars, look puzzled at signs, shy away from phone booths … If someone bumps into you, draw your sword. Go with it – be creative.' My sword lay on my lap. The blade was filed off, inside the scabbard: I could draw about three inches of it.

Schlippenbach waved his arms with inspiration. But the driver was unmoved. As he dropped us off, he asked in a friendly way, 'So, what zoo did you escape from, pal?'

'Terrific!' Schlippenbach cried. 'We can use that line! Ready art!'

We got out of the taxi with the boxes. A minivan stood across the street. A young woman in jeans was pacing near it. My appearance did not interest her.

'Galina, you're a marvel,' Schlippenbach said. 'We start in ten minutes.'

'You are the bane of my existence,' she replied.

They puttered with the equipment for about twenty minutes. I walked up and down in the slush in front of the Kunstkamera. Passers-by examined me with interest. A cold wind blew from the Neva river.

Sergei Dovlatov, *The Suitcase* (1986)
translated by Antonina W. Bouis

✳ ✳ ✳

*From the hopeless fictional film-maker of Dovlatov's story we turn to a real one – the internationally recognised St Petersburg film director Alexander Sokurov, who is also an influential campaigner for the preservation of St Petersburg's historic city centre, and for the revival of the once great 'Lenfilm' studios – the oldest in the country. Sokurov, whose* Russian Ark *is entirely set in the Hermitage, speaks about the over-whelming presence of the arts in the city.*

'On the one hand, it is in some sense a government city, yes, it was the capital after all. But on the other hand, there is too much artistic vision invested here. In the planning, the buildings. There is too much pure art here, you know? Just pure art. And there were too many figures here, on the level of, say … Tchaikovsky, Shostakovich, if we're talking music … So these are people representing the highest achievements of all mankind, you could say. Absolute achievements. They were in this city, they lived here … What's more, we aren't separated from them in the way we are from an epoch like the Renaissance: their children, their direct relatives still live here. Including Dostoyevsky's.

Alexander Sokurov interviewed by Marina Samsonova and Catriona Kelly (2011) for the 'Cultural Memory and Local Identity in St Petersburg' project, translated by Maya Vinokour

# Leningrad

There was no proper night that night: just the day nodding off for a second, like a soldier on the march who keeps in step but for whom dream and reality merge. In the rosy mirror of the canals there doze upside-down trees, windows and columns – St Petersburg. Then, suddenly, with the lightest breeze, St Petersburg melts away and in its place is Leningrad. On the Winter Palace a red flag stirs in the wind, and by the railings of the Alexandrovsky Park a policeman stands, armed with a rifle.

Yevgeny Zamyatin, 'The Lion' (1935)
translated by I. Silver

✻ ✻ ✻

Petersburg-Leningrad is a city of tragic beauty, unique in the world. Without understanding this, it is impossible to love Petersburg. The Peter and Paul Fortress is the symbol of tragedies, the Winter Palace on the opposite bank is the symbol of captive beauty.

Petersburg and Leningrad are totally different cities. Not in all respects, of course. In various ways they 'gaze into one another.' Leningrad is discernible in Petersburg and Petersburg, in its architecture, could be glimpsed in Leningrad. But the similarities only underscore the differences.

Dmitry Likhachev, *Reminiscences* (1995)
translated by Maya Vinokour

❋ ❋ ❋

*The revolution that transformed St Petersburg/ Petrograd into Leningrad (the name was officially changed in 1924) did not really happen overnight, of course. There had been many years of discontent, assassinations, demonstrations and civic unrest as the old Imperial regime came under increasing scrutiny. For some, the influence of Rasputin on the Imperial family was the final straw, though many of those involved in government tried everything to effect the much needed changes by evolution – reforming the laws – rather than revolution.*

*One of the most famous books on the Revolution is John Reed's* Ten Days that Shook the World. *This extract is a vivid account of the 'storming of the Winter Palace' ... and shows why so many of its treasures survived.*

We went towards the Winter Palace by way of the Admiralteisky. All the entrances to the Palace Square were closed by sentries, and a cordon of troops stretched clear across the western end, besieged by an uneasy throng of citizens. Except for far-away soldiers who seemed to be carrying wood out of the Palace courtyard and piling it in front of the main gateway, everything was quiet.

We couldn't make out whether the sentries were pro-Government or pro-Soviet. Our papers from Smolny had no effect, however, so we approached another part of the line with an important air and showed our American passports, saying, 'Official business!' and shouldered through. At the door of the Palace the same old *shveitzari*, in their brass-buttoned blue uniforms with the red-and-gold collars, politely took our coats and hats, and we went upstairs. In the dark, gloomy corridor, stripped of its tapestries, a few old attendants were lounging about, and in front of Kerensky's door a young officer paced up and down, gnawing his moustache. We asked if we could interview the Minister-President. He bowed and clicked his heels.

'No, I am sorry,' he replied in French. 'Alexander Fyodorovich is extremely occupied just now …' He looked at us for a moment. 'In fact, he is not here …'

'Where is he?'

'He has gone to the front. And do you know, there wasn't enough gasoline for his automobile. We had to send to the English Hospital and borrow some.'

'Are the Ministers here?'

'They are meeting in some room – I don't know where.'

'Are the Bolsheviki coming?'

'Of course. Certainly they are coming. I expect a telephone call every minute to say they are coming. But we are ready. We have *yunkers* in the front of the Palace. Through that door there.'

'Can we go in there?'

'No. Certainly not. It is not permitted.' Abruptly he shook hands all round and walked away. We turned to the forbidden door, set in a temporary partition dividing the hall and locked on the outside. On the other side were voices, and somebody laughing. Except for that the vast spaces of the old Palace were as silent as the grave. An old *shveitzar* ran up. 'No, *barin*, you must not go in there.'

'Why is the door locked?'

'To keep the soldiers in,' he answered. After a few minutes he said something about having a glass of tea and went back up the hall. We unlocked the door.

Just inside a couple of soldiers stood on guard, but they said nothing. At the end of the corridor was a large, ornate room with gilded cornices and enormous crystal lustres, and beyond it several smaller ones, wainscoted with dark wood. On both sides of the parqueted floor lay rows of dirty mattresses and blankets, upon which occasional soldiers were stretched out; everywhere was a litter of cigarette butts, bits of bread, cloth, and empty bottles with expensive French labels. [...]

The place was all a huge barrack, and evidently had been for weeks, from the look of the floor and walls. Machine-guns were mounted on window-sills, rifles stacked between the mattresses. [...]

For a while we stood at the window, looking down on the Square before the Palace, where three companies of long-coated *yunkers* were drawn up under arms, being harangued by a tall, energetic-looking officer I recognized as Stankievich, chief Military Commissar of the Provisional Government. After a few minutes two of the companies shouldered arms with a clash, barked three sharp shouts, and went swinging off across the Square, disappearing through the Red Arch into the quiet city.

'They are going to capture the Telephone Exchange,' said someone. [...]

It was getting late when we left the Palace. The sentries in the Square had all disappeared. The great semi-circle of Government buildings seemed deserted. We went into the Hotel France for dinner, and right in the middle of soup the waiter, very pale in the face, came up and insisted that we move to the main dining-room at the back of the house, because they were going to put out the lights in the café. 'There will be much shooting,' he said.

When we came out on the Morskaya again it was quite dark, except for one flickering street-light on the corner of the Nevsky. [...]

Here the streetcars had stopped running, few people passed, and there were no lights; but a few blocks away we could see the trams, the crowds, the lighted shop-windows and the electric signs of the moving-picture shows – life going on as usual. We had tickets to the ballet at the Mariinsky Theatre – all the theatres were open – but it was too exciting out of doors. [...]

Carried along by the eager wave of men we were swept into the right-hand entrance, opening into a great bare vaulted room, the cellar of the east wing, from which issued a maze of corridors and staircases. A number of huge packing cases stood about, and upon these the Red Guards and soldiers fell furiously, battering them open with the butts of their rifles, and pulling out carpets, curtains, linen, porcelain, plates, glassware ... One man went strutting around with a bronze clock perched on his shoulder; another found a plume of ostrich feathers, which he stuck in his hat. The looting was just beginning when somebody cried, 'Comrades! Don't take anything. This is the property of the People!' Immediately twenty voices were crying, 'Stop! Put everything back! Don't take anything! Property of the People!' Many hands dragged the spoilers down. Damask and tapestry were snatched from the arms of those who had them; two men took away the bronze clock. Roughly and hastily the things were crammed back in their cases, and self-appointed sentinels stood guard. It was all utterly spontaneous. Through corridors and up staircases the cry could be heard growing fainter and fainter in the distance, 'Revolutionary discipline! Property of the People!'[...]

'*Pazhal'st'*, *tovarischi!* Way, Comrades!' A soldier and a Red Guard appeared in the door, waving the crowd aside, and other guards with fixed bayonets. After them followed single file half a dozen men in civilian dress, the members of the Provisional Government. First came Kishkin, his face drawn and pale, then Rutenberg, looking sullenly at the floor; Tereschchenko was next, glancing sharply around; he stared at us with cold fixity ... They passed in silence; the victorious insurrectionists crowded to see, but there were only a few angry mutterings. It was only later that we learned how the people in the street wanted to lynch them, and shots were fired but the sailors brought them safely to Peter-Paul ...

In the meanwhile unrebuked we walked into the Palace. There was still a great deal of coming and going, of exploring new-found apartments in the vast edifice, of searching for hidden garrisons of *yunkers* which did not exist. We went upstairs and wandered through room after room. [...] The old Palace servants in their blue and red and gold uniforms stood nervously about, from force of habit repeating, 'You can't go in there, *barin*! It is forbidden –' We penetrated at length to the gold and malachite chamber with crimson brocade hangings where the Ministers had been in session all that day and night, and where the *shveitzari* had betrayed them to the Red Guards. The long table covered with green baize was just as they had left it, under arrest. Before each empty seat was pen, ink, and paper; the papers were scribbled over with beginnings of plans of action, rough drafts of proclamations and manifestoes. Most of these were scratched out, as their futility became evident, and the rest of the sheet covered with absent-minded geometrical designs, as the writers sat despondently listening while Minister after Minister proposed chimerical schemes. I took one of these scribbled pages, in the hand-writing of Konovalov, which read, 'The Provisional Government appeals to all classes to support the Provisional Government –'

All this time, it must be remembered, although the Winter Palace was surrounded, the Government was in constant communication with the front and with provincial Russia. The Bolsheviki had captured the Ministry of War early in the morning, but they did not know of the military telegraphy office in the attic, nor of the private telephone line connecting it with the Winter Palace. In that attic a young officer sat all day, pouring out over the country a flood of appeals and proclamations; and when he heard the Palace had fallen, put on his hat and walked calmly out of the building.

John Reed, Ten Days that Shook the World (1919)

*Debra Dean in the follow-up to this: the Imperial treasures now belong to everyone.*

Inside the Winter Palace, at the foot of the Jordan Staircase, one might believe that time has indeed stood still, that nothing has changed for centuries. The stone pillars rise regally up into the painted sky inhabited by the gods of Olympus, and the mirrored walls seem to hold the glittering reflections of generations of imperial soldiers, their sabres glinting in the dim light, and elegant women in huge satin skirts, their bosoms draped with fat pearls, their faces hidden behind sweeping fans. Marina ascends the marble steps, up, up, up, and stops on the first landing to catch her breath.

This is where the tour begins. For two years, she guided groups of schoolchildren or factory workers through the Hermitage. They would gather here at the start of the tour, and she would welcome them to the museum and begin by noting how many visitors had passed up these stairs before them. 'This staircase was designed in the eighteenth century by architect Francesco Bartolomeo Rastrelli. Notice the lavish use of gilded stucco mouldings, the abundance of mirrors and marble. And above us' – she would direct their gaze to the intricately painted ceiling fifteen metres up – 'the Italian painter Gaspare Diziani has depicted the Greek gods on Olympus.

'All this Baroque splendour was intended to overwhelm visiting dignitaries with the might and wealth of Russia. But this is merely the entrance. The State Museum of Leningrad comprises four hundred rooms in five contiguous buildings: the Winter Palace, where we stand now, the Small Hermitage, the Old Hermitage, the New Hermitage, and the Hermitage Theatre. The architecture is, as you can see here, magnificent. But what is even more remarkable is what these buildings contain, the most precious collection of art in the entire world.

'In pre-Marxist society, this was considered the private property of the ruling class, but after the Great Socialist Revolution, it was liberated and returned to the workers who created it.' Her sweeping gesture would direct their eyes down the grand staircase and back up again to the soaring ceilings.

'Comrades, all this is yours.'

This is the official welcome, lines scripted by some party functionary, but for her it is not empty propaganda. She herself is still amazed: they are her paintings. She is like a lover who still sees her beloved in the trembling golden light of their first meeting.

Debra Dean, *The Madonnas of Leningrad* (2006)

✻ ✻ ✻

*H. G. Wells had been in Russia in 1914. Returning for two weeks in 1920, he records his impressions of post-Revolutionary St Petersburg.*

The dominant fact for the Western reader, the threatening and disconcerting fact, is that a social and economic system very like our own and intimately connected with our own has crashed.

Nowhere in Russia is the fact of that crash so completely evident as it is in Petersburg. Petersburg was the artificial creation of Peter the Great; his bronze statue in the little garden near the Admiralty still prances amidst the ebbing life of the city. Its palaces are still and empty, or strangely refurnished with type-writers and tables and plank partitions of a new Administration which is engaged chiefly in a strenuous struggle against famine and the foreign invader. Its streets were streets of busy shops. In 1914 I loafed agreeably in the Petersburg streets – buying little articles and watching the abundant traffic. All these shops have ceased. There are perhaps half a dozen shops still open in Petersburg. There is a Government crockery shop where I bought a plate or two as a souvenir, for seven or eight roubles each, and there are a few flower shops. It is a wonderful fact, I think, that in this city, in which most of the shrinking popula-tion is already near starving, and hardly anyone possesses a second suit of clothes or more than a single change of worn and patched linen, flowers can be and are still bought and sold. For five thousand roubles, which is about six and eight pence at the current rate of exchange, one can get a pleasing bunch of big chrysanthemums. […]

All the great bazaar-like markets are closed, too, in Peters-burg now, in the desperate struggle to keep a public control of necessities and prevent the profiteer driving up the last vestiges of food to incredible prices. And this cessation of shops makes walking about the streets seem a silly sort of thing to do. Nobody 'walks about' any more. One realises that a modern city is really nothing but long alleys of shops and restaurants and the like. Shut them up, and the meaning of a street has disappeared. People hurry past – a thin traffic compared with my memories of 1914. The electric street cars are still running and busy – until six o'clock. They are the only means of loco-motion for ordinary people remaining in town – the last legacy of capitalist enterprise. They became free while we were in Petersburg. Previously there had been a charge of two or three roubles – the hundredth part of the price of an egg. Freeing them made little difference in their extreme congestion during the home-going hours. Everyone scrambles on the tramcar. If there is no room inside you cluster outside. In the busy hours festoons of people hang outside by any handhold; people are frequently pushed off, and accidents are frequent. We saw a crowd collected round a child cut in half by a tramcar, and two people in the little circle in which we moved in Petersburg had broken their legs in tramway accidents.

The roads along which these tramcars run are in a frightful condition. They have not been repaired for three or four years; they are full of holes like shell-holes, often two or three feet deep. Frost has eaten out great cavities, drains have collapsed, and people have torn up the wooden pavement for fires.

H. G. Wells, *Russia in the Shadows* (1921)

✳ ✳ ✳

*Married to a Russian, Englishman Lancelot Lawson had lived in the country for many years before the Revolution and visited the city shortly after its renaming in 1924.*

The contrast between Moscow and Petrograd, now renamed Leningrad, was always marked – Moscow with its air of 'the big village', so typical of Russian disorderliness; Leningrad, an Imperial capital, with broad streets and Western aspect. But today the contrast between the two cities is still more striking; for it is the contrast between life and death itself. Leningrad is a dying city. Never did I feel so depressed as during my stay there. […]

Today Leningrad reminds one of a beautiful woman suffering from neglect. It is still beautiful, very beautiful; but so inexpressibly sad. As one approaches the city in the train one sees lines of deserted factories with smokeless chimneys. […]

In Leningrad, as in all Russian towns, the streets have been renamed; the Nevsky has become the October Twenty-Fifth Prospekt! (the date of the Bolshevik Revolution); other streets are named after famous revolutionaries; one street, for example, in memory of the man who assassinated Alexander II, a second after Rosa Luxembourg; and a third after Robespierre.

Then there is a 'Street of Young Proletarians,' a 'Place of Communards', a 'Street of Brotherly Love,' and a 'Bridge of Freedom'. If one went only by the names of many of the streets one might well imagine one was strolling in the highways of Paradise itself.

Lancelot Lawson, The Russian Revolution, 1917–1926 (1927)

✳ ✳ ✳

*Some more changes, noted in his diary by composer Sergei Prokofiev on returning to the city in 1927.*

Wednesday 9 February

We arrived in front of the Winter Palace. Some changes here: the railings encircling the garden have been taken down and the garden is open to the public. But the disappearance of the railings does not spoil how it looks; quite the contrary, the square becomes more spacious. Shcherbachev explains that the much enlarged Hermitage now occupies more than half the rooms of the Winter Palace.

The building of the General Staff Headquarters is painted bright yellow, with white columns. This is new – in the past it used to be dark red, the Palace as well. Is that good? I liked it dark red. But Shcherbachev explains that the original colour was different.

We got to the Neva at sunset. It is fantastic, pink all over; even the river and snow and the walls of the buildings are pink. Lit up like this the Neva and the fortress of Peter and Paul are amazingly beautiful. We walk along the embankment and turn into Zimnaya Kanavka.

Sergei Prokofiev, Soviet Diary 1927 and Other Writings (1991)<br>translated by Oleg Prokofiev

✻ ✻ ✻

*In Victor Serge's powerful portrayal of the city at the time of the Civil War, the narrator is urged to look out over Petrograd[1] whose air is now crystal clear – a sinister symptom for an industrial city.*

Not a single chimney was smoking. The city was thus dying. And, like shipwrecked men on a raft devouring each other, we were about to fight among ourselves, workers against workers, revolutionaries against revolutionaries. If the Great Works succeeded in carrying along the other factories, we would witness a general strike pitting the populace of the dead factories against the Revolution. It would be the revolt of despair against the stubborn, wilful organised revolt which still had hope. It would be the fervid and unthinking treason of some of the best, ready to ally themselves with the famine against the dictatorship because they couldn't understand that the faith of millions of men can also die for lack of bread, that we are less and less free men, more and more, in an exhausted, besieged city, an army in rags whose safety lies in terror and discipline.

Victor Serge, *Conquered City* (1932)
translated by Richard Greeman

✻ ✻ ✻

*Novelist Andrei Bitov recalls growing up in Leningrad.*

For those of us born under the new order, the concept of 'before the Revolution' was pushed as far back as 'before Christ'. Yet I was born when the Soviet powers were not even twenty years old. At that time many things, and even more people, from THAT epoch were still around. […] In this city everything corresponds to something that came before: Venice of the North, Palmyra of the North, second Paris, but not the second Moscow … Here I

---

1   The city's name was changed to Petrograd at the time of the First World War as 'Petersburg' was considered too Germanic. (Petrograd is simply the Russian equivalent.) (Ed.)

learned to walk on the second largest square in Europe (Dvort-sovaya), to see the largest cathedral after St. Peter's (St. Isaac's), to contemplate one of the largest mosques (this time, for some reason, not the second, but the third in the world) … If it couldn't be the first, then it had to be the biggest. But what are words here! Across from my family home grew, as far as we knew, the biggest palm tree in Europe (among those growing in greenhouses); the tree, like the only elephant (probably also the biggest, at least among those living on the 60th parallel), was hit by a bomb during the blockade … The palm tree and the elephant perished on the periphery of my childhood consciousness, but Petersburg made it out intact again – Peter and Paul Fortress, Winter Palace, Bronze Horseman, and the rostral columns, and the sphinxes (which, though ancient Egyptian, were definitely the most north-erly)… – in any case, PETERSBURG, where 'perhaps I, too, was born,' inhabited by Pushkin, established by Peter, Petersburg, whose classicism and baroque will be, somehow, slightly more exact, slightly more classical and slightly less baroque, where the endeavour to catch up encoded a suppressed 'we must surpass.' And there's this sense that this city, invented and imposed upon Russia, is eternal, that it's no longer in tune with its young age (some two to three hundred years). (Incidentally, some black architectural humour: 'What'll be left if an H-bomb falls on Leningrad?' 'Petersburg.')

Andrei Bitov, *Life in Windy Weather* (1991)
translated by Maya Vinokour

✶ ✶ ✶

*Moving on to Leningrad in the 1950s, there are some surprises in store for Truman Capote and the American opera company with whom he travels to the city. They are there over the Christmas period and are surprised to find that religious practices are not entirely banned under the Soviet regime.*

Somewhat back from the Nevsky Prospekt, there is an arcaded building bearing a marked resemblance to St. Peter's. This is the Kazan Cathedral, Leningrad's largest anti-religious museum. Inside, in an atmosphere of stained-glass gloom, the management has produced a Grand Guignol indictment against the teachings of the church. Statues and sinister portraits of the Popes follow each other down the galleries like a procession of witches. Everywhere ecclesiastics leer and grimace, make, in captioned cartoons, satyr suggestions to nun-like women, revel in orgies, snub the poor to cavort with the decadent rich. *Ad infinitum* the museum demonstrates its favourite thesis; that the church, the Roman Catholic in particular, exists solely as a protection to capitalism. One caricature, an enormous oil, depicts Rockefeller, Krupp, Hetty Green, Morgan and Ford plunging ferocious hands into a mountainous welter of coins and blood-soaked war helmets.

The Kazan Cathedral is popular with children. Understandably so since the exhibition is liberally sprinkled with horror-comic scenes of brutality and torture. [...]

Anti-religious museums were not among the sight-seeing projects their hosts had lined up for the *Porgy and Bess* cast. Quite the contrary, on Sunday, Christmas Day, the Soviets provided the choice of attending a Catholic Mass or a Baptist service. Eleven members of the company, including Rhoda Boggs, a soprano playing the part of the Strawberry Woman, went to the Baptist Evangelical Church, whose Leningrad parishioners number two thousand. Afterwards, I saw Miss Boggs sitting alone in the Astoria dining-room. She is a round, honey-coloured, jolly-faced woman, always carefully groomed, but now her little Sunday best hat was slightly askew, the handkerchief she kept dabbing at her eyes was wet as a dish-cloth.

'I'm tore to pieces,' she told me, her breasts heaving. 'I've been going to church since I can walk, but I never felt Jesus

185

like I felt Jesus today. He was plainly written on every face. He was singing with us, and you never heard such beautiful singing.'

Truman Capote, The Muses Are Heard (1957)

❊ ❊ ❊

*And an example of 30s Soviet architecture – Leningrad's Palace of Culture. Truman Capote again.*

On Monday morning, the day of the première, the cast met at Leningrad's Palace of Culture for a final dress rehearsal with full orchestra. Originally the Soviets had intended housing the production in the attractive Mariinsky Theatre, but the demand for tickets convinced them that they could double their profit by transferring the opera to the huge Palace of Culture. The Palace, a pile of muddy-orange concrete, was slapped together in the 'thirties. From the outside it is not unlike one of those decaying examples of supermarket architecture along Hollywood and Vine. Several things about the interior suggest a skating rink. Its temperature, for one. But Davy Bey, and the other children in the company, thought it was 'a grand place', especially the vast backstage with its black recesses for hiding, its fly ropes to swing on, and where the tough backstage crew, strong men and stronger women, caressed them, gave them candy sticks and called them '*Aluchka*', a term of affection.

Truman Capote, The Muses Are Heard (1957)

❊ ❊ ❊

*Another famous writer visiting the city just a few years after Capote was Simone de Beauvoir, in the company of Jean-Paul Sartre. She loved the city and relished a visit to some of its literary locations.*

One night by train took us to Leningrad, one of the most beautiful cities in the world. It was a stroke of genius on the part of Catherine II to order Rastrelli to bring the Italian Baroque to the banks of the Neva, where it has made a perfect marriage with the pinks and blues and greens that clothe it here in the pale Nordic light. Like Rome, Leningrad is an enchantress; above all in the immense square glittering with the windows of the Winter Palace. Superimposed by my memory on its mysterious majesty lay black and white scenes from the 'ten days that shook the world' and from the revolts that heralded them. A bustling crowd hurried up and down the Nevsky Prospect: I recalled a photograph showing the roadway and the sidewalks piled with dead and dying. In the middle of the Neva Bridge, I saw a horse-drawn cab: the bridge rose; horse and vehicle went tumbling down, caught in the deep silence of those old films. Smolny. The Admiralty. The Fortress of Peter and Paul. Oh, the reverberation of those words inside me as I read them for the first time when I was twenty. During the day, it was Lenin's city I was walking in (and that other's, who is never named).

And then, in all its brightness, came the night. 'The White Nights of St Petersburg'; in Norway, in Finland, I had thought I knew what they were like; but the magic of the night-time sun needs this ghost-haunted, petrified décor from the past to complete its spell.

We had dinner at the home of the writer Guerman, his family, and also Heifitz, the director of *The Lady with a Dog*. We knew that he had escaped deportation to Siberia only by going into hiding and also, in part, thanks to Ehrenburg. 'Not once did I write the name of Stalin,' he told us, piling our plates with Siberian ravioli. We talked about the cinema and about theatre; he told us some of the things he remembered about Meyerhold. Heifitz's wife and twenty-year-old son arrived in time for coffee. They had been to see *Rocco and His Brothers*; she was very stirred and delighted. Young Heifitz and Guerman's children compared the merits of Voznesensky and Yevtushenko; he preferred the former, they the latter. Sartre had a long discussion with Mme Heifitz on the relations of children with their parents; he based some of his remarks on Freudian theories that she opposed passionately. There were lovers kissing on the benches in the fresh smell of early morning, young people playing the guitar and groups of boys and girls walking along laughing.

Two days later, we met them again in a restaurant at about eleven, after the theatre. They took us by car to see the Dostoyevsky neighbourhood by the light of the pale sky: his house, the place where Rogojine had lived, the courtyard of the old woman moneylender killed by Raskolnikov, the canal where he disposed of the axe. On the way we glimpsed the window of the room where Essenin killed himself. They showed us the very first place where Peter the Great had lived, and the first canals. On the outskirts of the town, at the spot where Pushkin came to fight the duel in which he was mortally wounded, we drank vodka to his memory.

Simone de Beauvoir, *Force of Circumstance* (1963)
translated by Richard Howard

❋ ❋ ❋

*Some reminiscences of a Soviet Leningrad childhood.*

The elephant-grey concrete mess that is the Palace of the Pioneers. The house where I was born on Vasilievsky Island, with its bridges over the Neva all raised at night so the large ships can pass, only to have their metal teeth bite into each other again in the early morning hours, primeval dinosaur necks against the continuously pink skies of the white nights. Confusing extended family relations. The national hymn in nursery school: we played 'Lenin Returns Home' and handed out papier-mâché flowers. My dark brown school uniform, whose resemblance to a bourgeois governess's outfit I did not notice until after I'd been in Vienna for a long time. My October

Child badge is still stuck on my jumper. The red bouquets for the parades, and the shop shelves swept clean. Our communal apartment with its varied tenants. Schenya, my first love, whose nose I had, not long before, bloodied by pushing him into a tree out of jealousy. The stories I grew up with, which accompanied me night after night into the future: 'The Mistress of Copper Mountain', who can change herself into a lizard and who richly rewards good men with jewels and crushes the bad between the walls of her mountain. She is green-eyed and mysterious. Baba Yaga, who wades through the swamp in her little hut on chicken legs. Sometimes she helps people who seek her out because they have no other choice; sometimes she devours them, depending on her mood. Splithead, who lives off the thoughts and feelings of others, an impassive vampire, watchful, invisible, menacing, but who is still unpleasantly personal, a private monster, custom-made and set upon our family.

My aunt Ljuba told her children that there was a bottle in the cellar with a hellhound in it. Now my cousins won't even go near the cellar door out of fear that the sound of their footsteps could wake the monster. But in their cellar are only a few cases of home-made liquor, hidden under old newspapers. This hellhound – always ready to jump out of his bottle – can be found in almost every communal apartment building. [...]

Our communal apartment is equipped with a chief spy in the reserves who has not recovered from being put into retirement and is, in any case, a fertile source for the most absurd reports to officials. Suffering agonies of stupefying meaninglessness, this Hero of Labour perches for hours in front of the communal telephone and transcribes into a file kept for just that purpose all of the conversations conducted unfazed right before his nose. He sits there in the half-dark and sweats moral responsibility to the fatherland from every gleaming pore.

Julya Rabinowich, Splithead (2009),<br>translated by Tess Lewis

# City under siege

*The most tragic period of Leningrad's history was the almost 900-day siege during which Hitler's forces surrounded the city, starved it, and subjected it to continual bombardment. Anna Reid on the background to the Siege in her recent, ground-breaking study,* Leningrad: Tragedy of a City Under Siege, 1941–44.

On 22 June 1941, the midsummer morning on which Germany attacked the Soviet Union, Leningrad looked much the same as it had done before the Revolution. A seagull circling over the gilded needle of the Admiralty spire would have seen the same view as twenty-four years previously: below, the choppy grey River Neva, lined by parks and palaces; to the west, where the Neva opens into the sea, the cranes of the naval dockyards; to the north, the zigzag bastions of the Peter and Paul Fortress

190

and grid-line streets of Vasilievsky Island; to the south, four concentric waterways – the pretty Moika, coolly classical Griboyedov, broad, grand Fontanka and workaday Obvodny – and two great boulevards, the Izmailovsky and the Nevsky Prospekt, radiating in perfect symmetry past the Warsaw and Moscow railway stations to the factory chimneys of the industrial districts beyond.

Appearances, though, were deceptive. Outwardly, Leningrad was not much altered; inwardly, it was profoundly changed and traumatised. It is conventional to give the story of the blockade a filmic happy-sad-happy progression: the peace of a midsummer morning shattered by news of invasion, the call to arms, the enemy halted at the gates, descent into cold and starvation, springtime recovery, victory fireworks. In reality it was not like that. Any Leningrader aged thirty or over at the start of the siege had already lived through three wars (the First World War, the Civil War between Bolsheviks and Whites that followed it, and the Winter War with Finland of 1939-40), two famines (the first during the Civil War, the second the collectivisation famine of 1932–3, caused by Stalin's violent seizure of peasant farms) and two major waves of political terror. Hardly a household, particularly among the city's ethnic minorities and old middle classes, had not been touched by death, prison or exile as well as impoverishment. For someone like the poet Olga Berggolts, daughter of a Jewish doctor, it was not unduly melodramatic to state that 'we measured time by the intervals between one suicide and the next'. The siege, though unique in the size of its death toll, was less a tragic interlude than one dark passage among many.

The tragedy arose from the combined hubris of Hitler and Stalin. In August 1939 they had astonished the world by putting ideology aside to form a non-aggression pact, under which they divided Poland between them. When Hitler turned on France the following spring Stalin stood aside, continuing to supply his ally with grain, metals, rubber and other vital commodities. Though it is clear from what we now know of Stalin's conversations with his Politburo that he expected to be forced into war with Germany sooner or later, the timing of the Nazi attack – code-named Barbarossa or 'Redbeard' after a crusading Holy Roman Emperor – came as a devastating shock. The new, poorly defended border through Poland was overrun almost immediately, and within weeks the panic-stricken Red Army found itself defending the major cities of Russia herself.

Chief victim of this unpreparedness was Leningrad. Immediately pre-war, the city had a population of just over three million. In the twelve weeks to mid-September 1941, when the German and Finnish armies cut it off from the rest of the Soviet Union, about half a million Leningraders were drafted or evacuated, leaving just over 2.5 million civilians, at least 400,000 of them children, trapped within the city. Hunger set in almost immediately, and in October police began to report the appearance of emaciated corpses on the streets. Deaths quadrupled in December, peaking in January and February at 100,000 per month. By the end of what was even by Russian standards a savage winter – on some days temperatures dropped to −30°C or below – cold and hunger had taken somewhere around half a million lives. [...]

The following two siege winters were less deadly, thanks to there being fewer mouths left to feed, and to food deliveries across Lake Lagoda, the inland sea to Leningrad's east whose south-eastern shores the Red Army continued to hold. In January 1943 fighting also cleared a fragile land corridor out of the city, through which the Soviets were able to build a railway line. Mortality nonetheless remained high, taking the total death toll to somewhere between 700,000 and 800,000 – one in every three or four of the immediate pre-siege population – by January 1944, when the Wehrmacht finally began its long retreat to Berlin.

Anna Reid, *Leningrad: Tragedy of a City Under Siege, 1941– 44* (2011)

❊  ❊  ❊

*An important historical document that captures the desperation and determination of a government facing the terrible situation of the Siege is this official proclamation by Leningrad Defence Chiefs and Soviet Party Leaders: it was posted all around the city.*

# TO ALL WORKERS OF THE CITY OF LENINGRAD

## A proclamation by Leningrad Defence Chiefs and Soviet and Party Leaders

Comrades of Leningrad, dear friends!

Our beloved native city is threatened with the direct assault of the German Fascist armies. The enemy is trying to force his way into Leningrad. He wants to destroy our homes, seize our factories and workshops, loot the people's property, flood the streets and squares with innocent blood. He would degrade the peaceful inhabitants and enslave the free people of our country. But that shall never be! Leningrad, the cradle of the proletarian revolution, the industrial and cultural centre of our country, has never been and will never be held by an enemy. We have not given our lives and labour to our beautiful city, and built its mighty factories with our own hands, for it to fall into the clutches of the German Fascist robbers.

That shall never be! This is not the first time that the people of Leningrad have been called upon to resist an invader, and this time, too, the cunning schemes of the enemy will fail. The Red Army is bravely defending the approaches to the city; the Navy and the Air Force are repelling and defeating the enemy's attacks. Nevertheless, he is not yet broken, his resources have not yet been exhausted, nor has he abandoned his piratical designs on our city.

So that we may not be taken unawares, we must realise the enemy's intentions and set against them our determination to defend Leningrad, our freedom, our children and our homes.

The people of Leningrad in their thousands are bravely fighting at the front. We appeal to them to be exemplary soldiers of the Red Army. We say to them: 'Be firm! Rally our fighting comrades by your example! Foster in them the spirit of fearlessness, courage and devotion to the fatherland!'

To help the Red Army in action let us form new detachments of the People's Militia, who will be ready to defend Leningrad with weapons in their hands. Let us draft into these detachments our best forces, the boldest and bravest of our comrades – workers, office staffs and intellectuals. The detachment of the People's Militia must immediately set about mastering the business of warfare, and quickly, learn to use a rifle, machine-gun and grenades, and prepare themselves to defend the city.

All the workers of Leningrad must do their utmost to support the detachments of the People's Militia.

Young men, join the ranks of the detachments of the People's Militia!

People of Leningrad, the Red Army looks to you for more and more equipment. It is the first task of all who are forging our victory at the lathes, in the factories and workshops to ensure that the soldiers at the front are amply provided with armaments and munitions.

Workers, engineers and technicians of Leningrad, strengthen the defence of your native country and of your native city with even greater self-sacrifice. Work on production unremittingly, with a thorough realization of the urgency of the moment. Increase the production of equipment and munitions for the front, comrades of Leningrad!

The malignant, dastardly enemy does not hesitate, in his fanatical hatred of our country and people, either to bomb peaceful cities or to shoot women and children. The Hitlerite bandits are preparing to use even more abominable means, such as poison gas. Let us make all the necessary preparations for the anti-aircraft and anti-gas defence of the city. Let us check up time after time whether everything possible has been done by each one of us, by each works and each institution, in the way of anti-aircraft and anti-gas defence. There must not be a single inhabitant of Leningrad who is unable to use the means of defence against aircraft and gas.

Comrades, the enemy is cruel and ruthless. There is no limit to his crimes. By organization, fortitude, valour and the merciless extermination of the Fascist murderers we can and must put a stop to the bloody slaughter of Soviet people by the Germans, and ward off the terrible danger that is threatening our city.

Let us rise like one in defence of our city, our homes, our families, our honour and freedom. Let us fulfil our sacred duty as Soviet patriots and let us be unswerving in the struggle against the ferocious enemy. Let us be vigilant and ruthless in dealing with cowards, panic-mongers and deserters. Let us establish the strictest revolutionary order in our city. Armed with iron discipline and Soviet organization, let us meet the enemy with courage and inflict on him a shattering defeat.

The Leningrad City Soviet of Workers' Deputies and the City Committee of the All-Union Communist Party (Bolsheviks) are firmly convinced that the Leningrad workers and all working people of the city of Leningrad will fulfil with honour their duty to the fatherland, will not allow the enemy to take them unawares, will devote all their energies to the task of defending Leningrad and, faithful to their glorious revolutionary traditions, will utterly smash the insolent and reckless enemy.

Let us be steadfast to the end, not sparing our lives. Let us grapple with the enemy, smash and annihilate him!

Death to the German Fascist bandits!

Victory will be ours!

*Commander-in-Chief:* Marshal K. Voroshilov
*Secretary of the Leningrad City Committee of the All-Union Communist Party (Bolsheviks):* A. Zhdanov
*President of the Executive Committee of the Leningrad City Soviet of Workers' Deputies:* P. Popkov

195

✳ ✳ ✳

*The citizens of Leningrad responded with unsurpass-*
*able heroism. They fought and died at the front, dug*
*trenches, tied themselves to their machines in factories*
*when they were too exhausted and hungry to stand,*
*and did everything humanly possible to maintain and*
*protect their way of life. Schools remained open, as did*
*theatres. Many risked – and sometimes gave – their*
*lives to protect their city's art and architecture. One of*
*the most remarkable feats of the Siege was the evacu-*
*ation of the contents of the Hermitage – recreated in*
*Debra Dean's novel,* The Madonnas of Leningrad,
*through the memories of an elderly woman, a former*
*Hermitage guide.*

In the Hermitage, they are packing up the picture gallery. It is past
midnight but still light enough to see without electricity. It is the
end of July 1941, and this far north the sun barely skims beneath
the horizon. *Belye nochi*, they are called, the white nights. She is
numb with exhaustion and her eyes itch from the sawdust and
cotton wadding. Her clothes are stale, and it has been days since
she has slept. There is too much to be done. Every eighteen or
twenty hours, she slips away to one of the army cots in the next
room and falls briefly into a dreamless state. One can't really call
it sleep. It is more like disappearing for a few moments at a time.
Like a switch being turned off. After an hour or so, the switch
mysteriously flips again, and like an automaton she rises from
her cot and returns to work. [...]

Sunday morning, Germany attacked without warning. No
one, not even Stalin it seems, saw this coming. No one except
Director Orbeli, the head of the museum. How else to explain
the detailed evacuation plan that appeared almost as soon as
news of the attack came over the radio? On this list, every
painting, every statue, nearly every object that the museum
possesses, was numbered and sorted according to size. Even
more astonishing, wooden crates and boxes were brought up

from the basement with corresponding numbers already sten-
cilled on their lids. Kilometres of packing paper, mountains of
cotton wool and sawdust, rollers for the paintings, all these
appeared as if preordained.

She and another of the museum's tour guides, Tamara, have
just finished removing the Gainsborough from its frame. It is not
one of her favourites. The subject is a pampered woman with
powdered hair rolled and piled ridiculously high, and topped
with a silly feathered hat. Still, as Marina is about to place
the canvas between oiled sheets of paper, she is struck by how
naked the figure looks out of its frame. The lady's right hand
holds her blue wrap up protectively over her breast. She stares
out past the viewer, her dark eyes transfixed. What Marina has
always taken to be a vacant-eyed gaze looks suddenly sad and
calm, as though this woman from a long-ago ruling class can
envision how her fortunes are about to change again.

Debra Dean, *The Madonnas of Leningrad* (2006)

✳ ✳ ✳

*And then the bombs begin to fall …*

In early September, the first Hitlerite shells descended – graceful
and even hesitant from their high loft. Then Junkers rose and
fell, rose and fell, leaving behind deposits of incendiaries like so
much fatal silt.

When they hit the Badayev warehouses, the cramped lines of
wooden buildings burned fast, and the fats stored within their
boards radiated red heat, turning the close sky to embers and
filling the air like summer cooking.

What did not burn were a few thousands tons of sugar, which
instead melted through the floor planks to survive, shaped
and imprinted by the cellars, as a hard candy. This candy was
broken into chips that would be prized and sold for money and
sex in the months that followed.

Elise Blackwell, *Hunger* (2004)

❊ ❊ ❊

*Dutch travel writer Geert Mak interviews someone who lived through it all.*

'I've lived in St Petersburg all my life,' says Anna Smirnova. 'I was twenty-one when it all started, on Sunday, 22 June, 1941. It was a beautiful day, and I remember how angry I was when I was awakened early that morning by the droning of whole swarms of planes. I wanted to sleep! After breakfast, we heard on the radio at noon that the war had begun. We weren't even surprised. We had talked about it a great deal, the Finnish war was already over, blackout drills had already been held. All the older people had been through a war before, and we all knew that we would experience one or more wars in the course of our lives. But this time my parents were terrified. My father said: "This is horrible. This is disgusting. This is death." He sensed it beforehand.

'There was a huge run on the shops that same afternoon. Whenever anything happens, of course, Russians expect a food shortage, so everyone started stockpiling matches, salt, sugar, flour, things like that. And six weeks later there really was nothing left in the shops. The war was approaching fast. In July the air-raid sirens went off all the time, we didn't have any bomb shelters, so we crawled under a couple of stone archways in the garden. We had to help dig anti-tank trenches outside the city, thousands of people were out there with shovels. Meanwhile, at the theatre school, classes went on as usual.

'On 8 September, the Germans reached the ring around our city, and the siege began. There were two million of us packed in there, closed off from everything else. You had to be in line at the bakery by 5 a.m., by 11.00 there was no bread left. It wasn't easy to walk around when you were starving, you had to drag yourself along by force of will. If possible, you kept all your clothes on in bed. You lay there like a big ball of rags, you

198

forgot you even had a body. But, well, we were young Soviets, we had absolutely no doubt that we would be victorious. On the radio they said the whole war might last a year or two, but that the siege of Leningrad would soon be over. They kept saying that. And we believed it, what else could we do? No one told the truth. There were no newspapers, no letters arrived, all we had was the radio.

'Excuse me if I become a little emotional, I don't talk about this very often.

'The total lack of heat and water was the worst. Everyone who had a job tried to stay at work as much as possible, sometimes there was still a little heating there. The Mariinsky theatre never closed, but the ballet dancers had to wear special costumes because it was so cold. There was no more transport. And that winter was so incredibly cold, it has only rarely been that cold.

'I think that's what killed my father.'

Geert Mak, *In Europe: Travels Through the Twentieth Century* (2004), translated by Sam Garrett

✳ ✳ ✳

*We join the Hermitage guide, Marina, firewatching on the roof of the museum on the night the Germans bombed Leningrad's food stores.*

What she remembers is the acrid smell of burning sugar. The way it singed the lining of her nose.

When Marina emerges from the stair well onto the roof, she can already hear the low rumble of the approaching Junkers. Schlisselburg fell on Monday, and so Leningrad is completely surrounded now, cut off from the outside world. Two nights ago, the Germans began dropping incendiary bombs, setting fires around the city. Wardens, armed with shovels and buckets of sand, have been posted in the various halls and around the perimeter of the roofs of the museums. Marina is a fire spotter, one of a pair posted to each observation platform on the roofs of the Hermitage.

She climbs the dozen steps up onto a small wooden platform. Olga Markhaeva, a curator of Netherlandish painting, is already up there. Her husband, Pavel Ivanovich, is in the same Volunteer division as Dmitry. Olga greets Marina and then hands her a pair of binoculars, which Marina hangs around her neck.

'Look,' Olga commands, pointing to the south.

Through the binoculars, Marina follows the droning sound and finds a slowly approaching shadow against the clouds. All summer there have been planes, tiny specks like mosquitoes circling and diving over the city. But this is different. She cannot make out individual planes, only a menacing phalanx of darkness.

It is not quite dark and, standing up here on this platform, Marina feels exposed to the sky like a mouse. There is no place on the vast expanse of the roof to hide. Cold with dread, she eyes the door leading back down to the hall below. Were it not for Olga Markhaeva's presence, she doubts she would be able to resist retreating back down into the safety of the museum.

The Hermitage can't possibly be a military target, but that is no comfort. There is no sense to any of this, nothing a sane person can understand. Though in the abstract, everyone knew that the Germans were close, when the first shells came screaming into the city a few days ago, it was like a fantasy, surreal and outrageous. Stunned, people looked at each other, disbelieving. This could not be. Not here, not in Leningrad. It is lunacy. They fire long-range missiles into the city, killing women and children and old people at random. For what? And why try to burn down a city? What good is victory if there is nothing left to claim?

Marina thinks of Dmitry and his love of rational argument. What would he do with this? Perhaps there is a logic to this that can be seen only from a cool distance: the two and a half million inhabitants of Leningrad a pin on a map from somewhere in Berlin. But here she is too close to see any pattern. Looking at the horrific swarm bearing down on them, it is easier to believe the explanation on the radio: that the enemy is uniquely evil. [...]

The drone of the Junkers is louder. They are clearly visible now, a dozen, two dozen, maybe more. They move methodically in formation. The ack-ack guns sputter wildly, and she hears the thudding of explosives to the south. Through the binoculars she picks out a burst of flame near the edge of the city, out by the Vitebsk railroad depot, then several more clustered together. Then the fires are sprouting in a straight line across the dark landscape of the city, springing up like a row of orange tulips. The thunder of engines envelopes her, and suddenly bombs are bursting in the Neva, fountains of spray blooming up the length of the river. The platform shudders in the wake of each explosion. A searchlight sweeping the sky catches one plane after another in its path, and Marina sees the swastika on a wing directly above her. [...]

There are a dozen fires within a kilometre's radius of the museum. She relays them one by one to Olga, trying to be accurate.

'On the far side of the Moika, near the Stroganov Palace, I think. No, wait ...' As she is watching, she spots a fire truck already rattling down Nevsky toward the fire. But it races right past the fire and turns south onto Vladimirsky. Other trucks are moving down the avenues, their bells ringing, passing fires that burn unchecked. They are all heading south. When Marina turns her binoculars in that direction, she finds an enormous column of smoke. The plume rises high into the sky above the city. At its base, it is tinged with red.

'My god.'

'What is it?' Olga is standing at her shoulder.

'I don't know. It's near the Vitebsk station.' She unstraps the binoculars and hands them to Olga.

Later, she will find out that what they are witnessing is the burning of the Badayev warehouses, where the food supplies for the entire city are stored. Or maybe they know this already; maybe Sergei has reported back to them the rumours already circling the city. Tomorrow, the worst of those rumours will be confirmed. Three thousand tons of flour, thousands of kilograms of meat, a molten river of sugar flowing into the basements of the charred warehouses. She cannot know this now, but lodged in Marina's mind, as real as anything else, is the chilling certainty that they are witnessing a catastrophe. [...]

Up and down the long series of roofs, wardens stand watching the distant conflagration and the smaller fires dotting the city. Their silhouettes blend into the rows of green copper statues that line the perimeter of the Winter Palace roof, warriors and gods that have vigilantly guarded the palace for nearly two centuries.

Debra Dean, *The Madonnas of Leningrad* (2006)

✳ ✳ ✳

*Duncan Fallowell has a conversation with survivors of the Siege.*

I:  Before the Revolution our family had a flat of eight rooms. Then workers were dumped on us to live in it and they hated educated people like us. The flat was in a large building on Ulitsa Nekrasova. All the flats were large and therefore many many people came to live on our staircase. But of the whole staircase, only four people survived the Siege.

D:  How long did it last?

A:  Nine hundred days. 1941 to 1944. It is impossible to calculate but you could say over a million lives were lost from bombardment, hunger and disease. Altogether our country lost twenty million in the war – excuse us if we are sometimes suspicious of foreigners. [He smiles].

I:     Whole families died. I was on the verge of dying at one point and had to lie on my bed because I couldn't walk. We waited for food in queues down to minus forty-two degrees centigrade sometimes, hoping a car might turn up with something, a piece of bread. That is why I now become very afraid when I feel cold. We had a small stove in our kitchen and everyone sat there to keep warm. A whole generation of my aunts died except one. She managed to survive – and was then arrested. That is a tragic story. I shall tell you later. There was no telephone, no transport, walking was difficult. So it was impossible to know who is alive, who is not. There is a cemetery where all the tourists are taken – Piskariovskoye – an awful place now with musicians and souvenir-sellers. We had to dig it with our hands to bury the masses of dead.

D:     My landlady was evacuated. Why were you not?

I:     Because Mother said we must stay – otherwise we shall never be allowed to return to our home, although … you know, in Russia we do not have this very strong addiction to *things*. Of course we like to have nice things and I love my gold ring but if I lose it I shall say, 'Oh well, that's life.' During the Siege my mother gave a boy a precious stone because the boy said he could bring us potatoes and we hadn't seen potatoes for two-and-a-half years. We did not see the boy again. But Mother was not angry because she said maybe the boy was killed or had a great problem.

D:     Yes, I understand that.

I:     There was a Jewish man called Ezrakh who built up a great art collection in this way during the Siege because when people are dying of hunger they will give a painting for a loaf of bread.

(The telephone rings. Before picking it up Alexander asks his wife in Russian 'Are you at home?'

'Niet,' and she serves up more tea.

'No, she's not at home.'

'Oh, is that X?' and she crosses to the phone for a cosy little chat with X.)

D:   What happened to that collection?

A:   Disappeared!

I:     No, no. Some is in the Russian Museum. Some at Pavlovsk, I think. If you are starving you cannot think of anything else – I could not sleep for it and the rats came under my blankets because it was so cold for them too.

A:   You see the bare spines of those leather-bound books? All eaten away by rats during the Siege. The city was gnawed away. Sometimes the rats ate children.

I:     You cannot imagine how *ugly* the Siege was, so very very ugly. People were swollen up and afterwards went very thin. People walked like this. [She demonstrates a stiff backward-leaning shuffle.] People were dirty – there was no clean water. I worked as a washer in a chemist shop and would put snow in a bucket and when it melted I could wash the medicine bottles – which was very hard work because I had no strength. Do you know what kept me going? My mother had a picture which she had bought in England of a woman, an Edwardian beauty with firm plump arms and a big hat and a pretty dog. I looked at it every day to remind myself of how things could be, that things could be better.

D:   I know all the cats and dogs were eaten. Was there cannibalism?

I:     … I don't know what to say about that.

A:   Yes, there was!

I:     The chemist where I worked was opposite the morgue and we saw … things taken away, bodies for food. A friend of mine had a daughter of three years old who looked very healthy. She disappeared one day, taken, probably eaten …

Duncan Fallowell, *One Hot Summer in St Petersburg* (1994)

✤ ✤ ✤

*Elise Blackwell's novel,* Hunger, *vividly recreates the dreadful realities of starvation and the 'innovations' in food production that became necessary.*

The bakeries produced a bread made of five parts' defective rye flour and one part each of salt cake, cellulose, soy flour, hack dust, and bran. By November, the official ration for this vile loaf fell to 250 grams per day for manual workers, half of that for clericals and children.

No tree in the city had bark below the reach of the tallest man. It had all been stripped off and boiled down for whatever nutrients it might contain and used as a salve for stomach pain.

All manner of animals – dogs and cats, sparrows and crows, rats and mice – and then their excrement were eaten. Soups were made from tulip bulbs stolen from the soil of the Botanical Gardens, pine needles, nettles, rotten cabbage, lichen-covered stones, cattle-horn buttons torn from once fine coats. Children were fed hair oil, petroleum jelly, glue. Root flour and floor sweepings were baked into scones. Dextrin appeared in fritters, cellulose in puddings. Pigskin machine belts and fish glue were spirited from closed factories and boiled into jellies.

People did anything to feed their children. They traded away the valuable and sentimental. They killed and cooked beloved pets. They peddled their flesh. They peddled the flesh of their children needing to be fed. They stole, connived, and killed. They starved their spouses. They starved themselves. [...]

A few blocks from my flat with Alena, in the direction of the institute, stood a posting board where people wanting to sell and buy could find one another. Before the siege, rectangles of paper, large and small, offered to sell all manner of things, from bicycles to purebred cats to cookware. As the siege took hold and day followed day, the papers were most often tattered scraps. And food became the board's only subject.

By late November, no one found odd the little card offering a grand piano as payment for half a loaf of bread, though few were in the position to trade away anything that could be eaten for anything that could not – no matter how rare, fine, or beautiful.

There were other cards as well, offering more than musical instruments, referring outright to bodies and souls.

I saw a woman, thin as everyone, spit in disgust upon reading such a notice. But its author plainly understood something the woman did not. The bravery to survive is a ruthless one. Martyrdom leads, by its very definition, only to the cold ground.

The only thing that struck me as truly strange about these postings was that they were not pulled down when the whole city ached for kindling. Neither was the poster of a woman holding a small, dead child that declared: DEATH TO THE KILLERS OF CHILDREN, though people risked the capital crime of picking up the flyers dropped by German planes, the flyers that outlined our surrender and prodded us to kill our leaders, give up, and eat again.

My own Alena brought home these flyers to start our small fires, telling me she would rather risk death and burn Hitlerite propaganda than set fire to even one page of her beloved books.

Of course the books would go too, one page at a time, from the title page of a less-favoured novel and the dessert section of a cookbook after sugar could not be had to the dearest segments of the most precious classics [...]

And everywhere the hunger stories seeped, sewagelike, from office to office, home to home. Stories were told of tremendous sacrifice and honour. The man who gave up his own parcel of bread and oil to save an old woman's ration card from thieves. The mother who ate nothing for three weeks so that her children might take a bit more nourishment.

I took these stories with, so to speak, a grain of salt. I could see with my own eyes that deprivation debases more often than it ennobles.

I was more inclined to believe the stories of murder and cannibalism, however farfetched they might have sounded one year earlier. I believed the story of the man who killed his own brother for his ration card and then cooked him for meat. The story of the woman who self-amputated her foot for food. The story of the mother who starved her dullest child so that she might survive with her bright favourite.

I believed, in short, the stories about people who did things worse than I did, the stories about people less human (or perhaps more human) than I was.

Elise Blackwell, *Hunger* (2004)

✳ ✳ ✳

*Anna Reid's historical account of how the city tried to survive provides further details of what the population was reduced to eating.*

Within the city, institutions involved in food processing and distribution were ordered to search their premises for forgotten or defective stocks that could substitute for conventional flours in the production of bread. At the mills, flour dust was scraped from walls and from under floorboards; breweries came up with 8,000 tons of malt, and the army with oats previously destined for its horses. (The horses were instead fed with birch twigs soaked in hot water and sprinkled with salt. Another feed, involving compressed peat shavings and bonemeal, they rejected.) Grain barges sunk by bombing off Osinovets were salvaged by naval divers, and the rescued grain, which had begun to sprout, dried and milled. (The resulting bread, Pavlov admitted, reeked of mould.) At the docks, large quantities of cotton-seed cake, usually burned in ships' furnaces, were discovered. Though poisonous in its raw state, its toxins were found to break down at high temperatures, and it too went into bread. Altogether these substitutions, together with successive ration reductions, reduced Leningrad's consumption of flour from over 2,000 tonnes a day at the beginning of September to 880 tonnes a day by 1 November.

As autumn turned to winter the substitutions became more exotic, and the resulting foodstuffs, distributed in place of the bread, meat, fats and sugar promised on the ration cards, less nutritious. Flax-seed cake found in the freight yards, ordinarily used as cattle food, was used to make grey 'macaroni'. Two thousand tonnes of sheep guts from the docks, together with calf skins from a tannery, were turned into 'meat jelly', its stink inadequately disguised by the addition of oil of cloves. From the end of November onwards bread contained, as well as ten per cent cotton-seed cake, another ten per cent hydrolysed cellulose, extracted from pine shavings according to a process devised by chemists at the Forestry Academy. Containing no calories, its purpose was solely to increase weight and bulk, making it possible notionally to fulfil the bread ration with a smaller quantity of genuine flour. The resulting loaves, which had to be baked in tins so as not to fall apart, were heavy and damp, with a clayey texture and bitter, grassy taste. To save on the two tonnes of vegetable oil used each day to grease the tins, an emulsion of water, sunflower oil and 'soapstock' – a by-product of the refinement of edible oils into fuel – was devised. It gave the loaves, Pavlov conceded, an odd orange colour, 'but the qualitative flaws were quite bearable, and the oil saved went to the canteens.' Another of the Forestry Academy's inventions was a 'yeast extract', made out of fermented birch sawdust, which was distributed to workplace kitchens in sheet form and served up, dissolved in hot water, as 'yeast soup'. [...]

As the official ration dwindled and private stocks ran out, Leningraders also sought out their own, increasingly desperate, substitute foods. The commonest of these were *zhmykh* and *duranda* – the husks of linseed, cotton, hemp or sunflower seeds, pressed into blocks and normally fed to cattle. Grated and fried in oil, they could be turned into 'pancakes', the elaborate preparation of which helped give the comforting impression of a real meal. Also near-universally eaten was joiner's glue, made from the bones and hooves of slaughtered animals. Likhachev found eight sheets of it at Pushkin House, which his wife soaked in several changes of water then boiled with bay leaves to make a foul-smelling jelly, which they forced down with the help of vinegar and mustard. They also cooked up the semolina used to clean their daughters' white sheepskin jackets: 'It was full of strands of wool and grey with dirt, but we were all glad of it.' An art teacher searched the flats of evacuated friends: 'I rummaged in all the cupboards and took rusks of any kind – green, mouldy, anything … Altogether I collected a small bagful. I was extremely pleased to have got quite a good amount. Later one of my students brought me oilcake – three blocks this size. That was something tremendous – three blocks of oilcake! He also ate linseed oil and fish glue, used for mixing paints and priming canvases.

Substitutes were often dangerous. Even if not poisonous in themselves, they could cause diarrhoea and vomiting, or damaged thinned stomach linings. Anything, though, was better than nothing. Glycerine contained calories, Leningraders discovered, as did tooth powder, cough medicine and cold cream. Factory workers ate industrial casein (an ingredient in paint), dextrine (used to bind sand in foundry moulds), tank grease and machine oil. At the Physiological Institute, Pavlov's slavering dogs were eaten; at another, scientists shared out their stocks of 'Liebig extract' – a dried meat broth made from the embryos of calves and used as a medium for growing bacteria. One father brought home the maggoty knee of a reindeer, an air-raid casualty at the zoo.

Eaten also were the vast majority of household pets. 'All day long,' a wife wrote to her husband at the front, 'we're busy trying to find something to eat. With Papa we've eaten two cats. They're so hard to find and catch that we're all looking out for a dog, but there are none to be seen.' One family, to save themselves embarrassment in front of neighbours, referred to cat meat by the French *chat*. Others swapped pets so as not to have to eat their own animal, or bartered them for other necessities. A teacher brought a handwritten advertisement, which she had found pasted up in the street, into her staff room. Reading 'I will trade 4.5 metres of flannel and a primus for a cat', it sparked a 'long argument – Is it moral to eat cats or not?' Such squeamishness soon faded.

Anna Reid, *Leningrad: Tragedy of a City Under Siege, 1941–44* (2011)

✻ ✻ ✻

*Despite all the efforts of the authorities – and individuals – the rate of death from starvation was horrendous. Suffering on such a vast scale can scarcely be contemplated or described. The story of one family, told simply by a child, Tanya Savicheva, can stand for many.*

On display in St Petersburg's Municipal Museum is the thin, light-blue diary of eleven-year-old Tanya Savicheva. The only entries for 1941–2 are these:

Zhenya died, 28 December, 12.00 a.m. Grandmother died, 25 January, 1942, 3 p.m.

Leka died, 17 March, 5 p.m. Uncle Vasya died, 13 April, 2 p.m. Uncle Aleksei, 10 May. Mama died, 13 May, 7.30 a.m. The Savicheva family is dead.

Following page: 'They are all dead.' Following page: 'I am here alone.'[1]

---

1 The child diarist, Tanya Savicheva, often writes in the third person, giving a chilling objectivity to the terrible events she witnessed. In the original Russian, the last line actually reads 'Only Tanya is left'. The diary is on display at the Museum of Leningrad History; a copy can be seen at the Piskariovskoye Memorial Cemetery. (In 1971, a minor planet discovered by a Soviet astronomer was named in honour of her.) (Ed.)

Tanya was evacuated and died in an orphanage in 1944.

Geert Mak, *In Europe: Travels Through the Twentieth Century* (2004)
translated by Sam Garrett

✻ ✻ ✻

*One of the most famous 'events' during the Siege was
the performance of Shostakovich's Seventh Symphony.
It's said that some of the audience dressed up for the
occasion, while the specially assembled band of musicians wore a motley collection of sweaters, waistcoats,
old shirts – simply whatever they had. The situation
was reflected in the concert hall itself which still had
velvet curtains and chandeliers, despite bomb damage
and boarded-up windows. Four pieces on the event,
starting with a brief memory.*

'When we were in the city we went to plays and concerts to
keep up our feeling of normalcy and self-respect. Shostakovich's Seventh Symphony had its première in Leningrad on 9
August, 1942, and it was dedicated to the suffering city. That
was a remarkable event, none of us will ever forget it. Listen to
that music again and imagine how we listened to it, with our
skinny bodies, in our tattered rags, we all stood there weeping.
At the close we heard our artillery pounding along with the
music. They had to keep the Nazis from shelling the concert
hall.'

(Mak quoting the words of Anna Smirnova.)

Geert Mak, *In Europe: Travels Through the Twentieth Century* (2004)
translated by Sam Garrett

✻ ✻ ✻

*Sarah Quigley's novel,* The Conductor, *is a fiction-
alised account of the events leading to the writing
of the Seventh Symphony and the preparation of its
performance under the baton of Karl Eliasberg. In*

*this extract we see the starving, motley band of musicians in the first rehearsals for what was to become an historic concert.*

Elias watched the makeshift orchestra tuning up. There was old Petrov, who had somehow recovered and survived the winter, though he was nothing but skin and bone. And Nikolai, lifting his bow as if it were made of concrete – but so many musicians gone! Their replacements, still unknown to Elias, handled their instruments with the jerky mechanical movements of wind-up toys. Within three months, with this roomful of skeletons, he had to produce an inspired rendition of the largest ever Shostakovich symphony! If he hadn't been so tired, he might have laughed at the absurdity of it.

Tuning up, warming up: the processes that had once seemed interminable were over in less than a minute. Then the room was quiet once more, while far away the restless mutter of gunfire continued, as familiar and constant as hunger.

Elias raised his arms. Pain flared in his back, and his shoulders trembled. 'Friends,' he said, although he knew fewer than a quarter of them. 'Friends, I know that you're weak, and you're starving. But we must force ourselves to work. Let's begin.'

He brought down his baton. The musicians stirred, seeming ready to play – but nothing happened. It was as if, moving as one body, they were paralysed from nerves, fear, or extreme fatigue. This was as bad as Elias's very first rehearsals, when he'd been so green and nervous the orchestra resisted his every move. There was no derisive laughter now, just an unnerving silence. Exhaustion seemed to be spreading through the room.

'Comrades!' He thought back to the way Shostakovich's hands had pounded at the piano keys, hammering out the opening to a work he wasn't yet certain about. 'Comrades! I command you to raise your instruments. It's your duty.'

The musicians sat upright; their eyes flickered towards him.

He raised his arms again. Over the sea of heads, he caught sight of Nikolai, gripping his violin with his bony left hand. His eyes were fixed on Elias with the intensity of someone about to go over the top into battle.

Elias looked away before sentiment could weaken him. 'Let's begin.' He brought down his arms.

He'd heard the first chords of the symphony so many times, playing them out in his imagination as he lay in bed, clutching his coat around him. The reality was completely different. A few straggling chords, the inadequate rattle of a snare drum, a tiny tapping of bows on strings. It was the smell of food without taste, or the promise of sustenance without delivery. He was grasping at thin air.

He rapped on his music stand, and the musicians straggled to a halt. Already the mouths of the woodwind and brass players were reddened, their scabby lips bleeding. Some of the faces raised to Elias had the white-green tinge of the dead. Then, as he watched, the lead flautist slid out of his chair and onto the floor.

'What shall we do with him?' The second flautist knelt beside the collapsed man, calling his name in a voice high with fear.

'Take him outside. Lay him in the corridor. Cover him with a coat.' Was the flautist alive or dead? He had no idea, no energy to find out.

It took three percussionists to drag the man out. The disruption seemed to go on forever: the rest of the orchestra simply sat where they were, many of them with their eyes closed. They were bundled in threadbare scarves and overcoats, and wore woollen gloves with the fingers cut off, but most were shivering. Elias stared fixedly at the page in front of him. The black notes looked like heavy chunks of granite.

It was time to start again. He took a deep breath. 'This isn't good enough. You're making a mockery of our great composer. The music must be barbaric, it must be brilliant. Remember, you're fighting off the enemy!'

213

But the musicians before him were neither barbaric nor brilliant: they were close to collapse, incapable of fighting off a horde of mosquitoes, let alone brutal invaders. The symphony crawled instead of marching. [...]

Day after day, the orchestra returned to the chilly, dusty room. 'From now on,' announced Elias, 'rehearsals will run for three hours, beginning at ten and finishing at one.'

'Three hours! That's impossible,' objected Katerina Ginka. Her cheeks were hollow, and all traces of ruddiness had drained from her face, but still she had the strength to argue. 'We can't play for even three minutes without fainting – or dying.'

Elias flushed. The flautist who'd collapsed had been taken to a military hospital and no one knew if he'd survived. *It wasn't my fault*, he protested silently. *The man was skin and bone, he had pleurisy, he'd been giving all his food rations to his wife.* Yet the sharp bark of guilt made him snap at Katerina. 'There's one word I won't tolerate. *Can't* is no longer a part of the Radio Orchestra vocabulary.'

He waited, expecting protests. Would any of the original members dispute the fact that a mismatched bunch of amateurs was now the Radio Orchestra? But no one said a word; even Katerina looked defeated. 'And if anyone is late,' he continued, 'whatever the reason, they'll lose their bread ration for the day.'

There was a muted gasp. Petrov's eyes watered, Katerina opened her mouth and then closed it again.

'Now, from the top,' ordered Elias. Even this brief exchange had left him exhausted; raising his baton felt like a monumental effort.

Sarah Quigley, *The Conductor* (2011)

✳ ✳ ✳

*Orlando Figes fills out the historical and cultural context.*

214

The symphony was resonant with themes of Petersburg: its lyrical beauty and classicism, evoked nostalgically in the moderato movement (originally entitled 'Memories'); its progressive spirit and modernity, signalled by the harsh Stravinskian wind chords of the opening adagio; and its own history of violence and war (for the *Boléro*-like march of the first movement is not just the sound of the approaching German armies, it comes from within.) [...]

For it to achieve its symbolic goal it was vital for that symphony to be performed in Leningrad – a city which both Hitler and Stalin loathed. The Leningrad Philharmonic had been evacuated and the Radio Orchestra was the only remaining ensemble in the city. The first winter of the siege had reduced it to a mere fifteen players, so extra musicians had to be brought out of retirement or borrowed from the army defending Leningrad. The quality of playing was not high, but that hardly mattered when the symphony was finally performed in the bombed-out Great Hall of the Philharmonia on 9 August 1942 – the very day when Hitler had once planned to celebrate the fall of Leningrad with a lavish banquet at the Astoria Hotel. As the people of the city congregated in the hall, or gathered around loudspeakers to listen to the concert in the street, a turning point was reached. Ordinary citizens were brought together by music; they felt united by a sense of their city's spiritual strength, by a conviction that their city would be saved. The writer Alexander Rozen, who was present at the première, describes it as a kind of national catharsis:

> Many people cried at the concert. Some people cried because that was the only way they could show their joy; others because they had lived through what the music was expressing with such force; others cried from grief for the people they had lost; or just because they were overcome with the emotion of being still alive.

Orlando Figes, *Natasha's Dance: A Cultural History of Russia* (2002)

✣  ✣  ✣

*In his memoirs, Shostakovich tells us more of what
the symphony was really about.*

I wrote my Seventh Symphony, the 'Leningrad', very quickly. I
couldn't help but write it. War was all around. I had to be with
the people, I wanted to create the image of our country at war,
capture it in music. From the first days of the war, I sat down at
the piano and started work. I worked intensely hard. I wanted
to write about our time, about my contemporaries who spared
neither strength nor life in the name of victory over the enemy.

I've heard so much nonsense about the Seventh and Eighth
Symphonies. It's amazing how long-lived these stupidities are.
I'm astounded sometimes by how lazy people are when it comes
to thinking. Everything that was written about those symphonies in the first few days is repeated without changes to this
very day, even though there has been time to do some thinking.
After all, the war ended a long time ago, almost thirty years.

Thirty years ago you could say they were military symphonies, but symphonies are rarely written to order, that is, if they
are worthy of the name symphony. [...]

The Seventh Symphony had been planned before the war
and consequently it simply cannot be seen as a reaction to
Hitler's attack. The 'invasion theme' has nothing to do with
attack. I was thinking of other enemies of humanity when I
composed the theme.

Naturally, fascism is repugnant to me, but not only German
fascism, any form of it is repugnant. Nowadays, people like to
recall the pre-war period as an idyllic time, saying that everything was fine until Hitler bothered us. Hitler is a criminal,
that's clear, but so is Stalin. I feel eternal pain for those who
were killed by Hitler, but I feel no less pain for those killed on
Stalin's orders. I suffer for everyone who was tortured, shot, or

starved to death. There were millions of them in our country before the war with Hitler began.

Dmitry Shostakovich, *Testimony* (1979)
translated by Antonina W. Bouis

* * *

*Finally, the end of the Siege is in sight.*

When the Leningrad front offensive was officially announced, all the lucky citizens of Leningrad could feel that the blockade would soon enough be broken, could feel like a pulse the trembling of the ground caused by the Soviet naval guns, continuous, nearly subliminal, and life preserving.

Every day the radio chanted and droned the names of the liberated communities: Krosnoye Selo, Ropsha, Peterhof, and Duderhof; then Uritsk, Ligovo, Strelna, and Novgorod. All places where people lived, I thought.

We heard reports of the sappers who, with their trained dogs, searched for mines in the liberated outlying areas of Leningrad, all now treeless, covered with only the lowliest vegetation.

Soap was being made again, and the piano factory would soon be running. Also, every day, both morning and afternoon, came the radio committee's advertising for trumpeters and piccolo players. The dead still had not been replaced. Forgotten perhaps in a necessary amnesia, but not replaced.

Pushkin and Pavlovsk were liberated on the twenty-fourth of January, and then, three days later, Leningrad, emancipated, rejoined the living world.

Elise Blackwell, *Hunger* (2004)

* * *

*As a child, art historian Mikhail German had been one of those evacuated from the city. He recalls the return at the end of the war.*

August 1945 saw the return from evacuation.

I recognized familiar places, was thrilled by the buses (only two bus routes were running), and by the trolleybuses that I had completely forgotten as they silently rushed through the city, and the trams with boarded up windows, just like the houses (that forgotten electrical smell of the trams, was it heated metal, ozone?), the few cars and even the carts – there was still a lot of horse-drawn transport – the movie posters ('can we go to the cinema tomorrow?'), the windows of the special shops where you could buy insanely expensive goods without ration cards, the kiosks filled with the joys of our pre-war childhood – happiness such as fizzy water and ice-cream; the 'metropolitan' way of life we had forgotten. It was strange, on a quiet peaceful day, to see the many notices: 'Citizens, during artillery fire, this side of the street is more hazardous' (many years later they painted replica markings on the walls, but they were a good metre higher, and not very realistic).

Then, in August 1945, the sun shone as it had done in the summer of '41, the Neva flowed as blue and huge as then, but the city itself seemed emptier, more subdued, and nothing like as noisy as it had been before the war. It was a weary, exhausted splendour. The impressive façades were mutilated with shrapnel and too quiet; many windows were boarded up. The houses seemed dead, as though covered in scars, like the stony faces of soldiers blinded in the war. The Winter Palace was grey and faded.

Mikhail German, 'City Chronotopes' in
*St Petersburg in Cinema* (2011)
(ed. Lubov Arkus) translated by Sergei Afonin and Alice Jondorf

✳ ✳ ✳

*Those who survived the Siege were, it was said, like*
*a race apart once the Siege was over. But if the city*
*thought its heroism would be rewarded, it was to be*

218

*sorely disappointed. Two extracts from novels that deal with what happened next, the first from* The Betrayal – *Helen Dunmore's sequel to* The Siege – *and the second from Andreï Makine's* The Life of an Unknown Man.

People said that Leningrad's heroism would be rewarded. No other city had held out for so long. Paris had fallen in forty days. Leningrad had held out for nine hundred, and had never fallen, no matter how many shells rained down on it. They had starved in thousands, and then in hundreds of thousands, but in the end it had been the Germans who retreated.

It seemed impossible now that they had really done the things they'd done. That they'd lived, let alone continued to work and fight.

But so soon after, the signs of hope began to disappear. Exhibitions that showed the life of the city under siege were dismantled, and the exhibits scattered. Plays were written but never put on. Memoirs were put away in drawers. *What has happened to you is not as important as you think. We intend to tell this story in a different way.*

The visionary reconstruction was a pipe dream. Money was needed elsewhere, and Leningrad must accept that there were other priorities. It was a provincial city and due for relegation. If Leningrad thought it deserved better, it was naïve. *We don't mind hearing about the battles and the shells, but the appalling details of starvation are not required. Besides, it raises unpleasant questions. Please keep your personal stories where they belong, inside your heads.*

Every hope had been smashed.

But maybe some time, in the not too distant future, things would start to get easier. 'No one can live for ever,' they whispered to each other. Even now, when they're alone, they go no further than that. *He* is an old man, even though his polished-up photographs make him look young as he presides over the great parades. Over seventy now.

'Georgians live for a long time,' said Andrei once.

'Only if they stay in Georgia,' Anna replied.

Helen Dunmore, The Betrayal (2010)

✻ ✻ ✻

On this September day Mila went into Leningrad to hand in a notebook at the Blockade Museum: it had been found on a sandy slope by the shore, notes in German. When she made her way into the courtyard of the building she thought at first it must be a fire, then an anarchic demolition site, then a brawl taking place amid a conflagration. It was all these things at once. A bonfire was blazing in front of the entrance to the warehouse which served as the exhibition hall. Military personnel (those 'army officers' from State Security) were actively thrusting back the employees of the museum who seemed to be trying to leap into the flames. There was little shouting and this absence of words made the scene all the more distressing. But these women were not trying to immolate themselves, their hands were reaching into the fire to extract objects in order to save them. And the agents of State Security were hurling humble items into the blaze, which they had just snatched from the exhibition hall: bundles of letters, clothes, photographs ... The struggle was fierce. Elderly women were battling against a wall of fists and rifle butts, falling, picking themselves up, rushing towards the fire.

It was not the bloodiest day in the history of the regime holding sway in that country. It was its day of greatest shame. And when, decades later, they opened the archives on the killings and repressions, they did not always dare to mention this deadly bonfire ...

Mila was not aware how she found herself in the middle of the battle [...]

Hysterical shouting suddenly broke out at the exhibition

220

hall's exit. A plump man of small stature appeared, surrounded by his entourage. Mila quickly recognised him from official portraits in the newspapers: Malenkov, a member of the Leader's praetorian guard. The uniforms stood to attention, breaking off the massacre.

'Aha! The factionalists in hiding!' he bellowed. 'They've spun themselves a web of rampant reaction here! They've fabricated a myth of a Leningrad fighting all alone, without the leadership of the Party! They've left out the vital role of the great Stalin, father of our victory! Everyone out! All this stale rubbish to the fire! Quick! Move!'

The uniforms went into action again and this time, assisted by Malenkov's henchmen, they seized the staff and hurled them into a van waiting in the street. Mila grasped a bundle of letters and escaped, taking advantage of a thick trail of smoke given off by the flames as they devoured fresh armfuls of documents.

She went home on foot. [...]

They came looking for her an hour later.

Andreï Makine, The Life of an Unknown Man (2009)<br>translated by Geoffrey Strachan

❊ ❊ ❊

*But, of course, there are memorials.*

More than half a million victims of the blockade are buried in the expansive Piskariovskoye Memorial Garden. More than half a million, mostly civilians. These bones that were people are gulped by mass graves – a hundred and eighty-six slightly raised mounds that conceal much.

The bronze figure of a woman, symbol of the mother country, leans towards them, hips rounded, grieving but herself ample.

Elise Blackwell, Hunger (2004)

❊ ❊ ❊

221

*In a recent interview, the great film-maker Alexander Sokurov reflects on the sacrifice of the citizens of Leningrad in defending their city.*

*Interviewer*: I think it's in *Russian Ark* you have something about people who remained in the Museum [the Hermitage] during the blockade....

*Sokurov*: Yes, yes. And there we are given a number – something like two million perished here. And the hero of the film, the Interlocutor says: 'No, no, no, it's too much. You can't pay such a price for a city. A city is not worth two million lives.' It's not worth it. Of course, no city is worth it. No, no city is worth such sacrifices. And maybe the Lord, when He summons me, will punish me for these words. No city is worth such sacrifices. But they happened. All the sacrifices happened and so, of course ... But it's difficult to contemplate this subject, and perhaps even sinful, too. But they happened, and one can only lament the fact.

Leningrad atmosphere is inseparable from these sacrifices, from this horrible price that the city paid for its existence. And you cannot forget about it ... And that is why all the beauty here has something like a reverse side. You cannot disregard it, it is always in the subconscious ...

Alexander Sokurov interviewed by Marina Samsonova and Catriona Kelly (2011) for the 'Cultural Memory and Local Identity in St Petersburg' project, translated by Maya Vinokour

# The Sleeping Beauty wakes

*And so to post-Soviet St Petersburg – still in many respects the country's 'window onto Europe' of Peter the Great's vision. When Gorbachev sought to introduce reforms – his twin policies of restructuring (perestroika) and openness (glasnost) in 1985, he began by visiting Leningrad – the city most likely to give a warm reception to his policies. This visit in many ways marked the resurrection of the city and of long-standing Petersburg values.*

Under Gorbachev the old Petersburg culture rose up in an explosion of pent-up feelings and pride to overcome the discredited Brezhnevite culture. The city's history and culture could now be researched and discussed openly, and a wealth of new publications about the city began to come out. *Mir iskusstva*[1] and the entire Silver Age[2] enjoyed a revival. The works of the Symbolists, Acmeists, and Futurists were again published, as were those of Zoshenko[3] and the Serapion Brothers[4], and of Kharms[5] and the *oberiuty*[6]. Silver Age and avant-garde paintings were brought up from the cellars of the Russian Museum and displayed, with Filonov[7] in particular proving a revelation. Akhmatova again became a public idol, and in 1989 a museum dedicated to her opened in her old apartment at Fontanka House. *Requiem* was published, as was *Poem without a Hero*[8]. Films of the Lenfilm director Alexei German, *Checkpoint on the Road* and *My Friend Ivan Lapshin*, which had not passed the censors and had been shelved for years, were now shown and received warmly. The eminent scholar and writer Dmitry Likhachev, who had lived through the 1917 revolutions and the blockade and was a fountain of knowledge about the city, became the city's elder statesman and unofficial ambassador.

---

1 Magazine and art movement (including Diaghilev's circle) influential in the development of the arts in Europe in the early twentieth century. (Ed.)

2 Period of rapid development of the arts in Russia in the first quarter of the twentieth century. (Ed.)

3 Mikhail Zoshenko (1895–1958) Member of the Serapion Brothers. Widely read in the 1920s but increasingly in trouble with the Soviet authorities. (Ed.)

4 Literary group taking its name from a story by Ernst T. Hoffman about an individualist devoted to free and radical art. (Ed.)

5 Daniil Kharms (1905–1942) Highly eccentric, 'absurdist' innovative writer. Arrested and imprisoned in a psychiatric ward where he died, probably of starvation, during the Siege of Leningrad. Widely known for his much-loved works for children. (Ed.)

6 An avant-garde collective (the Union of Real Art). (Ed.)

7 Pavel Filonov (1883–1941) Innovative, influential painter. Actively involved in the 1917 Revolution but later increasingly disapproved of by the authorities. Died of starvation during the Siege of Leningrad. (Ed.)

8 Isaiah Berlin, to whom Akhmatova read 'Poem Wihout a Hero' in 1945, described it as a 'kind of final memorial to her life as a poet and the past of the city – St Petersburg – which was part of her being.' (Ed.)

The art and writings of Petersburgers who had flourished in emigration now also appeared in the city. Nabokov was published. Balanchine's ballets appeared in the Kirov's repertoire in 1989, and Makarova and Nureyev returned to dance on the Kirov's stage. Stravinsky's music enjoyed a revival. But the greatest watershed and source of city pride was Brodsky's receipt of the Nobel Prize for Literature in 1987. It vindicated the city's many writers and intelligentsia who had not been allowed to work or publish in the postwar era, confirming to the world that their art was worthy of international recognition.

Arthur George with Elena George, *St Petersburg: A History* (2003)

✳ ✳ ✳

*But, for some, the freedom so long wished for has come at a price.*

The House of Friendship is a government international-liaison organisation, the legacy of Soviet days, and is housed in the nineteenth-century Shuvalov Palace. Mmm, very nice – the building has cherubs along the frieze and is on that part of the Fontanka where the canal (which they call a river) gently bends and passes under the equine statuary of the Anichkov Bridge, making blond perspectives to bewitch the soul: lines of pillared palaces crinkle in a heat-haze above bronze-coloured water ...

Within the Shuvalov, Mrs Podnak in a big red blouse takes charge of me. 'The first thing I want to tell you,' she says, jabbing a ball-point into a notepad, 'is that Nevsky Prospekt was not like this before. All these traders are not typical.'

'Shouldn't they sell things?'

'They feel they can stand there and sell anything! They should all be put in a *special place*. It's ugly.'

'I do love it.'

She goes blank for an instant behind her spectacles, then

lunges forward. 'But our city is not this – it is a museum city!'

'It's falling down.'

'Jolly well right there. And the problem also is the mafia.'

'Yes, freedom can be messy.'

'We have gone from total protection to total exposure. They throw us off a cliff and say fly!'

Duncan Fallowell, *One Hot Summer in St Petersburg* (1994)

✳ ✳ ✳

*For many years, Australian teacher and writer Gail Ford has been taking parties of students to Russia and has witnessed first hand the changes in the country since the end of Communism. She records them – along with many other experiences and insights – in her book* The Lure of Russia. *This extract recounts the time she visited the city soon after the fall of Communism.*

The city seemed to be in a great hurry to cast off its grey communist past and take on the richness and extravagance of the court – and nearly everyone seemed tsar-happy. It was shortly after our visit in September 1991 that the people decided, by popular vote, to restore their city's original Imperial name of St Petersburg.

The fervour to turn back the clock was no doubt a reaction to the hardships and denials of the communist years, mixed with a rose-tinted nostalgia for the elegance of the past. But, however bad the Soviet system had been, many people seemed to be conveniently forgetting that, even though life had been incredibly luxurious for the few at the top in Imperial Russia, it had been pretty tough for everyone else.

The tsarist mood hit us on our second night in Leningrad when we went to an extraordinarily moving choral concert held in the magnificent Smolny Cathedral, designed by Catherine the Great's architect, Rastrelli – a spectacular ensemble with twin blue wings, ornate pale blue and white ornamentation and an imposing dome. Its interior, which, like so many of the country's cathedrals were 'de-churchified' and converted into a concert hall, had been whitewashed – putting it in stark contrast with the ornate decoration of the active Russian cathedrals we had seen in Moscow.[...]

My biggest surprise, however, was when I was wandering around the cathedral during the interval and came upon a large display of chinaware and other memorabilia that had belonged to various royal and noble families. *Where had all this stuff been?* It had been just a month since the fall of communism and all this had appeared out of nowhere. Similarly, a few nights later, when I turned on the television, a huge church procession was being televised with dozens of priests decked out in full, highly ornate regalia. How did they come up with all of those mitres, capes and so forth so quickly – had they been lurking somewhere not too far underground all those years, just waiting to be brought into the open?

Also symptomatic of this tsar-fever was the outpouring of grief with the exhumation of the bones of the last royal family and the wish to sanctify all of its members. In 1918, with heavy fighting between the Red and White Russian armies across the country, it had been vital to the Bolshevik cause that there was no possibility of the restoration of any member of the royal family then, or in the future. So it could well be argued that for the revolution to succeed, it had been imperative that the whole royal family had to perish. The uncaring regimes of the last tsars had resulted in countless deaths, including many thousands of children. It seemed to me that Nicholas II and the tsarist regime were just as responsible for the fate of his family as the Bolsheviks who had carried out the executions. But now it seemed that the family members were all martyrs – even saints.

Not quite everyone, however, harboured such tsarist fantasies and there were still pockets of people who believed fervently in the communist ideals, even in Leningrad. One such group was a straggly number of communist supporters who did their best to uphold the faith, bravely waving their red hammer-and-sickle flags outside the Gostiny Dvor Metro Station on Nevsky Prospekt, a popular place for anyone with a cause to wave their banners and make speeches.

My most lasting image of total disenchantment with the new order, however, was a brief encounter on a bus with an elderly woman who was probably well into her eighties. When asked if she had any spare bus tickets we could buy, she replied vehemently, 'If I can't buy bread in the shops, I'm not going to buy tickets to ride on the bus.' This was her practical way of showing her disapproval of, and reaction to, the failure of the current government! She then looked quizzically at us and asked where we were from.

'Afstralia.'

The bus fell silent, all eyes on us, and though I tried to fade in with the crowd I felt as though I was being scrutinised like a rare zoo animal.

'Afstralia, Afstralia,' they whispered; one may as well have come from the moon. But then came the elderly woman's resounding response, said with such intensity that I will never forget her tone of voice, or the words, as they were translated for us:

'Why would anyone want to come HERE? In my youth it was a great country, but now it is NOTHING!'

She spat the last word out, seething with an emotion that was shattering. Presumably she was thinking of the Stalinist era, when her country had had great clout – and now it had been shown up for the failure of that very system that had brought its people such pride. I felt for this elderly citizen of the failed Soviet state. Not only was her country now regarded as a lame duck but, for the older people especially, life under the new capitalist system was getting worse and worse.

We wound and bumped our way through the streets of Leningrad and I looked out of the bus window at the wonders and majesty of that great city. Why would anyone come here … how could anyone resist coming to what was still one of the most beautiful cities in the world?

All of the elegant old buildings were still there, although in an even more dilapidated state than they had been two years earlier and, sadly, some of the less attractive aspects of capitalism were already evident. One wonderful thing about Leningrad in the communist days had been the total lack of billboards, flashing signs, and the other trappings of the competitive free-enterprise system, but the city landscape was already changing. This was most apparent along Nevsky Prospekt, surely one of the world's great avenues.

This great thoroughfare angles its way through the centre of Leningrad across a wide loop in the Neva River, going from the strikingly elegant golden spire of the Admiralty to Ploschad Vosstania. In the middle of this frenetically busy square stands a gigantic granite pillar, and when you look along Nevsky Prospekt you see this column in one direction, and the Admiralty Spire in the other, like soaring exclamation marks in either direction. However, one evening, when walking along Nevsky Prospekt with Tania, one of the host teachers, I was stunned to see that, towering behind and completely dominating the great column in Ploschad Vosstania, there was a huge new rotating billboard with flashing lights screaming, 'Marlboro, Marlboro, Marlboro' and then 'Pepsi, Pepsi, Pepsi' in lurid rotation. I stopped in my tracks.

'That is the ugliest thing I have seen since I arrived,' I said.

'What?' Tania asked puzzled.

'That huge advertisement!' I replied, pointing.

'But isn't that what capitalism is all about?'

Unfortunately she was right, but it seemed so wrong in that particular place.

'I just hope I don't find a big 'M' straddling St Basil's when I am next in Moscow,' I said sadly. Fortunately, there has been some discretion about where advertisements are placed, but the big neon monstrosity still dwarfs the column outside the Moskva Station.

The shops, too, were showing signs of a new commercial era, coming to life as though they had been hibernating for over seventy years. Imported goods were beginning to appear, and shopkeepers were beginning to make a little effort at tempting displays to attract customers. A few were actually introducing the supermarket style of shopping instead of the laborious old Russian system. There was also a slow change in attitude by some of the younger sales assistants – possibly due to the fact that a few were 'doing time' at international food chains where service is mandatory, and they now showed at least some effort to serve. The more enterprising people out on the streets flogging their wares had also become pushier. However, in reality, many of the shops were still fairly empty. One night, as we drove home with Tania and her husband Arnold, I commented on all of the brightly lit shops compared with our visit only two years earlier, to which Arnold replied ruefully,

'Yes, though there is nothing in the shops but light.' Then, after a long pause, he added, 'But light is enough,' perhaps sadly epitomising the fortitude and optimism of the Russian people.

Gail Ford, The Lure of Russia (2010)

✳ ✳ ✳

*Another view of the changes from Communist to post-Communist times from journalist and broadcaster Miranda Sawyer who visited St Petersburg with her mother in 2011.*

My mum has been to St Petersburg before: in 1981, when she was a teacher in Manchester, she took a group of schoolgirls. 'Everyone kept wanting to buy our jeans and coats,' she remembers. 'And we went to a circus. That had *vultures*!' Before that, in the summer of 1965, she and my dad *drove* to St Petersburg in a Mini. They went via Finland. I really can't believe they did this, but there are photographs.

The main difference between 1965 St Petersburg and the city of forty-six years later is, says, Mum, the cars. Back then, people formed crowds around the Mini, and ooh-ed and aah-ed over its transverse engine; during the Communist years, no foreign cars were imported into Russia. Now, Ford, GM and Toyota all have factories close to St Petersburg and the centre sometimes locks into a static traffic jam.

Also, she says, in 1965, 'there were no signs'. In order to do anything – visit sites, check into a hotel, change money, get petrol tokens – they had to get authorisation from the In-Tourist office. They had the address but couldn't find it and had to beg a sailor, who understood a little English, to take them to the door. When they got there, it was entirely anonymous. No plaque, no display, no indication from the outside of what was within.

Now, St Petersburg has plenty of signs. Not that we can read them, though some words are easy to guess: КОФЕ for coffee, РЕСТОРАН means restaurant, says my mum, and we go to a Ukrainian one, where the waiters wear billowing silk trousers and everyone smokes. I ask for a vodka and tonic and the waiter is puzzled. He brings me a glass of vodka, to be knocked back in one go, and a bottle of tonic for afters.

His trousers are fancy. Ours are not. Not one person asks us if they can buy them. This is because there are clothes shops everywhere and because our trousers are not desirable. Today's Russian woman is tall and gorgeous and dressed like a Selfridges Christmas tree. There is no part of her clothing that is plain: everything is stonewashed, or appliquéd, or has diamanté dangly bits, or is made out of actual leopard. Heels are killer. Make-up can be viewed at a hundred paces. Our trousers – and us – are just too dull.

I wonder where these Swarovski-studded glamazons go when they hit thirty-five. Because it appears they have been kidnapped and swapped for small, stout, grumpy lady trolls. After a while, I realise all Russian women contain within their DNA both ravishing supermodels and Rosa Klebb – like St Petersburg; like Russia itself. On the way from the airport, we passed mile upon mile of concrete housing blocks: relics of the Communist era and still the places most locals live. And yet, in the city centre, all is a Big Fat Gypsy Architect's wet dream.

Miranda Sawyer, 'Back in the USSR', *The Observer*,
20 November 2011

❊ ❊ ❊

*Cultural tourism is big business all over the world and St Petersburg is a prime destination for those who love art, architecture, literature and the performing arts. Some literary visitors may feel the spirit of Dostoyevsky still haunting the city ...*

I'm not sure why I'm here, but we've certainly done our proper literary duties: been to the Pushkin House, the Nevsky monastery-graveyard, the huge marble tomb of Dostoyevsky, laying a flower on the grave of the writer who best caught this city in its misery. We've then walked the streets in this neighbourhood, the area where he lived once and where he set the urban miseries of *Crime and Punishment*. A persistent sombreness of the kind he depicts still lies over everything in this city.

Malcolm Bradbury, *To the Hermitage* (2000)

❊ ❊ ❊

*A 'Dostoyevskian' sense of threat and brooding uncertainty can be found in parts of Edward Docx's novel,* Self Help.

232

Arkady and Henry emerged into the deepening twilight of the northern sky and set off along the potholed street that ran between the six other dilapidated tower blocks similar to their own. With the exception of three old women, their heavy hand-cart full of cheap fizzy drinks and expensive fake mineral water, weaving oddly on their invisible route through the worst of the ruts – everybody else was drunk: the half-dozen old men sitting opposite on the weedy verge around their upturned crate on oddly legless chairs – seating ripped from abandoned cars; the heavily made-up girl now leaving Block Two with her infant child in an improvised sling, her three-year-old and her five-year-old – all in sullen attendance and ready for the ride into town and another night working together with the tourist-bar spill; the gang of boys, nine- or ten-year-olds, standing around some old metal drum that they had somehow managed to ignite on the corner and every now and then reaching in with tar-caked hands to chuck fume-spewing fire bombs at each other or any passer-by they did not recognise, then swapping their vodka-spiked drink tins from hand to hand so they could blow cool air on their blackened fingers.

The two turned right, away from the few feeble street lamps that would have taken them in the direction of Primorskaya metro station. Instead, they walked towards the Smolensky ceme-tery – a woodland, half wild, half kempt, with winding paths, dense thickets and sudden glades that sat square in the centre of Vasilievsky Island – a short cut on their way into town. [...]

He went on – through the most dead Vasilievsky streets, stray cats all that he saw, until he reached the river. Then he slowed his jog to a brisk walk and crossed the Neva on the Leytenanta Bridge[1]. The river black tonight as liquid obsidian.

Entering the central districts, he stiffened a little, continuing at a more casual pace, ready to appear drunk should a car slow

---

1  The Leytananta Shmidta Bridge (now Blagoveshchensky). (Ed.)

or show undue interest. Soon enough he was sloping along the banks of the Kruykova Canal by the filthy pitch water of New Holland[1] – a derelict place, unvisited by all save small-time criminals, addicts and the gangs of homeless insane. Though he kept his head down and his gaze to the pavement in front of him, he was listening – meticulous ear primed for the slowing note of an engine or the fall of another step. He knew well that it was in these dead hours (when Petersburg slipped off its creamy European robes and revealed itself a mean and swarthy peasant once more) that the real business of Russian life got done. Boy and man, he had seen it: the black Mercedes rolling down the half-lit street, the tinny police car idling, smear-faced street girls slipping like sylphs along the railings of the canals, and the drugged and drunk always watching from their darkened doorways, glass-eyed and desperate, crawling back and forth between heaven and hell, one scabby knee at a time. And all of it dangerous. He glanced up.

A figure had appeared on the pavement ahead.

Edward Docx, Self Help (2007)

✳ ✳ ✳

*Particularly since the tercentenary celebrations in 2003, the city has seen an explosion of all kinds of arts activity. Although visitors still go there to see the amazing art, artefacts and architecture of the past, the contemporary art scene is very much alive and kicking. Journalist and St Petersburg resident Tim Stanley tells us what's going on now.*

For a brief period in the early twentieth century, Moscow and St Petersburg/Petrograd/Leningrad stood alongside Paris and Berlin as some of the most important incubators of a revolutionary new artistic movement, the avant-garde. There seemed

---

1   Used by the Ministry of Defence until 2004, New Holland Island is now being transformed into an arts and entertainment area. (Ed.)

to be something in the combination of political stagnation, evolving social unrest and pockets of huge economic wealth which sparked a creative flame that found expression across a range of artistic forms – fine arts, design, architecture, drama, ballet, film, poetry. The avant garde movement soon splintered but elements managed to survive the revolution and civil war which followed, only to morph into a new aesthetic, socialist realism, created to meet the objectives of the new society of which it was now a part. Soviet art was directed by party functionaries from Moscow. With few exceptions, the country's public artistic endeavours gradually calcified; anything innovative and not officially approved was driven underground or abroad.

Most people would agree that since the end of Soviet rule it is Moscow that has dominated Russia's cultural landscape, although today the reasons for this are economic rather than political. In contemporary art terms the sheer number and scale of its galleries is unrivalled, and landmark projects such as Strelka, Garazh and Winzavod look set to extend this dominance still further.

But something is happening in St Petersburg, the country's second largest city and 'northern capital' which may be about to challenge Moscow's pre-eminence. The last few years have seen a whole slew of new contemporary art museums and galleries open up in venues across the city, perhaps seeking to capitalize on its proximity to Europe, its cultural and historical appeal, and the huge numbers of domestic and international visitors who arrive each year. Since the turn of the twenty-first century, about a dozen or so new institutions have been founded, many by local businessmen keen to diversify their interests, create a legacy and to give something back to their home city. September 2010 was surely the high-point of this trend, when not one but two contemporary art museums – Erarta and Novy (New) Museum – both opened on Vasilievsky ostrov[1] that month.

---

1   Island (Ed.)

What is behind this sudden northern renaissance? It is tempting to suggest that the same factors which made the city a centre for early twentieth-century avant garde (political stagnation, social unrest and pockets of extraordinary wealth) may be at play a century later.

'There was a sudden energy, but of course these institutions do not just appear overnight. They are often the result of a natural process which gathers pace over many years. For a long time there was a lot of talk in the city about the need for a contemporary art space. When public sector initiatives failed to materialize, the private sector stepped in,' according to Mikhail Ovchinnikov, director of Erarta Museum of Contemporary Art on Vasilievsky ostrov.

Erarta's mission is to collect, exhibit and popularize original contemporary art from St Petersburg and, increasingly, from regions across the country. One of the reasons the city attracts some five million visitors a year is the fact that its historical centre remained largely unspoiled by the ravages of the twentieth century, with all its revolutions, civil war, Nazi bombardment, even Soviet town-planners. The city's inhabitants consequently see themselves as proud and stubborn defenders of a unique aesthetic legacy. 'The city has its own artistic schools and traditions which developed over the twentieth century, independent of what was coming out of Moscow. It's a harmonious town, but also quite focused on itself and its own history,' Ovchinnikov believes.

And this combination of regional pride and self-consciousness can be seen in many of the works exhibited in the museum's permanent collection, regardless of whether the form of the painting is abstract, realist, or naïve. While the theme of the city is a constant in the collection, Erarta has also spotted an opportunity to broaden the collection to works by artists from the regions, and includes, for example, an extensive holding of works by the prolific Soviet artist Petr Gorban, from Stavropol.

'We're trying to extend the collection to include what artists across Russia are doing. Last time we looked, the museum collection included works of artists from more than twenty towns across Russia,' says Ovchinnikov. 'Similarly, we've been working on bringing exhibitions from cities across the country – Samara, Perm, Novosibirsk, Krasnodar – to exhibit here in the museum. Next step will be exhibiting our collection in these cities.'

The permanent collection may be characterized by regional pride, but there is also a lot of colour and humour too. Nikolai Kopeikin's elephants series replaces the figure of Peter the Great on horseback with a pachyderm in a take on Falconet's iconic Bronze Horseman statue, and Nikolai Sazhin's 'Catherine II and her Favourites' presents a stylized version of the great monarch famed for her prodigious amorous appetite, alongside a list of her lovers and the amount of money she spent on them, in what may be a sly allusion to the excesses and whims of political authorities.

The museum has also created installations it calls U-Spaces, providing sensory and emotional experiences popular with children and adults alike, and has a regular programme of cultural and educational activities. 'Part of the democratic concept of the museum is to help our visitors to find the artist within themselves. On our first anniversary we removed every single exhibit from the museum walls and replaced them with canvas on which visitors could create their own art. We had children, artists, businessmen, housewives, students, pensioners – in all over seven hundred works were created.'

Many believe art has a responsibility to provoke and challenge social as well as artistic conventions. As if any reminder of this was needed, the day I met with Ovchinnikov he had just returned from Krasnodar in the south of Russia where he had been attending the opening of a controversial exhibit put together by Marat Gelman, a leading figure in the Russian

237

contemporary art scene. The Icon Expo includes works by a number of contemporary artists, self-confessed Christians and atheists alike, designed to show examples of how iconography can remain relevant even in non-traditional forms. In spite of receiving the tacit approval of the Russian Orthodox Church, the exhibit opening was marked with bad-tempered protests from local priests and Cossacks who were offended by the exhibition, including personal verbal attacks on Gelman and even a bogus bomb threat which shut down the exhibition for a few hours.

At the same time, members of female punk rock band Pussy Riot were recently jailed for staging an anti-Putin protest in Moscow's Cathedral of Christ the Saviour, unofficial seat of the Orthodox Patriarch and something akin to St Peter's Rome for Russian Orthodox Christians. I asked Ovchinnikov his opinion about the relevance of contemporary art to post-Soviet Russia. 'One way to interpret the [Pussy Riot] action was not as an artistic or political gesture, but as an act of desperation. I agree with Anatoly Osmolovsky [a leading Russian artist and art theorist] on this point. Of course a church is not an appropriate place for activism, but maybe there are no other suitable places – if it had happened anywhere else, it would have seemed less extreme.'

St Petersburg is also home to Banksy-supported art collective Voina (meaning 'War'), which has staged a number of sexually and politically provocative actions over the last few years designed to outrage. These included a kind of mass 'fuck-in' in a Moscow museum, and the drawing of an enormous phallus on a drawbridge in front of the St Petersburg headquarters of the FSB, one of the KGB successor agencies. 'The role of museums and museum curators is to turn artistic activities like these into statements which can be comprehended by a wide audience. We want our museum to be a part of a normal civil society to be built in Russia. I think all cultural institutions in

Russia have a very important historical mission to help create that society.' [...]

The State Hermitage Museum, grande dame of the city's artistic institutions and one of the world's greatest museums, is working on a project it calls Hermitage 20/21 in which galleries of modern and contemporary art will be located in the recently acquired halls of the General Staff Building, opposite the Winter Palace on Palace Square. This represents something of a strategic shift for the Hermitage – although their extensive collection includes a large number of works by modernist greats including Picasso, Matisse, Malevich and Kandinsky, these artists have never been a priority for the museum. The collection will include sculpture and graphic arts, as well as video and new media.

Some in the city might feel threatened by such a strategic shift on the part of its anchor artistic institution, but not Ovchinnikov. 'This development by the Hermitage will be mutually enriching. The task of new generations of museums, funds, and curators is to integrate our authentic Russian art into a wider contemporary context.' He pauses, then repeats: 'We are on a historical mission.'

Tim Stanley, 'Contemporary Art in Petersburg:
A Historical Mission' (2012)

❊ ❊ ❊

*But let's enjoy St Petersburg in carnival mood, celebrating itself and its history, with this description – from a novel by Andreï Makine – of some of what was to be seen during the tercentenary, for which so much work on the once neglected city was accomplished.*

The energy of this new life is pleasantly contagious, a euphoriant drug that Shutov encounters again in the street in ever stronger doses. He feels rejuvenated, almost mischievous, leaps up to catch the balloon a child has let go of, favours its mother with a wink. Buys himself an ice cream, gives directions to two young female tourists who are lost. And having reached Nevsky Prospekt, attests to the miracle: he feels completely at one with the carnival crowd making its way towards the Winter Palace, and it is a physical belonging, a bodily adherence. [...]

The music from several bands creates such a din that people communicate by facial expression and gesture. Besides, the only message to be shared is one of permanent amazement. A giant inflatable cow with eight legs floats above the crowd, its enormous udder sprinkles the onlookers, who yell, dodging the jets, opening their umbrellas. A little further on the human tide is cut in half by a procession of Peter the Great looka-likes! Military frock coat, three-cornered hat, moustache like an angry cat's whiskers, cane. Most of them are of a stature at least faintly evocative of the tsar's six foot six, but there are also some little ones and even a woman dressed as the tsar. At one crossroads this regiment gets mixed up with a squad of near-naked 'Brazilian dancers', adorned with feathers. The tsars' uniforms brush against long, bronzed thighs, graze the hemispheres of plump buttocks. And quickly these give way to courtiers in periwigs, the avenue is awash with crinolines, sunlight dancing off the high, powdered coiffures. The whipped cream of their attire is succeeded by a new inflatable monster. A dinosaur? No, a ship. Shutov reads the name on its stern: *Aurora*. 'That was the cruiser in the October Revolution,' a mother explains to her son of about twelve years ... If that historic gunshot, which children in the old days would have come across at primary school, now has to be explained, this really is a new era ... The forgetfulness is refreshing: yes, spare them your wars and revolutions!

The loudspeakers cutting through the musical hullabaloo seem to be in agreement with Shutov: 'Welcome to the launch of the Great May Revolution. Everyone to Palace Square. The Mayor of St Petersburg is going to have his head cut off.'

240

Laughter erupts, masks scowl, another Peter the Great, this time on horseback, towers above the crowd.

And down below, almost on the ground, a shrill voice rings out: 'Let me through, I'm late! Make way!' A dwarf, an elderly man, dressed as a king's fool, or rather a tsar's fool. This waddling figure scurries along, pushing the crowd aside with his short arms. One of the 'Brazilian dancers' is with him, clearing a passage for him, shaking her feathers and her bracelets. Clearly they are expected at Palace Square and their disarray is both comic and touching. [...]

Once at Palace Square, Shutov begins to grasp what lies at the heart of the changes. A geyser of energy, held in check for a long time. The frenzied search for a new logic to life after the highly logical madness of dictatorship. He sees the mayor mounting the scaffold, yes, the Mayor of St Petersburg in person! (Would this be possible in Paris or New York?) The firecrackers explode, the crowd hoots noisily, the mayor smiles, almost flattered. An executioner brandishes ... an enormous pair of scissors, points them at the condemned man's neck, seizes his tie and cuts it off! A wave of delirium ripples across the square at the sight of the trophy displayed. A loudspeaker chokes with delight: 'A Gucci tie!' Shutov surprises himself by cheering with the others, slapping strangers' hands, physically bonded with these thousands of living beings. The little clown seen just now climbs breathlessly onto the throne and a magistrate in ceremonial robes declares him to be the governor of the city.

'A collective exorcism,' he thinks as he goes to his rendezvous with Yana. Three days of this burlesque May Revolution to undo decades of terror, to wash away the blood of real revolutions. To deafen themselves with the noise of firecrackers so as to forget the sound of bombs. To unleash these merry executioners into the streets so as to blot out the shadowy figures that came knocking at doors in the night not so long ago, dragging men out, still half asleep, throwing them into black cars.

Behind the Winter Palace a placard announces a 'family portrait'. Seated on folding chairs, a Peter the Great, a Lenin, a Stalin and, beyond an untoward gap, a Gorbachev, complete with birthmark painted on the middle of his bald head. Stalin, a pipe in mouth, talks on his mobile phone. A Nicholas II and a Brezhnev (the missing links) rejoin the group, laden with packs of beer. Laughter, camera flashes. The barker, a young woman in a miniskirt, moves among the crowd: 'Now then, ladies and gentlemen, spare a coin for the losers of History. We accept dollars too ...'

'They've managed to turn the page at last,' Shutov says to himself. And the thought of being left behind, like a dried flower, between the preceding pages, gives him the desire to hurry, to catch up. [...]

The Hermitage is open all night, it was announced on television. He goes there, is glad to mingle with the throng crowding in at the entrance, laughs at the quip repeated by several voices: 'So here we go, storming the Winter Palace again!' The memory of the carnival comes back to him, the tribal warmth, the hope of renewing links with that world on which he is twenty years in arrears. He will catch someone's eye in front of a painting, strike up a conversation ...

From his first steps inside he freezes, dumbfounded. The atmosphere is reminiscent of a railway station. People sitting on the floor, leaning against the wall, some of them asleep. Others, perched on the window ledges, are scanning the sky: a son et lumière spectacle above the Neva has been promised. Two adolescents stretched out behind a gigantic malachite vase are idly kissing. A tourist in shorts speaks very loudly in German to a female companion, clad in the same brand of shorts (but three times as wide) who nods as she bites into a thick sandwich. A group of Asians passes by, filming every picture in the room with highly disciplined synchronization. A husband explains to his wife: 'The Metro opens again at five. We might as well spend the night here.' Ladies in crinolines and moustached hussars materialize, like ghosts, in imitation of the ones who used to frequent the palace. But the crowd is too tired to pay them any attention.

Shutov walks on, observes, and his thoughts about Russia returning to the brilliant high road of her destiny seem to have been too hasty. For there is also a confusion of styles, the disappearance of a way of life and barely the first babblings of a new manner of being ... [...]

All that remains of the jubilant enthusiasm for the carnival is this indifferent clustering of the crowd as it moves from place to place in search of the last stray sparks of the festival. On Palace Square Shutov listens to the performance of a former dissident singer. A familiar repertoire: camps, prisons, blood. The human mass laughs, yawns, moves off and spills into Nevsky Prospekt.

Andreï Makine, *The Life of an Unknown Man* (2009)
translated by Geoffrey Strachan

❊　❊　❊

*A final look at the city in the company of journalist
Viv Groskop, returning in 2012 to the city where
she had been a language student twenty years before
and weighing up what has changed ... and what has
stayed the same.*

I first visited St Petersburg as a language student in the summer of 1992 and lived there for the best part of the next two years. It was a strange and wonderful time. I turned twenty-one when I was there, celebrating my birthday with a party on a canal boat with vodka and caviar. I lived in a communal flat, learnt to speak Russian fluently and went through several ill-advised boyfriends who were quite drunk a lot of the time.

So far, so student life. But in St Petersburg you also can't fail to soak up culture on every corner. This is the city of

Dostoyevsky, Tchaikovsky and Shostakovich. It is home to one of the greatest dance companies in the world, the Mariinsky Ballet (the Bolshoi's great rival). This is where Russia's greatest poet Pushkin wrote most of his major works – and was killed in a duel with his wife's lover. Twenty years ago I spent three hours travelling by tram in the snow to the exact spot where he died, only to discover that it was a patch of grass in the middle of a housing estate.

St Petersburg is seductive, charming, and a little eccentric. It was founded by Peter the Great in 1703 as an act of will – most of the city is built on swampland, with mosquitoes still a problem – and almost all of its original Baroque architecture remains intact. But the city is undergoing rapid renovation – and on the twentieth anniversary of my first visit, I've come back to see just how things have changed.

The first shock is when I find out where I'm staying: W Hotel, a design-led luxury venture, which would have been unimaginable in the 1990s. Its address? Vosnesensky Prospekt, number six. I used to live at number four. At first it's confusing. How could they turn that building into a hotel? It was all flats. But, of course, they've bought up the whole block. When I look out of my seventh-floor hotel room I can see my old courtyard – and my old window on the fourth floor opposite. When I lived there, there was a piece of cardboard across part of the window. It's gone. All the apartments look like they've been converted into luxury accommodation.

Later, I try to get into the courtyard, which used to be public, but it's all locked up. I wonder what happened to my flatmate, Sasha, who wanted to be a DJ but spent all day sitting in the kitchen smoking, his underpants hanging on a makeshift washing line above the stove.

As for the city itself, my first impression is that everything and nothing has changed. In the early 1990s, I had originally chosen St Petersburg, which was still often referred to as Leningrad, and not Moscow or Voronezh – the other cities British students were encouraged to visit – because it seemed most like Paris. Which it was – and still is. Paris with cobwebs, a nineteenth-century city preserved in an attic. The place it now also reminds me of is Havana. It's like a living museum. Some of it is still dusty and messy. If you step away from the main drag, you'll find half-ruined mansions and palaces crumbling under the weight of accumulated dirt. But it's pulling itself together – without destroying its old façades – and the city has an upbeat, forward-looking feel.

This was not the case twenty years ago. In those days the Soviet era was still very much alive, all bureaucracy and poverty. Life was not easy for Russians then. It's not necessarily easy now, but at least it is predictable. When I arrived this time, I spent an hour looking for somewhere to change money. No banks were open because it was Sunday and all the old 'exchange money' places I knew were long gone. I eventually gave up and went to the Grand Hotel Europe where a sweet young girl showed me how to operate the new hole-in-the-wall machines, which convert dollars into roubles. I was shocked. Two decades ago you could change money in virtually any shop and you never changed more than you needed for twenty-four hours because the exchange rate was so variable. When I tell the young girl this, she laughs. 'Wow. Instability. Horrible.' She shudders. She was not born then.

The times I remember are ancient history to someone like her. Years ago, when I first took a rickety Intourist bus from the airport down Moskovsky Prospekt, the road leading into the centre, the Soviet Union had virtually collapsed and Yeltsin's star was in the ascendant. I remember looking out of the window, bug-eyed with amazement that people were wearing 1970s clothes, including flares and corduroy jackets. They looked utterly grey and miserable. There were food shortages everywhere. I lived with host families at first, and a typical breakfast would be one boiled egg or one tomato. People constantly borrowed money from each other to get by and used blat (influence or contacts) to find out which shops had had a delivery of food. Once you got to know them, people were not unhappy, just poor. They were about thirty years behind the rest of the world culturally and always had a lot of questions about the Beatles.

Now St Petersburg is (almost) like any other European city. You can get a latte on every corner, there's free WiFi every-where and you're as likely to face a queue for food as you are to see a performing bear sitting in the passenger seat of a Lada (as I once did on my way to class). It was, is and always will be one of the most romantic cities on earth. For my money it wins that competition hands down. Its architecture is stunning, the palaces' faded pastel façades gleaming in the afternoon sunlight. This time of year it is at its most magical. Between the end of May and the start of August is 'the season of the midnight sun', when the sun never quite sets and there is daylight twenty-four hours a day. It's called the White Nights or Belye Nochi.

People tend to stay out partying all night, carrying bouquets of flowers and bottles of fizzy wine. The White Nights are a perfect time to explore by boat the city known as 'the Venice of the North'. You can rent water taxis all night – often they're the only way to get around, as the bridges over the River Neva legendarily stay up through the night, stopping overland traffic from passing between the islands that make up the city. It's one of the most pedestrian-friendly cities you will ever visit, too. The metro system is efficient, but St Petersburg is best explored by foot, and I spend most of the four days I'm there just walking around and reminiscing.

Virtually nowhere I know has survived. The old fish shop – which only ever sold herring – has become a lavish branch of Zara. The two bakeries I used to visit are still going but, instead of selling one kind of black bread, they now specialise in baguettes and French pastries. There's a Subway around the corner from my old flat and a McDonald's down the road. Part of me is sad that everything has become the same everywhere. But everyday life is now effortless rather than a slog and that can only be a good thing. [...]

One of the biggest pluses of the past two decades is that St Petersburg has become easier for tourists. There are more signs in English than ever, and far more English speakers. It's easy to find your way around on your own. In the early 1990s it was hard to visit without being part of a tour group. It was a pain getting into museums, galleries and theatres without pre-booked Intourist tickets. Now it's just like visiting any other European city. All the places I want to go to – The Russian Museum (for Russian Painters) and the Hermitage (for one of the best art collections in the world) – have efficient, informative websites (all in English), with opening hours and ticket prices listed.

Unfortunately for me, I can't quite shake off my post-Soviet mentality. I find myself walking down Nevsky Prospekt – St Petersburg's Oxford Street – in my usual brisk, suspicious manner, as if I'm being followed. Not because I was used to having a KGB tail but because, when I was younger, I would regularly be hassled and followed by youths and dodgy types who wanted to say hello or change money. What everyone wanted most was dollars. Those days are gone. The only way you'll get noticed for being a foreigner now is if you're woefully underdressed for the weather. One babushka in a fur coat and headscarf stops abruptly and makes the sign of the cross over her bosom while glaring disapprovingly at my hatless head. I smile. It's still Russia.

Viv Groskop, 'Back to St Petersburg'
British Airways 'High Life' magazine, June 2012

# The House of Romanov

The Romanov dynasty ruled Russia from 1613 until the Revolution of 1917. Below we give the order of succession, along with the dates during which the emperors and empresses ruled, and their relationship to each other.

**Michael 1613–1645**

**Alexis 1645–1676** (son of Michael)

**Theodore (Feodor) III 1676–1682** (son of Alexis by his first wife)

**Peter I (the Great) 1682–1725** (son of Alexis by his second wife)

**Catherine I 1725–1727** (second wife of Peter the Great)

**Peter II 1727–1730** (grandson of Peter the Great)

**Anna 1730–1740** (niece of Peter the Great)

**Elizabeth 1741–1761** (second oldest surviving daughter of Peter the Great and Catherine)

**Peter III 1761–1762** (son of Princess Anna, daughter of Peter I)

**Catherine II (the Great) 1762–1796** (wife of Peter III)

**Paul I 1796–1801** (son of Catherine the Great)

**Alexander I 1801–1825** (son of Paul I)

**Nicholas I 1825–1855** (younger brother of Alexander I)

**Alexander II 1855–1881** (eldest son of Nicholas I)

**Alexander III 1881–1894** (second son of Alexander II)

**Nicholas II 1894–1917** (son of Alexander III)

# Post-Revolutionary leaders of Russia

Vladimir Lenin 1922–1924

Alexei Rykov 1924–?Late 1920s (exact date disputed)

Joseph Stalin ?Late 1920s (exact date disputed)–1953

Georgy Malenkov 1953–1955

Nikita Khrushchev 1955–1964

Leonid Brezhnev 1964–1982

Yuri Andropov 1982–1984

Konstantin Chernenko 1984–1985

Mikhail Gorbachev 1985–1991 (instigated 'perestroika' and 'glasnost')

Boris Yeltsin 1991–99

Vladimir Putin 1999–2008

Dmitry Medvedev 2008–2012

Vladimir Putin 2012–

# Selective Index

* after name indicates a writer whose work is extracted in this anthology.

# Acknowledgements

Oxygen Books would like to thank the many people who have supported *city-pick ST PETERSBURG* with their enthusiasm, professional help, ideas for texts to include, and generosity. Among them we would like to mention particularly the permissions personnel in the many publishers and agencies we have dealt with, along with Andrew Furlow, Amanda Hopkinson, Galina Krupy, Wendy Sanford, Tim Stanley, Michael Geoghagan, Susan Thorne, our translators, many helpful librarians (especially staff at Shenfield Library), James Rann and the staff of Academia Rossica in London, Marina Samsonova in St Petersburg (whose meticulousness in finding material and checking translations, information, and the final text has contributed greatly to the quality of this book), and Eduardo Reyes for providing such delightful illustrations.

Astvatsaturov, Andrei *Skunskamera* (2010) published by Ad Marginem. Translation © Oxygen Books Ltd. Reprinted by kind permission of the author and publisher.

Bely, Andrei *Petersburg* (1916), translated by John Elsworth (2009), reprinted by permission of Pushkin Press.

Bitov, Andrei *Life in Windy Weather* (1991). By kind permission of the author.

Blackwell, Elise *Hunger* (2003) published by William Heinemann; reprinted by permission of The Random House Group Ltd.

Bradbury, Malcolm *To the Hermitage* (2000) Copyright © Malcolm Bradbury 2000. Reprinted by permission of Pan Macmillan, London.

Brodsky, Joseph 'Guide to a Renamed City' in *Less Than One: Selected Essays* (1986),
reprinted by permission of Penguin Books Ltd.

Capote, Truman *The Muses Are Heard* (1957) reprinted by permission of Penguin Books Ltd.

Chechot, Ivan 'Kupchina', in *Saint Petersburg as Cinema*, (2011) ed. Lubov Arkus, reprinted by kind permission of the Séance Workshop (http://seance.ru)

Coetzee, J. M. *The Master of Petersburg* (1994), published by Secker and Warburg. Reprinted by permission of The Random House Group Ltd.

Cross, Antony 'Homes by the Neva' (2003) in Rossica 10/11. Reprinted by kind permission of the author.

Dean, Debra *The Madonnas of Leningrad* (2006) published by Fourth Estate. Reprinted by permissions of HarperCollins.

de Beauvoir, Simone *Force of Circumstance* (1963), translated by Richard Howard, © 1963 The Estate of Simone de Beauvoir and Editions Gallimard; reproduced by kind permission of the estate of Simone de Beauvoir and Editions Gallimard, Paris c/o Rosica Colin Ltd, London.

Dimbleby, Jonathan *Russia: A Journey to the Heart of a Land and its People* (2008), published by Ebury Publishing, for BBC Books; reprinted by kind permission of The Random House Group Ltd.

Docx, Edward *Self Help* (2007) Copyright © Edward Docx, 2007. Reprinted by permission of Pan Macmillan, London.

Dostoyevsky, Fyodor *Crime and Punishment* (1866), translation © David Margashack, 1951. Reprinted by permission of Penguin Books Ltd.

Dostoyevsky, Fyodor *The Idiot* (1868/9) translation © David Margashack, 1955. Reprinted by kind permission of Penguin Books Ltd.

Dovlatov, Sergei *The Suitcase* (1986) translated by Antonina W. Bouis, © Alma Classics Ltd, 2011. Reprinted by permission of Alma Classics.

Dunmore, Helen *The Betrayal* (2010) Reprinted by permission of Penguin Books Ltd.

Dunmore, Helen *The Siege* (2001) Reprinted by permission of Penguin Books Ltd.

Eliseev, Nikita 'The leap' in *Saint Petersburg as Cinema*, (2011) ed. Lubov Arkus, reprinted by kind permission of the Séance Workshop (http://seance.ru).

Fallowell, Duncan *One Hot Summer in St Petersburg* (1995), published by Jonathan Cape, reprinted by permission of The Random House Group Ltd.

Figes, Orlando *Natahsa's Dance* (2002), published by Allen Lane, reprinted by permission of Penguin Books Ltd.

Ford, Gail *The Lure of Russia* (2010), published by Citrus Press; reprinted by kind permission of the author.

George, Arthur and George, Elena *St Petersburg: A History* (2003), published by Sutton Publishing. Reprinted by permission of The History Press.

# Acknowledgements

German, Mikhail 'Chronotopes' in *Saint Petersburg as Cinema*, (2011) ed. Lubov Arkus, reprinted by kind permission of the Séance Workshop (http://seance.ru).

Gogol, Nikolai *Nevsky Prospekt* (1835) in *The Collected Tales*, translated by Richard Pevear and Larissa Volokhonsky. Reprinted by permission of Granta Books.

Goncharov, Ivan *Oblomov* (1859) translation © David Margashak, 1954. Published by J. M. Dent, a division of The Orion Publishing Group Ltd. All efforts to trace the copyright holder through the publisher were unsuccessful.

Gostrop, Viv 'Back to St Petersburg', first printed in British Airways' *High Life* magazine, published by Cedar Communications. Reprinted by permission of David Higham Associates.

Karsavina, Tamara *Theatre Street* (1930) published by Dance Books. Reprinted by permission of David Higham Associates on behalf of the author's Estate.

Koeppen, Wolfgang *To Russia and Elsewhere: Sentimental Journeys* Published by Suhrkamp Verlag, 1986, (Nach Rußland und anderswohin. Empfindsame Reisen) in Wolfgang Koeppen: Collected Works in Six Volumes. Translation © Susan Thorne, 2012.

Kotelnikov, Oleg 'Kronstadt' in *Saint Petersburg as Cinema*, (2011) ed. Lubov Arkus, reprinted by kind permission of the Séance Workshop (http://seance.ru).

Kovalova, Anna 'Cinema in St Petersburg: St Petersburg in Cinema' in *Saint Petersburg as Cinema*, (2011) ed. Lubov Arkus, reprinted by kind permission of the Séance Workshop (http://seance.ru).

Likhachev, Dmitry *Reminiscences* (1995) translation © Maya Vinokour. Every effort has been made to contact the rights holder.

Lurie, Lev 'The Petrograd Side' in *Saint Petersburg as Cinema*, (2011) ed. Lubov Arkus, reprinted by kind permission of the Séance Workshop (http://seance.ru).

Mak, Geert *In Europe: Travels Through the Twentieth Century* (2004), translation © Sam Garrett, 2007. Published by Harvill Secker. Reprinted by permission of The Random House Group Ltd.

Makine, Andreï *The Life of an Unknown Man* (2009), © Éditions du Seuil Janvier 2009, translation © Geofreey Strachan 2010. Reproduced by permission of Hodder and Stoughton Limited.

Malvern, Gladys *Dancing Star* (1946) We have been unable to trace the copyright holder.

Morris, R. N. *A Gentle Axe* (2007) Published by Faber and Faber. Reprinted by permission of David Higham Associates on behalf of the author.

Morris, R.N. *The Cleansing Flames* (2011) Published by Faber and Faber. Reprinted by permission of David Higham Associates on behalf of the author.

Nabokov, Vladimir *Pnin* (1953). Copyright © 1953, 1955, 1957, Vladimir Nabokov. Used by permission of The Wylie Agency (UK) Ltd.

Nabokov, Vladimir *Speak, Memory* (1967). Copyright © 1947, 1948, 1949, 1950, 1951, 1967, Vladimir Nabokov. Used by permission of The Wylie Agency (UK) Ltd.

Piryutko, Yury 'Vasilievsky Island' in *Saint Petersburg as Cinema*, (2011) ed. Lubov Arkus, reprinted by kind permission of the Séance Workshop (http://seance.ru).

Prokofiev, Sergei *Soviet Diary 1927 and Other Writings* (1991), translation © Oleg Prokofiev 1991. Reprinted by permission of Faber and Faber Ltd.

Quigley, Sarah *The Conductor* (2011) published by Head of Zeus. Copyright © Sarah Quigley 2011. Reprinted by permission of the author and Head of Zeus Ltd.

Rabinowich, Julya *Splithead* (2009), reprinted by permission of Granta Books.

Reid Anna *Leningrad: Tragedy of a City Under Siege, 1941–44* (2011), © Anna Reid, 2011, reprinted by permission of Bloomsbury Publishing Plc.

Rolin, Olivier *En Russie* (1997), reprinted by permission of Editions de Seuil. Translation © Oxygen Books Ltd, 2012.

Savitsky, Stanislav 'Kolomna' in *Saint Petersburg as Cinema*, (2011) ed. Lubov Arkus, reprinted by kind permission of the Séance Workshop (http://seance.ru).

Sawyer, Miranda 'Back in the USSR', the *Observer* 20 November 2011, © Guardian News and Media Ltd 2011.

Serge, Victor *Conquered City* (1932), translated Richard Greeman. Copyright International Victor Serge Foundation.

Shostakovich, Dmitry *Testimony* (1979), translated by Antonina W. Bouis, reprinted by kind permission of Penguin Books Ltd.

Sitwell, Sacheverell *Valse des Fleurs* (1941) Reprinted by permission of Eland Publishing Ltd © *Estate of Sacheverell Sitwell*.

Slovo, Gillian *Ice Road* (2004) published by Virago, reprinted by kind permission of Aitken Alexander.

## Acknowledgements

Sokurov, Alexander 'Interview' (2011), translated by Maya Vinokour; reprinted by kind permission of Alexander Sokurov and Professor Catriona Kelly of the University of Oxford, organiser of the AHRC supported project 'Cultural Memory and Local Identity in St Petersburg'. Oxf/AHRC Spb-11 PF22 MS.

Stanley, Tim, 'Contemporary Art in Petersburg: A Historical Mission' (2012), by permission of the author.

Stratanovsky, Sergei 'Obvodny Canal' in *Saint Petersburg as Cinema*, (2011) ed. Lubov Arkus, reprinted by kind permission of the Séance Workshop (http://seance.ru).

Tolstoy, Leo *War and Peace* (1869), translation © Richard Pevear and Larissa Volokhonsky, 2007. Published by Vintage; reprinted by permission of The Random House Group Ltd.

Wells, H. G. *Russia in the Shadows* (1921) Reprinted by permission of A. P. Watt Ltd on behalf of Literary Executors of the Estate of H. G. Wells.

Every effort has been made to trace and contact copyright holders before publication. If notified, the publisher will rectify any errors or omissions at the earliest opportunity.

An exciting and unique travel series featuring the
best-ever writing on favourite world cities

# *NEW YORK*

'This sublime and 'literary' travel book operates on so many levels. For those who have never been in New York, here are some of the greatest writers painting the city in magical word pictures. For those who know and love the city, here are images so evocative you will feel as though you are there. And for those planning to visit, this is a compendium of everything that is special about the city.'
**Bruce Elder, *The Sydney Morning Herald***

'With more than 150 excerpts from fiction and non-fiction, Reyes succeeds in capturing the authentic flavour of the Big Apple ... this excellent addition to the city-pick series of urban anthologies'
***The Guardian***

'The latest in this excellent series of travel anthologies has Charles Dickens, Alan Bennett, Sylvia Plath and Martin Amis sharing their musings on this most loved of cities'
***Lonely Planet Magazine***

'A wealth of atmospheric literary snippets that evoke the 'crush and heave' of New York City – this gazette dips into a host of writers whose themes range through the city's history, jazz and architecture ... a prismatic, engrossing and skimmable work, the book suggests further intriguing tangents for further exploration – both on foot and on the page'
***Financial Times***

'The hubbub of clamouring voices covers the history of the city, the difference between the five boroughs, the architecture, the famous inhabitants, the experience of living in NYC and more ... the multitude of subjects and viewpoints gives a good impression of the heterogeneity and bustle of the great metropolis, and succeeds in painting it as a unique and thrilling place'
***The Irish Times***

'A slim volume, perfect for carry-on, the New York edition is a fast-paced powerwalk through different 'themes' or moods of the city ...City Pick: New York works both as an excellent, and imaginative, alternative travel guide, and as an easy way for wannabe Manhattanites to pop in and out of the city that never sleeps.'
**Katie Allen, *We Love This Book***

'Regroups the very best of literature written about the greatest cities on the planet from some of its finest authors. The New York edition is divided into 12 sections, including, 'On the Waterfront', 'Big Yellow Taxis etc' and 'Celebrity City', and offers insights into various aspects of The Big Apple as seen through those who have written about it'
***Easy Voyager***

£9.99   ISBN 978-0-9567876-1-3

# *BERLIN*

'A gem ... an elegant, enjoyable and essential book'

Rosie Goldsmith, **BBC Radio 4**

'This wonderful anthology explores what it is really like to be a Berliner by bringing together extracts about the city from a range of genres, including some specially translated. This was the city of Einstein, Brecht, George Grosz, and Marlene Dietrich. It was 'the New York of the old world', a melting pot of new ideas and lifestyles ... This collection is timely: on 9 November 20 years ago, Berliners tore down the hated wall'  *The Guardian*

'*city-Lit Berlin* gathers more than a hundred extracts from writers on aspects of Berlin's conflicted heritage ... the editors have trawled widely to try to capture the modern city's rule-bound yet permissive tone, as well as its persistent state of cultural and architectural renewal. The result is an eclectic pillow-book ... a stimulating intellectual tour of the idea of the city that would complement any guidebook's more practical orientation'  *Financial Times*

'This is a sublime introduction to the city'  *The Sydney Morning Herald*

'A welcome contrast to the many formulaic travel guides in print and online, *city-Lit Berlin* reveals the city as seen through the eyes of 60 writers of all description – ... a volume that has greatly enriched the field of travel books.'

**Ralph Fields, *Nash Magazine***

£8.99   ISBN 978-0-9559700-4-7

# *PARIS*

'It's terrific ... all the best writing on this complex city in one place'

**Professor Andrew Hussey, author of *Paris: The Secret History***

'Superb ... It's like having your own iPad loaded with different tomes, except that this slim anthology contains only the best passages, bite-sized chunks just perfect to dip into as you sip that pastis in a pavement café.'

*The Times*

'The ideal book for people who don't want to leave their minds at the airport'

**Celia Brayfield, author of *Deep France***

£9.99   ISBN 978-0-9559700-0-9

# LONDON

'For those visitors to London who seek to do more than bag Big Ben and Buckingham Palace, this is the ideal guide, a collection of writings that expose not only the city's secret places but its very soul ... I can't imagine a more perfect travelling companion than this wonderful anthology'

**Clare Clark, author of *The Great Stink***

'The latest offering in this impressive little series concentrates on the spirit of London as seen through the eyes of an eclectic selection of writers. Part of the joy of this collection is that the writers span several centuries, which means that multiple faces of London are revealed. It's an exciting selection, with unexpected gems from novelists, travel writers, journalists and bloggers. Keith Waterhouse, for example, writes with gentle pathos about the double life of a transvestite in Soho; Vita Sackville-West wryly observes a coronation in Westminster Abbey; Virginia Woolf promenades down Oxford Street; and Dostoyevsky strolls down the Haymarket'

**Clover Stroud, *The Sunday Telegraph***

' ... a frenzied orgy of London writing. You'll love it.'     ***Londonist***

'The second volume in this enticing new series includes extracts from the work of 60 wonderfully diverse writers, including Will Self, Monica Ali, Alan Bennett, Dostoyevsky, and yes, Barbara Cartland (writing about a West End ball)'

**Editor's Pick, *The Bookseller***

£8.99   ISBN: 978-0-9559700-5-4

# DUBLIN

'An elegant, incisive and always entertaining guide to the city's multitude of literary lives.'

***Lonely Planet Magazine***

'*city-pick Dublin* is the latest triumph of distillation. There's everything here from David Norris' defence of the significance of Joyce's *Ulysses* to Iris Murdoch's fictional treatment of The Easter Rising. You'll read about walking and drinking, being poor and being poetic, new wealth and newcomers, old timers and returning natives.'

**Garan Holcombe, Book of the Month, The Good Web Guide**

'From Sean O'Casey to Anne Enright – the best ever writing on Dublin has been specially published in a new book entitled *city-pick Dublin*'

**RTE**

'Bite-sized beauties ... You won't find pub recommendations or directions to art galleries in this little guide, but you will get a taste of Dublin's most important natural resource: stories.'

***The Dubliner***

£8.99   ISBN 978-0-9559700-1-6

# AMSTERDAM

'This engrossing book ... Some of the names in city-pick Amsterdam' – such as the historian Simon Schama – may be familiar to British readers, but there are plenty more contributions in translation from Dutch writers.'

*Lonely Planet Magazine*

'This latest addition to the excellent 'city-pick' series of urban anthologies weaves together fiction and non-fiction, including more than 30 specially translated extracts, to give an intimate portrait of one of Europe's most distinctive cities.'

*The Guardian*

'Charles de Montesquieu, David Sedaris and Cees Nooteboom walk into a bruin café. It's not the start of a bad bibliophile joke, but the portrait painted by a new breed of city guide ... It's a simple idea, presenting a metropolis in all its multifaceted glory through the words of great writers; and it's one so good it's astonishing it hasn't been done before. Split into loosely thematic sections, one of the nicest features of this collection are the 70-plus contributors – novelists, journalists, travel writers – span the centuries. There's a thoughtful selection of Dutch writers including not only literary heavyweights like Mak, who are widely known in translation, but also lesser-known authors – Meijsing, Stefan Hertmans, Jan Donkers – some of whom are translated into English for the first time. It makes for some delightful discoveries – even for those of us who think we know this city well'

*Time Out Amsterdam*

'The latest installment in this much-lauded series, city-pick: Amsterdam showcases all the qualities that have established city-pick as an innovative literary alternative to your average visitor's potted history or guidebook. Eclectic, challenging and deeply involved in its subject, it takes you to deeper, more diverse places than you could ever hope to go elsewhere.'

*Translated Fiction*

£8.99 ISBN 978-0-9559700-2-3

# VENICE

'The latest addition to this admirable series ... makes any visit to La Serenissima more flavoursome'

*The Bookseller, Editor's Pick*

' ... the latest literary treat from the city-pick series ... as a guide to the atmosphere and spirit of the city, it's unmissable.'

*Lonely Planet Magazine*

'For those who love Venice, this book is genuinely unmissable ... short extracts are seamlessly blended into a compelling narrative.'

*The Sydney Morning Herald*

£8.99   ISBN 978-0-9559700-8-5

www.oxygenbooks.co.uk